THE UNITY
OF
WESTERN CIVILIZATION

THE UNITY
OF
WESTERN CIVILIZATION

ESSAYS ARRANGED AND EDITED

BY

FRANCIS SYDNEY MARVIN

THIRD EDITION

Essay Index Reprint Series

BOOKS FOR LIBRARIES PRESS
FREEPORT, NEW YORK

First Published 1929
Reprinted 1970

INTERNATIONAL STANDARD BOOK NUMBER:
0-8369-1889-4

LIBRARY OF CONGRESS CATALOG CARD NUMBER:
77-128277

PRINTED IN THE UNITED STATES OF AMERICA

PREFACE TO THE THIRD EDITION.

ANOTHER seven years have passed and a third edition of this book is now called for. Happily nothing has happened in the interval to belie either the conclusions suggested in the original essays or the hopes expressed in the reissue of 1922. General peace has been maintained and all the changes to be noted are in the direction of greater unity in the world, especially in that Western world which was the immediate subject of the first Unity School. The interval between the first and the second editions was disturbed internationally by the Polish wars of 1920, by the occupation of the Ruhr, and the long-drawn and dangerous troubles of the Reparation question. The interval between the second and the third editions has witnessed the growing strength of the League of Nations, the transference of Reparations from the political to the financial sphere by the Dawes Commission and, above all, the final reincorporation of Germany in the comity of the West by the Locarno Treaties and her admission to the League in 1926. It is hardly possible to paint too brightly the change in colour that has thus emerged.

It is surely not a superficial optimism to trace the same process in wider spheres. The four greatest human aggregates not directly affected by these Western European arrangements are the United States, Russia, China and India. In each of these the same period has seen the growth of a pacifying

PREFACE TO THE THIRD EDITION

spirit. America, without joining the League, has assisted it by fathering the Kellogg Pact and is now seeking the safest way of joining the Court of International Justice at the Hague. China has found, earlier than was expected, a Central Government capable of recognition by other Powers and that Central Government is facing its long task firmly and with a welcome readiness to accept disinterested Western counsel. India has very generally co-operated with the Simon Commission and is awaiting its report without enthusiasm but with less signs of alienation than at any time since the War. Russia remains outstanding, distracted and distressed within, less a menace to the world than she was, probably in the near future the recipient of charity and careful handling from better-ordered nations.

It is, however, fundamental to this volume, and to all which have succeeded it in the Unity Series, that the strongest bonds of unity and the true springs of progress are to be sought rather in things of the spirit than in any political adjustments, however necessary these may be. In this view it must be noted that the recent period—since the issue of the second edition—has seen the intellectual schisms which followed the War practically disappear. All nations now meet again, as before, in scientific and humanitarian conferences, and the Committee of Intellectual Co-operation of the League of Nations has spread its unifying activities in ways which it would take a complete volume of specialist essays to describe. Science, too, the supreme unifier, has in the last years achieved some of its most amazing triumphs, in which—especially in physics and astronomy—the co-operation of nationals, divided twelve years ago by the War, is now more marked than ever. On this point nothing better could be said than one of the last utterances of Professor William Bateson, whose death has taken place since our last issue:

"Science by its operations has caused the earth to shrink so that a unity of public opinion once created can now be maintained which in the time of our grandfathers would have been impossible."

PREFACE TO THE THIRD EDITION

It is to strengthen this tendency that this volume is again issued, with a few verbal corrections only. The series of volumes of which it was the pioneer is described in the fly-leaves at the end of the book, and those who sympathize may be interested to hear that a ninth course will be held this summer at Danzig—one of the most international of towns—at which the progress of the World at Peace in the last ten years will be discussed in a similar set of lectures to these. The Editor will be glad to send details to any one who desires them.

F. S. MARVIN.

WELWYN GARDEN CITY,
March, 1929.

PREFACE TO SECOND EDITION.

Six years have elapsed since the first issue of this volume, and in one respect at least the hopes expressed in the first Preface have been fulfilled. Four other courses have followed on similar lines, and the subsequent books have been widely circulated as the " Unity Series," so called after this initial volume. The line of study has proved a fruitful one, and this year (1922) a fresh start will be made with a course on " Science and Social Progress," to be followed next year by one on " Art and Civilization." The desire to take wider views in history, and to approach all great problems from the historical point of view, is on the increase, and it is of good omen for our social stability and progress in the future.

When we look at the matter of this first volume in the light of the same six years our feelings will doubtless be more tinged with regret, but they can hardly differ much in general tendency from those we then expressed. The war, then beginning, concluded as we believed and hoped that it would. The League of Nations foreshadowed in Chapter XII is now in being. The whole world is now labouring painfully to restore and to extend that " Unity of Western—and Eastern—Civilization " of which we attempted to describe the outlines. We have learnt by sad experience how intimately our prosperity and even our life depends on the lives and prosperity of all other communities, and especially of those most closely linked to our own by kinship, by commerce, and by the restless intellectual life of modern times. These truths are all set out, or alluded to, in the essays which follow, and we reprint them just as they stand.

The pacification of Ireland, the new settlement in India, the League of Nations, with its recent replica in Washington, are all examples of the spread of the same spirit. Were we now to add another chapter, it would be to point out how much still remains to be done on these lines, and especially by the co-operation of the old leaders of modern Western civilization—of France and England—in healing the wounds of Europe, and, perhaps still more, in building up the bridge between West and East in Asia Minor and the Middle East. On this, as on other sides of human life, history offers us a foundation, a direction and a hope, but here, as elsewhere, man has in every age to strive afresh to make good the best of the past, and extend its dominion. Without the guarantee of history we should be fighting in the dark : without the constant struggle the hope would become a memory more and more remote.

F. S. MARVIN.

BERKHAMSTED,
21st January, 1922.

PREFACE

THE following essays are the substance of a course of lectures delivered at a Summer School at the Woodbrooke Settlement, near Birmingham, in August 1915. The general purpose of the course will be apparent from the essays themselves. No forced or mechanical uniformity of view was aimed at. The writers will be found, very naturally and properly, to differ in detail and in the stress they lay on different aspects of the case. But they agree in thinking that while our country's cause and the cause of our Allies is just and necessary and must be prosecuted with the utmost vigour, it is not inopportune to reflect on those common and ineradicable elements in the civilization of the West which tend to form a real commonwealth of nations and will survive even the most shattering of conflicts. That we on the Allied side stand fundamentally for this ideal is one of our most valuable assets.

The fact that the lectures were delivered at

a settlement for training persons for social work in a religious spirit, suggested to more than one of those who took part in the course, how similar is the task which now lies before us in international affairs to that which Canon Barnett initiated thirty years ago for the treatment of the social question at home. We need in both cases to associate ourselves mentally with others in order to realize the common elements which underlie the seeming diversity in the civilization of the West.

The method of the course was primarily historical, though certain essays have been added of a more idealist type. It is hoped that the point of view suggested, though prompted by current events, may be found to have some permanent value. It could obviously be applied to many other aspects of European life, e. g. morality and politics, to which conditions of space have only permitted indirect reference to be made in this volume.

F. S. M.

CONTENTS

		PAGE
I.	INTRODUCTORY: THE GROUNDS OF UNITY	17
	By F. S. Marvin.	
II.	UNITY IN PREHISTORIC TIMES .	35
	By J. L. Myres, Wykeham Professor of Ancient History, Oxford.	
III.	THE CONTRIBUTION OF GREECE AND ROME	69
	By J. A. Smith, Waynflete Professor of Mental and Moral Philosophy, Oxford.	
IV.	UNITY IN THE MIDDLE AGES . .	91
	By Ernest Barker, Fellow of New College, Oxford.	
V.	UNITY AND DIVERSITY IN LAW .	122
	By W. M. Geldart, Vinerian Professor of English Law, Oxford.	
VI.	THE COMMON ELEMENTS IN EUROPEAN LITERATURE AND ART .	137
	By the Rev. Dr. A. J. Carlyle, University College, Oxford.	
VII.	SCIENCE AND PHILOSOPHY AS UNIFYING FORCES	162
	By L. T. Hobhouse, White Professor of Sociology, University of London.	

CONTENTS

	PAGE
VIII. THE UNITY OF WESTERN EDUCATION By J. W. HEADLAM, late Fellow of King's College, Cambridge.	180
IX. COMMERCE AND FINANCE AS INTERNATIONAL FORCES By HARTLEY WITHERS.	198
X. INTERNATIONAL INDUSTRIAL LEGISLATION By CONSTANCE SMITH, sometime British Delegate on International Bureau for Industrial Legislation.	222
XI. COMMON IDEALS OF SOCIAL REFORM By C. DELISLE BURNS.	242
XII. THE POLITICAL BASES OF A WORLD-STATE By J. A. HOBSON.	260
XIII. RELIGION AS A UNIFYING INFLUENCE IN WESTERN CIVILIZATION By H. G. WOOD, late Fellow of Jesus College, Cambridge.	280
XIV. THE GROWTH OF HUMANITY By F. S. MARVIN.	301

ANALYSIS

CHAPTER I. THE GROUNDS OF UNITY

The appeal to history. Previous great schisms in Europe which have been surmounted give hope for the present. The Reformation. The Napoleonic Wars.

The two points of view. (1) Man's nature itself tending to unity through conflict. (2) The stages in the process developed in history.

In pre-history conflict and diversity are predominant, though the necessities of life prescribe certain uniformities. Consolidation comes in favoured physical conditions, especially great river-basins like the Nile and the Euphrates.

The possibility of a world-unity first consciously envisaged in the Greco-Roman world. Greece gives unity in thought, Rome in practice. Order with a solid intellectual foundation established with the Roman Empire. In the mediaeval world a unity mainly spiritual is reached in the same framework. The position of Germany in this development. The break-up of the fourteenth and fifteenth century. The enlargement of the known world and the growth of wealth and knowledge. This crisis still continues and has been recently accentuated by the birth-throes of nationalities. The supreme problem for international unity is now the reconciliation of national units with the interests of the whole. Underneath the superficial turmoil the great unifying forces of science and of common sentiments continue to grow and will ultimately prevail.

CHAPTER II. UNITY IN PREHISTORIC TIMES

Retrospect of the search for unity in man's affairs, in its political and scientific bearings.

The Unity of Man as an Animal Species. Ancient beliefs, doubts suggested by the practice of slavery, their solution, and the modern conception of a ' Human Family '

The unity of man as a rational animal struggling against nature for subsistence. Archaeological evidence as to the reasonableness of primitive culture on its material side ; doubts raised by man's irrational ' barbarities ' on the social plane. Lévy Bruhl's hypothesis of a ' savage logic ' and the Greek analysis of wrongdoing as rooted in ignorance.

Man's struggle with Nature in the N.W. Quadrant of the Old World. Unity here not to be found in the Food Quest. Prehistoric Europe shows variety of regimens, hoe-agriculture, pastoral nomadism. The wheel and the plough and the composite bread and cheese culture.

Race, Language, and Culture as Factors of Unity. The spread of the European Bread Culture is earlier than that of Indo-European Speech and probably than that of the ' Alpine ' type of man. Race in Europe has led not to unity but to discord, and linguistic affinity does not ensure mutual intelligibility.

CHAPTER III. THE CONTRIBUTION OF GREECE AND ROME

Contemporary history is the only genuine and important history, the present is the only object of historical knowledge ; what the present is and how, properly conceived, it gives history its unity and justifies the study of what is past (ancient history) ; all history is *our* history, and otherwise without meaning or value to us. The history of classical antiquity is the history of the youth of the modern world, of the formation of the now latent but still potent hopes, fears, designs, and thoughts which constitute the substratum of the European mind ; how this still unites a divided Europe and affords a ground of hope for a restored and deepened union. Our debt to the Greeks : (*a*) the very notion of civilization, (*b*) the idea of its realization through knowledge, (*c*) the ideal of freedom as the inner spirit of true civilization. How the Greeks failed to work all this out in both theory and practice, and how nevertheless they taught their lesson to the world ; the services of Greece to the world in the creation of Art, the Sciences, and Philosophy ; the Greek ideal of a life beyond ' civilized ' life, but rendered possible by it, and thus giving to civilized life a new and higher value ; defects and merits of this ideal.

The Romans are inheritors of all this ; how, while making it more prosaic, they rendered it more practical and more effectually realized it. All this most visible in the Imperial period. The

ANALYSIS

Roman ideal: (*a*) world-wide peace, (*b*) secured and maintained by a centralized system of laws issuing from and enforced by a single power. Influence of this ideal on later and modern thought and practice. Causes of its decline and fall: (*a*) ignorance of the economic substructure of civilized life, (*b*) neglect of opportunities to extend and defend it, (*c*) the rise of the idea of nationality. The Revolution as the last great attempt to reinstate the full Roman ideal in its outworn form.

Lessons still to be learned by us from the study of both the success and the failure of Greco-Roman civilization; how the consideration of these may at once sober our expectations and inspire us with hope in the present. The forces which created it still maintain it and show no signs of exhaustion. But that they may continue in effect we must study these forces and learn the lessons the ancient experience of their working conveys, exerting ourselves first to understand Greco-Roman thought and practice and then to better their instruction.

CHAPTER IV. THE MIDDLE AGES

I. The mediaeval world. Geographical extent. Economic structure: its features of uniformity and isolation: the effect of the rise of a national economy on mediaeval society. Linguistic basis. Mediaeval scheme that of a general European system of estates rather than of a balance of powers.

II. The unity of mediaeval civilization in its great period (1050–1300) ecclesiastical. The attempt of the Church to achieve a general synthesis of human life by the application of Christian principle. (1) The control of war and peace and the feudal world: the Truce of God and the Crusades: the papacy as an international authority: the mediaeval conception of war. (2) The control of trade and commerce and the economic world: just wages and prices: the mediaeval town. (3) The control of learning and education and the world of thought: reconciliation of Greek science and the Christian faith: allegorical interpretation of the world and its effects on natural science.

III. The mediaeval theory of society. The organic conception of society: mediaeval thought *naturaliter Platonica*. The one society of mankind. Hence (1) little conception of the State or sovereignty or State law; but the universal society has nevertheless to be reconciled in some way with the existence of different kingdoms. Hence, again, (2) no distinction of Church and State as two separate societies: these are two separate authorities, *regnum* and *sacerdotium*, but they govern the same society. The one society of mankind an ecclesiastical scheme uniting a great variety of personal groupings.

IV. The influence of law on the development of the kingdom into the state—a process begun early in England and France, but only generally achieved about 1500. The new conditions—geographical, economic, linguistic—which prepare the way for the new world of the sixteenth century. The gulf between that world and the old mediaeval world. The hope of unity to-day.

CHAPTER V. UNITY AND DIVERSITY IN LAW

The Problem in the Ancient World. Law universal and supreme over mankind (Sophocles, Antigone). Law arbitrary and varying from place to place (Herodótus). Nature and convention. The 'rightlessness' of the stranger in antiquity. The law was a 'law of citizens'. Admission of the foreigner to legal protection. Rome develops a law of the men of all nations (*ius gentium*), which reacts upon the law of citizens (*ius civile*), and ultimately coalesces with it. The law of nature.

The break-up of the Ancient World; the Middle Ages. The invaders bring their own law with them. In the kingdoms which they founded each man had his 'personal law'. Local Law. Feudal Law. The beginnings of National Law: England, France, Germany. Roman Law in the Middle Ages. The Canon Law.

The Modern World. The reception of Roman Law. State Sovereignty. The Modern Codes. Unity and diversity of law within the political unit. The world divided into territories of the English Common Law and lands where Roman Law conceptions prevail. Forces making for unity: the notion of a 'law of nature'; the pursuit of common ends. International law, private and public.

CHAPTER VI. THE COMMON ELEMENTS IN EUROPEAN LITERATURE AND ART

The question of the place of nationality in art and literature. It has little or no place in the Middle Ages. The mediaeval epic; its character. The mediaeval romance. Modern European art and literature transcends national conditions. The character-

ANALYSIS

istics of the new European literature of the fourteenth century: Dante, Boccaccio, Chaucer. The drama of England and Spain in the sixteenth and seventeenth centuries. Painting and sculpture from the fourteenth to the seventeenth century. The classical mind, and the principle of good taste and common sense. The realism of Defoe and Hogarth, and the Spanish Picaresque novel. Sentimentalism in the eighteenth century. The poetry and painting of nature. The great revolution and the romantic movement. Great literature and art are not national but human.

CHAPTER VII. SCIENCE AND PHILOSOPHY

Western civilization possesses a certain unity (1) in the sense of unity of character, (2) in the fact that it has a common origin, ultimately in the Greco-Roman civilization but more immediately in mediaeval Christendom, and (3) in the sense that its parts have maintained a constant intercommunication of ideas. (4) The different qualities of German, French, and English thinkers have in large measure complemented one another, (5) and the history of science and of speculative philosophy is largely a history of the interaction of distinct national schools. (6) The same thing is true of political thought. (7) Thus the world of thought forms a commonwealth which is superior to all national differences and, in spite of the war, remains a foundation of a very genuine unity.

CHAPTER VIII. UNITY IN EDUCATION

Distinction between Unity and Uniformity. Historical Unity; the origin of the School and the University. Both instruments of the mediaeval Church for maintaining a common system throughout Western Christendom. Importance of Latin as the universal language of education. Suppression of the vernacular and of national movements. The Reformation; a common European movement. Erasmus. The new teaching based on classical literature. Tendency to disunion; the influence of the Reformation and the national Churches. Growth of national literature. Political influences, the French Revolution, and the National State. The essential Unity still preserved, not merely in the study of the natural sciences, but in the historical unity given by Christianity and the spirit of Greece.

CHAPTER IX. COMMERCE AND FINANCE

Commerce and finance practical expressions of the instinct of self-preservation which is common not only tô all men, but to all living creatures. Early appearance of trading habit in boys. Early examples of trade. Abraham's purchase of a burying-ground from Ephron the Hittite. Solomon's trade with Hiram of Tyre. Herodotus, the first historian, opens his history with an allusion to trade. Trade is based on specialization, and is at once a cause of unity and of disunion. Its extension from individuals to communities. Foreign trade stimulated by variations of value in different communities. Specialization increases efficiency, but makes the worker a machine, and a speculator on the chance that others will want what he makes. International trade also promotes both unity and friction. On the whole, commerce a great promoter of unity. Likewise finance, or money-dealing. Its origin and development. London's catholic taste in foreign securities : sometimes prefers them to the home-made article. Effect of foreign investment on home production and consumption. Foreign finance and productive specialization.

CHAPTER X. INTERNATIONAL INDUSTRIAL LEGISLATION

Interdependence true of countries as of classes. A fact brought home to us by the European War. Importance of international action in relation to the raising of social and industrial standards. This truth perceived by Robert Owen a century ago. Work of Owen and his successors in the direction of an international minimum of labour conditions. Action of the Swiss Federal Council. The German Emperor calls the first Conference on workmen's protection 1890. Formal failure and substantial achievement of this Conference. Founding of International Association for Labour Legislation and International Labour Office. Constitution and work of these bodies. Biennial conferences of the association : subjects and methods. International Conventions of 1906, their scope and value. Subsequent labours of the Association. Its present position and future hopes.

ANALYSIS 13

CHAPTER XI. COMMON IDEALS OF SOCIAL REFORM

Ideals arise from perceived social evils. They have caused in recent years (*a*) Common action by European Governments and (*b*) action by separate Governments influenced by foreign experience. There has also been a growth of sentiment, not yet embodied in law or institutions, with regard to (i) the position of women and children, (ii) social caste, and (iii) the increase of common action for reform by civilized states.

CHAPTER XII. THE POLITICAL BASES OF A WORLD-STATE

The nineteenth century has made three great contributions towards the possibility of International Government, the political realization of nationality, the growth in substance and method of international law, and the progress of federalism. In other fields outside politics, especially in commerce and finance, a network of international co-operation has grown up. Closer political union is needed for three purposes: first, the consolidation, extension, and improved sanctions of existing international law; secondly, the settlement of differences between nations; thirdly, positive co-operation for the common good. This progress involves some further diminution of 'sovereignty' and 'independence'. But these concepts have no absolute validity. In the Hague Conventions and other intergovernmental instruments the rudiments of international government already exist. In order to establish effective security for peace, what is needed is a general treaty providing that all disputes be submitted to arbitration or conciliation, with such guarantees for acceptance of the award as will establish confidence. The test of confidence is the voluntary reduction of armaments. Internationalists differ as to the nature and rigour of the sanctions. Some rely entirely on a 'moratorium' and the pressure of public opinion: others would compel the submission of all issues, but not the acceptance of awards: others, again, would apply force, diplomatic, economic, or military, to both processes.

Internationalism, to be effective, would require a machinery for dealing with new issues before they ripened into disputes. How

14   ANALYSIS

far will the state of mind following this war assist this progress of internationalism ? Is a spiritual conversion, corresponding to the process of biological mutatism, possible or probable ?

CHAPTER XIII. RELIGION

The history of Europe suggests that, though the Church exerted a considerable influence on the growth of a common type of civilization in the West, in modern times religion has proved a divisive rather than a unifying factor. During the last generation or two, however, there has been a decline of the dogmatic and sectarian tempers. This change is largely due to the growth of the scientific spirit, and, as in other realms of inquiry so in the study of religion, international co-operation has steadily developed. Both literary criticism and psychological analysis have contributed to the widening of sympathy. The better understanding of certain elements in the Christian ideal and the Christian hope must also be taken into consideration as a factor making for a new catholicism which finds expression in movements like the Adult School Movement and the Student Christian Movement, and in the ever-growing demand for closer co-operation in missionary work.

Beyond this, partly through the comparative study of religions, we are conscious that religious thought in the West possesses some common characteristics, notably, faith in the solidarity of mankind and in the reality of progress. Of themselves, these two convictions do not constitute any very close bond of union, and both beliefs need to be defined and enforced by the sense of sin and the consciousness of God which the West has learned from Jesus.

CHAPTER XIV. THE GROWTH OF HUMANITY

The need of a basis of right sentiments even greater than that of improved political machinery to secure international union. We must start from patriotism and enlighten and enlarge it. Of the three Western nations which lead in the arts and sciences, France and England through the war become closely allied in defence of a policy of the union of free and pacific people throughout the world. The position of Italy, Russia, and the United States. The increase of arbitral methods and the formation of

ANALYSIS 15

leagues of peace or even of a world-state are matters calling for earnest thought ; but the spread of the notion of humanity, the co-operation of all mankind in a common work is more fundamental and may be begun by any one at home. This idea, starting with the Stoics, is fully developed with the advent of modern science. It shows itself in many forms and the spread of exact science is its most powerful aid. This is entirely independent of nationality and will be increasingly concerned with the alleviation of human suffering and the improvement of life.

The final test of a high international aim is the joint effort of the stronger peoples to protect and assist the weaker and less advanced. The case of Africa and the Brussels Conference of 1889. Analogy with the treatment of the young at home.

I
THE GROUNDS OF UNITY

In face of the greatest tragedy in history, it is to history that we make appeal. What does it teach us to expect as the issue of the conflict ? How far and in what form may we anticipate that the unity of mankind, centring as it must round Europe, will emerge from the trial ?

Only two occasions occur to the mind on which, since the break up of the Roman Empire, a schism so serious as the present has threatened the unity of the Western world. The first was the Reformation and the war which it entailed down to the Peace of Westphalia. The second was the struggle against Napoleon, terminated a hundred years ago. The latter was in many respects a closer parallel. It was a struggle of the independent nations of Europe against the overweening ambition and aggression of one Power. It united them in an alliance which achieved its purpose and survived the successful issue of the war for some years. Some such course, with a comity of nations far wider and more enduring than the Holy Alliance as its sequel, we hope and predict for the present war.

The struggle at the Reformation was less like the present, either in its causes or its course, but it has some features which make it a useful point for a survey of the permanent unifying elements which hold and will hold the West together in spite of occasional cataclysms and the clash of rival interests and passion. A man like Erasmus, trembling before the catastrophe, willing to make immense sacrifices to avoid an open breach, uncertain of any final readjustment which might restore the harmony of the world, was not unlike some among us who hoped against hope that the enemy might be appeased, who thought that almost any peace was better than any war, who still fear that the breach in unity is vital or irreparable for generations.

And the issue three hundred years ago may also inspire us with a cautious optimism, a strong though not unmeasured trust. The right cause triumphed, fully in the end. Freedom was secured, both for churches and for individuals, throughout the world. The evil features in the papal system, against which the attack was really levelled, quietly but completely disappeared, and the institution survived, itself reformed. Lefore a hundred years were out the world had moved on to the conquest of new vantage points and the establishment of a wider unity on a firmer base.

Both previous occasions are therefore full of hope. The European system is, as we shall see throughout these essays, the necessary nucleus of any civilized order embracing the whole world; and the great convulsions which have hitherto continued to occur in it from time to time are moments of especial value for the study of the conditions under which it exists. They are the pathological experiences which reveal the strength and the weaknesses of the normal functions. We strive and hope for a more lasting state of general health, and do not despair of the patient even in this grave attack. He has survived even more serious illness. For though the present war is the most gigantic that the world has ever seen, its very greatness is the result of some of those modern developments—scientific skill, improved communications, national cohesion—on which ultimately the better organization of the whole common-

I THE GROUNDS OF UNITY

wealth of nations will be built. *Passi graviora* ; we have weathered the storms of the sixteenth and seventeenth centuries, when the old Roman order and its sequel in the Catholic Church were at their weakest and the recuperative power of science and social reform and nationalism had hardly begun its work. We shall not fail with our greater forces of the present to regain and create a Europe freer, stronger, and more united than that which now seems to be shaken to the depths.

The process of gaining a greater unity among the leading nations of the world, like all the aspects of human evolution, must be regarded from two points of view, distinct in theory, inextricable in life. What does the nature of man itself demand ? How has this nature expressed itself, and been affected in history by the external conditions, the geography, climate, conflict and commingling of races, which the theatre of its appearance has imposed ?

Looked at in itself, so far as we can isolate it from its surroundings, man's nature is distinguished from that of lower animals by two features, both of them essentially social and tending to unity. He is more deeply and permanently attached to members of his own species, by affection, sympathy, veneration, tradition, than any other creature. And he is a reasoning being, reason itself requiring the contact and agreement of various minds. The incomparably greater force which he has acquired in the world, over all other species and over nature itself, is due to the working of these two factors. At starting he was physically less strong than many other creatures, and if he fought with others of his own kind, other animal species did the same. He was ahead of them by his reason, and reason acted, and must act, through the concert of thinking beings. This concert is not merely, or even mainly, an attachment among those living at the

same time to co-operate for some common end; it is
with man a conscious sequence of one generation on
another. Sometimes the movement of adaptation is
slower, sometimes quicker, but in every case the living
are carrying on the work of the dead, and their co-operation in time as well as space is due to the working of the
same qualities of attachment and reason, the social
factors, by which at any moment a community of men
is bound together.

Still looking at the matter *a priori*, it is clear that the
vast community of mankind, though it has come more
closely in contact in recent years over all the planet, yet
acts, and must act, habitually and momentarily, through
many smaller aggregates. Of these the leading types are
the family and the country or nation. The former is not
directly relevant to our inquiry, the latter plays a leading
part in it. The former is less dependent on external
conditions of land-formation and the like, and is in
consequence more universal, more purely human. The
latter has been shaped by geographical conditions, by
racial qualities, by the apparent accidents of history.
Its relation to the larger units of human society raises
the most difficult, fundamental and unavoidable questions.
To curb aggressive nationalism is the root-problem of the
present war. To reconcile permanently nationalism with
humanity would be to establish the everlasting peace.

Western society, indeed the whole community of mankind, is built up of these smaller units, the family and the
nation, with their various intermediate groupings, but the
historical process has by no means conformed at all
exactly to this logical order. Society has not been made
in orderly fashion by forming families and then combining families to make hundreds, and hundreds to make
counties, and counties nations, and so on to the whole.
This is the *a priori* way, but the way of nature

and history was less perfect. The minor forms of human association have been taking shape, being altered and on the whole improved, throughout the process. At one point, of high importance for our argument, a larger form of association was achieved before the necessary constituent elements were articulated. This was the Greco-Roman world encircling the Mediterranean and completed in the Roman Empire of the second century A.D. It was the nucleus from which the Western world of modern civilization has been developed; yet it was there, settled in its main outlines, before the national units which it required for internal harmony and cohesion had taken any definite shape. It is to the difficulties of their growth and mutual adjustment that we owe most of the conflicts of modern history.

We shall in this book go back first to a still earlier stage, a stage of pre-history, to a time when no one, not gifted with superhuman insight and prescience, could have foreseen the course which human civilization would pursue. All over the world, for tens of thousands of years, a culture persisted, associated with stone implements, and marked by a similarity which is often extremely striking, in races and tribes widely severed by distance and climatic conditions. The raw material of the human product in science, art, and invention was alike in texture although often exuberant in detail and imagination. But it had not yet the unity of an organic whole, knit by a common purpose and conscious of itself.

To gain the cohesion of large numbers of men by whom wealth could be created and sufficient leisure and independence secured for an intellectual life, not dictated by the necessities of existence, a special concurrence of favourable physical conditions was required. The rich and secluded river-basins of many parts of the world provided this, and in consequence we find similar large communities arising at the end of the Stone Age in such places as China, Peru, Mexico, and above all in Mesopotamia and Egypt. The last named derived their special importance for the sequel from their proximity to the Mediterranean, which was to act as the great meeting-place and training-school for adventurous spirits and inquiring minds. From the busy intercourse of these land-locked waters arose the civilization called Minoan, or Aegean, centring in Crete, itself to be surpassed by the trading activity of the Phoenicians and the art and science of the Greeks.

It is with the advent of the Greek that the seal is placed upon the claim of the Mediterranean to be the birthplace of the highest type of human civilization, the centre from which a unity of the spirit was to spread, until, by material force as well as by the conquering mind, the European or Western man was recognized as in the forefront of the race. The supremacy of the Greek lay in his achievement in three directions, as a thinker, as an artist, and as the builder of the city-state. For our present purpose the first and the last are the most important and the first the most important of all.

The city-state was important as the first example of a free, self-governing community in which the individual realized his powers by living—and dying—with and for his fellows. This new type of human community was of the highest moment in the sequel. In many points it was a model to the Romans, and thus became a fulcrum for the upward movement of the Western world. In the works, too, of the Greek philosophers, especially of Plato and Aristotle, it inspired the earliest and some of the deepest reflections on the nature of social life and government. But it never acquired the permanence of the political units needed to build up the European Commonwealth. For this nations were required, and the

Greeks were a race and not a nation. The πόλις lacked the size, the variety of elements, and the territorial basis on which a modern nation rests.

It is rather in their achievements as thinkers and as artists, above all in their science and philosophy, that we find the most fundamental and lasting contribution of the Greeks to the unity and progress of mankind. When these became allied to the tenacity, the organizing and legal genius of the Romans, a firm centre of civilized life was established, which has survived the shocks of two thousand years of growth and conflict and will survive the upheaval of the present. The Greek unification was in the world of thought and art; the Roman attempted a corresponding work of organization in the human world which lay nearest to him in the countries round the Mediterranean Sea. Both efforts were of priceless value and continuing effect, but both were, from the conditions of the problem, imperfect solutions, the brilliant but precocious sketches of adolescent genius. The Greek, working at first on the material accumulated by generations of Chaldean and Egyptian priests, discovered from their crude, unorganized, and inexact observations of geometry and astronomy the elements of unity in diversity which constitute science. Inquiring for causes, comparing and correcting individual facts, he arrived at the first equations in mathematics, the first laws of nature. His work in this sphere and in that of medicine went on continuously until after the Roman occupation of the Mediterranean world was complete. It died out gradually in the theological atmosphere of Alexandria, and on the purely human side ended in Stoicism with an amalgam of universal philosophy and Roman law. The Stoic Empire of the second century A.D. was the high-water mark of the joint efforts of Greeks and Romans to attain unity and humanism in thought and practice. Its brilliance while it lasted, the nobility of its leading men, the persistence of the main lines of its structure, are the measure of our debt to the builders of the Greco-Roman world.

The Roman contribution to the result which in the end so perfectly combined both movements was, in its origin and nature, singularly unlike the Greek. The Roman did not analyse his conceptions. He accepted what came to him, either from his ancestors or from other peoples, without scrutiny, except so far as to see that new matter could be worked into old forms without a dislocation in practice. He was the pragmatist, the Greek the idealist. This instinct of adaptation and sequence made the Roman the pioneer in law as the Greek was the pioneer in science. It rendered possible the holding together in one political system of the multifarious territories and peoples from the Tigris to the Solway Firth for long enough to enable the greater part of that area to be permanently civilized on Roman lines. But, like the artist's sketch of his picture, the whole was outlined before the parts were worked out in their final form: and the sketch itself was seriously imperfect in more than one point. The set-back which Augustus received on the eastern side of the Rhine was never made good, and the Germanic tribes therefore remained un-Romanized until the Church in the seventh and eighth centuries resumed the work on other lines. This defeat of Varus and the legend of Hermann became to the German a symbol of national greatness in a sense which none of the other national conflicts with Rome ever assumed. To us Boadicea is a barbarian, and we trace with gratitude and pleasure the signs of civilization left by the Roman occupation. To us the Roman was for centuries a defence against barbarism, and we regret that we had to do over again many of the things which he had once taught us. But the Roman Empire, when the German accepted it, was no longer the Empire

I THE GROUNDS OF UNITY

which had founded the unity of Europe. It was a German Empire, and though the ancient world fired his imagination, he always saw it through German eyes.

The next stage in unity was the mediaeval Church, which inherited the framework of the Roman Empire and extended the area of moral and civilized life which Rome had initiated.

In this Germany was included, and she played a distinguished part. Roman missionaries, some by way of England and Ireland, went further than the Roman legions had attempted, and the sword of Charlemagne did the rest. Germany in the later Middle Ages was perhaps the most valued of all the Pope's domains, and her prince-bishops his greatest lieutenants. The moral and religious effect of the Catholic discipline, appealing to sides of human nature which Greece and Rome had left untouched, was nowhere more deeply felt than by the Germans. Spiritually they were thus lifted at least to the level of the rest of Western Europe, but politically they remained unincorporated, the most feudal and military nation of the West.

The growth of nations was, on the political side, the main achievement of the Middle Ages. Rome had given the framework of a great system, and into this had poured barbarians from North and East, Goths, Franks, Huns, Moors, Lombards, tribes at the level of the Homeric Greeks when they swept down to the Aegean. They came as migrant hordes, and in the area civilized by Rome and the Catholic Church they settled down as nations, mingling with the earlier population and divided up by the geographical configurations of the Continent. Among them France and England had the advantage. They gained their unity as nations earlier than any other countries of the West—England in a form which has lasted substantially unaltered for six hundred years.

Spain, which had been torn asunder by the Moors, was not consolidated fully till the end of the fifteenth century, in time to send the last of the crusaders under Columbus in quest of fresh worlds to conquer across the Atlantic. But Italy and Germany—and especially the latter—remained disintegrated until our own time. Both gained their union about the same time, fifty years ago, but by different methods and in a different spirit. Italy, naturally a compact geographical unit, was welded by a democratic enthusiasm, of which Cavour and Mazzini were the soul and Garibaldi the right arm. Germany, vast in power and numbers, lay strongly entrenched in the central area of the Continent, but failed to kindle into national life at the same democratic moment. She was fashioned into political existence by a Thor's hammer, which, as it rose and fell, dealt shattering blows on friends as well as foes, in Austria as well as France, on Danes and Poles, on Liberals and Socialists, on little kings and great ecclesiastics. And now this Frankenstein creation among states offers the most serious problem in adjusting national claims with European unity. We have to check and to assimilate—if the world is to live as one—the one Power which has hitherto developed most persistently and successfully its own resources, but least in subordination to the interests of the whole.

There are those who would regard all national barriers and organization as somewhat of an obstruction, who would prefer a simple internationalism to the world as we know it, with its pent-up passions and attachments, its constant liability to explosion, its slow progress by tortuous channels towards the larger view and the surer hold. Many reformers, from Plato downwards, have taken up a similar attitude in regard to the smaller institution, the family, which is often found to be an obstruction in the way of short cuts to social utopias at

I   THE GROUNDS OF UNITY

home. Kant's ideal of a cosmopolitan constitution as the goal of all human effort rather leans to this side of the balance. But a due balance must be kept and the full value both of family and nation maintained against theories or tendencies which would roll us all out into cosmopolitan items. A glance at other elements which go to make up the unity of European society will tend to correct the perspective.

The unity of the Roman Empire was mainly political and military. It lasted for between four and five hundred years. The unity which supervened in the Catholic Church was religious and moral and endured for a thousand. Less binding on one side, it was more searching and pervasive on others, and though now broken, it still remains in full force over many millions of minds, while the Roman political and legal structure has to be sought for in formal institutions which have absorbed its spirit and transformed its letter. But beyond the actual fabric of the Church itself we have the multitude of cognate and derivative institutions which have served the cause of unity in the moral and intellectual sphere. We shall speak later of the more perfect and lasting unity of science. The universities in the Middle Ages and the Renascence tended to the same end, using a material in philosophy and theology which was bound to wear out with the spread of knowledge and the flux of time. But in their prime they succeeded in producing a more complete community of scholars than has perhaps been ever witnessed in Europe before or since. Then as always the realm of the genuine love of truth, or even of honest disputation, was independent of differences of race or political boundaries, and the scholar went from Oxford to Paris, or from Rotterdam to Bologna, solely to widen his mind or to sit at the feet of some world-famous teacher.

And the wandering scholar was by no means the only

social link. Many of the trade-routes surprise us by the length and adventurousness of their course. Amber from the Baltic found its way to the south of Italy and Spain, while small boats from Ireland were brought into the mouths of the Loire and the Garonne when the coasts of the Channel were impassable through barbarians from the North.

Mediaeval Europe was, in fact, much more of a unity than the modern traveller would expect, and this was mainly due to the influence of the Church. The spiritual unity went deep on one side of man's nature, and when a man like Erasmus surveyed the prospect at the beginning of the sixteenth century we can well understand his horror, and his determined abstention from any step which would precipitate the break-up of the one organized body which represents the old united culture of Christendom and might check the new forces which were threatening selfishness and disorder in ever-widening circles on the globe. For it must be noted that new forces of expansion were making themselves felt, as the unity of the Church was being threatened from within. Explorers were extending, East and West, the sphere in which the European was to impose his influence for good and evil on other peoples, and the sixteenth century thus becomes one, perhaps the most critical, of all the turning-points in the history of the West. Danger was mixed with hope, disorder with new knowledge and fresh power, and the crisis has not yet been surmounted. But we have gained by now some insight into the nature of the new forces and see that they should, and one day will, work more fully in the direction of unity in the civilized world, of healthy independence in the parts and a growing harmony in the whole. Little of this could have been seen by the observer at the outbreak of the Reformation.

Nationalism, democracy, colonial expansion, religious

THE GROUNDS OF UNITY

change, the growth of knowledge and its application to industry and social reform, these are the salient features which distinguish our modern from the mediaeval world, and we have to consider how far they make for the unity of mankind.

The sixteenth century saw both the strengthening of national governments and the beginning of European colonization. England, France, Spain, Portugal, Holland, all settled down under a central government stronger and more independent than they had previously enjoyed, and pegged out estates for themselves beyond the seas. In each case wars have been entailed in the process, and, as we know, the backwardness of Germany at this period has been visited upon the rest of Europe tenfold in recent times. National expansion thus appears to be an eminent provocation of international strife. It is with no intention either of ignoring facts or minimizing dangers that one turns here to the other side of the account. Where was the spark actually fired which led to the present conflagration? In that part of Europe where the national units were least stable and developed, where the conditions of government and social order are most remote from our own. Who can doubt that if in the Balkans the Turks had been able to establish even the sort of government we maintain in India, or if, still better, the Balkan States, apart from the Turks, had gained their own independence in a federation like the Swiss, the aggression of the Central Powers would have been checked? The compact, well-established national unit is not in itself a danger, but there is a danger in weak, oppressed, or disjointed nationalities, who have not found safety and offer a bait to their expansive neighbours.

Thus strong and independent nations, as Kant postulates in his *Perpetual Peace*, are guarantees of peace, stones in the Temple of Humanity. Another consideration not generally recognized, strengthens this conclusion. In recent years all leading and progressive nations have been devoting their first thought to social reform. This has been conspicuously the case with ourselves, with the French, with the United States, with the smaller, more advanced countries in Europe. Germany, too, though her first energies have been given to organizing war, has had in this matter two distinct souls. Her social democrats and part of her governing class have been consistent and successful in working for the amelioration of the condition of the people, and have often anticipated other nations in her process. It is self-evident, first, that a strong national government is needed to carry out wide social reform, second, that in proportion as governments devote themselves whole-heartedly to this, their energies are less likely to be devoted to molesting their neighbours. Germany, unfortunately for herself and the world, had no government which could speak for the whole people and be responsible to it. A truly national government in Germany, or anywhere else, would not have willed this war.

The colonial expansion which was connected with the outburst of national sentiment in the sixteenth century, and has led to frequent conflicts between European nations ever since, also appears in a different light if we study it in view of facts not dreamt of in the sixteenth and seventeenth centuries. The Americas, which appeared to the early navigators as rich estates to be cultivated for the benefit of proprietors at home, have developed into powerful and independent countries, eminently pacific (except for internal brawls), looking forward to producing new types of life and government, hoping perhaps to hold the balance in a long-drawn contest of the Old World Powers. The circle, therefore, of the Mediterranean world which was enlarged by the discoveries of the sixteenth century, finds its completion to-day in new states across the Atlantic, which are on the whole enormously preponderant on the side of peace, and wish to hold their own in Western civilization by force of wealth and industry, and not by arms. To us, too, it is clear, and will be one day to the Germanic Powers, that the British Empire, the largest political aggregate on the globe, is essentially a league of free peoples, under no compulsion from the centre, but responsive to attack upon their power or liberty by any third party, strong from their general contentment with the conditions and institutions of their life, and not through any systematic regulations imposed from above. Even India and other protected states and dominions, though not yet self-governing, are moving steadily in the direction of responsibility and of willing association with the British Empire or Commonwealth as a whole.

Such is the much vaster community of nations which has succeeded to the Western Europe of the sixteenth century; and no mention has been made of the place of Russia or the countries still further east. The picture does not suggest a welter of conflicting passions and ambition throughout the world. On the whole a mass of men and women labouring with fair contentment at their daily task, not concerned that their state or nation should extend its boundaries, least of all that it should provoke attack; little conscious of the historic debt of nations to one another, but wishing well to others except when they cross the path of a personal desire; gaining rapidly more sense of actual community among living men, but hardly realizing yet how man's power has been built up in the past and how infinitely it might be advanced and the world improved by harmony and steadily directed efforts in the future. That the sense of brotherhood has gained ground in the world, especially since the middle of the eighteenth century, is certain. Voices of protest reach us even from Germany through the storm of hatred. But the vague sympathy, the desire for peace and shrinking from the horrors of war need to be enlightened, to have a reasoned basis in the belief that all nations, and especially those of the vanguard, are partners in a common work and essential one to another, above all, perhaps, to have institutions which tend to co-operation and make a sudden and disastrous breach as difficult as possible. Many of these instruments of peace were being forged when the war broke out. Many of the most profound ties between nations are not understood or are kept in the background by nationalist teachers or a nationalist press.

Of all the modern steps towards international unity, the most indisputable, the most firmly based and furthest-reaching, is science, and the various applications of science, both in promoting intercourse between different parts of the world and in alleviating suffering and strengthening and illuminating human life. The more prominence, therefore, that we can secure for the growth of science in the teaching of history, the larger place humanity, or the united mind of mankind, will take in the moving picture which every one of us has, more or less full and distinct, of the progress of the world. For some hundreds of years, culminating in the three or four centuries A.D., the dominant feature in the picture was of a triumphant city-state, Rome, gradually subduing and embracing the world. Then for some thousand years the picture was of a religious organization leading the civilized world, and nationalities were only emerging as somewhat dim and ill-defined figures. Then, with the rupture in the Church and the upspringing of other religious bodies and forms of thought, national figures become predominant in the scene, and attract nearly all the attention, which is given, except by a few curious persons, to the study of history.

THE GROUNDS OF UNITY

Nationalism, once in defect in Western Europe, has been for some time in excess. The remedy is not directly to attack it, except in the case in which it gave us no choice, but to supply the limiting and controlling ideas. Of all these, science fits the case most exactly, because, as science, it can know no distinction between French or German, English or Russian. There is no French physics or German chemistry, and if we are told that the Prussians have their own theory of anthropology, based on the predominance of a particular type of skull which other anthropologists dispute, we are quite sure that in that case science has not yet said her last word.

We put physical science first because it contains the largest number of certain and accepted laws. The further we get from mathematical exactness the more liable we are to differences of opinion, which may, as in the case of anthropology, cluster round some question of national pique. But it would be easy to trace through all the sciences, and into philosophy and religion, a growing unity of method and result before which national differences often resolve themselves into a difference of style. The style is the nation's, but the truth is mankind's.

We could not, indeed, be sure that if every one in Western Europe were a trained scientist, wars would cease from the earth : certain professors have taught us too well for that. But in so far as men come to recognize that the great body of organized knowledge is a common possession, due to the united efforts of different nations, and that it can only be increased by joint action and may be increased to such a point that the whole of life is a happier and nobler thing, so far they will be averse to war. And in its various applications, to increasing production and quickening communication, to lengthening life and healing sickness, to protecting workers and cheapening food, men see the natural fruits of an activity whose basis is common thought and its ultimate purpose the common good.

It has been said with truth that it is easier to trace the growth of science as a joint product of co-operating minds, than to find a growth of common sentiments among the men and the nations who have created it. True among individuals, it must be at least as true among groups and nations. We may work successfully with some one at a problem or learn from a teacher or a companion when we dislike him personally and do not seek his society apart from the needs of our common work. It has often happened, and will happen again in private and public. But though particular antipathies may increase, the tendency to dislike others is a diminishing quality among civilized men. In the long run common sense and necessity will prevail. We are born to live a while before we die; and we must live on the same planet, sometimes next door to those who have sworn a never-dying hate.

II [1]

UNITY IN PREHISTORIC TIMES

THE new perspective, with all its shift of values, which is forced on us by the war, touches the past no less than the present and the future. However objectively we try to present to ourselves the data of history, we cannot emancipate ourselves from the need to present them from a point of view which must in the last resort be our own. We may bring ourselves by training and criticism nearer to the centre of things, more intimate with essential factors and remote from the trivial periphery; but it is a matter of degree, and historical study an affair after all of mental triangulation. Like a surveyor in the field, we are safest in our determination of any third position if we have already knowledge of two, and of how the third looks from both of them. And even if we were indeed at the centre of things, I suppose we might take our round of angles quite uselessly, unless we had also some divine gift of judging distances.

So the historian accepts his limitations as the rules of the game, and sets out to see unity askance. It is his rare chance, if events shift *him*, and set him gazing at a world in which, as now, half his own career is inside the picture; not perhaps very easy to find in a moment—as one might fail to recognize oneself in a group-photograph—but none

[1] This chapter has not had the advantage of Prof. Myres's revision, in view of the rest of the book which he has not seen. Being for some time abroad on war-work, it was impossible to communicate with him; and it is therefore thought best to print his paper just as it was written some months before the lectures were delivered.

the less there, and intelligible only in relation to its actual surroundings.

Looking back, indeed, over the course of anthropology and prehistoric archaeology, much of which lies in the years since 1870, and nearly all of it since 1815, the first thing which strikes us now is the frequency and delicacy of its response to contemporary thoughts and aspirations. A few of the greatest men have recognized this at the time. I quote from Karl Ernst von Baer, the founder of comparative embryology, and in great matters the master of men as different as Huxley, Spencer, and Francis Balfour. He died in 1876, when political anthropology was still young; but in his great book on Man he ' appeals to the experience of all countries and ages, that if a people has power, and attempts wrongdoing against another, it also does not omit to conceive the other as very worthless and incompetent, and to repeat this conviction often and emphatically ' (*Der Mensch*, ii. 235). It is easy for us to dot the *i* and cross the *t* here; less easy perhaps to realize that what troubled von Baer was the persistence of British and American ethnologists in the polygenist heresy, which he traced (and rightly) to their reluctance to treat their ' black brother ' as if he were their relative at all. Judgement in that ethnological controversy went by default, with the victory of the North in the American Civil War; and in 1871 the lion lay down with the lamb, even in London; inveterate foes in the Ethnological Society and the Anthropological merging their fate in one Anthropological Institute. In 1915 the reluctance of the ' tall fair people who come from the north '—I borrow a phrase from Professor Ridgeway—to fraternize with mere brunettes, beyond Rhine and Danube, comes in its turn before the same tribunal as polygenism in 1862.

Our subject, ' Unity in Prehistoric Times ', embraces three main topics: (1) the unity of human effort and reason everywhere in Man's struggle with Nature and with his Fellow-man ; (2) the special conditions which favoured or hindered unity of prehistoric culture in what has been called elsewhere the 'north-west quadrant' of the Old-World land-mass west of Ararat and the Median hills and north of Sahara, the cradle and nursery of the modern 'western world'; and (3) the convergent lines of advancement within that region, which can be traced through the centuries before Roman policy let Greek culture penetrate almost as deep into peninsular Europe as Alexander's conquests had opened to it the inlands of the Near East.

When we speak of unity in human affairs, and particularly just now, when the supreme unity seems to some to be nationalism, and to others the negation, or rather the supersession of nationalism, we mean the rather complex outcome of several distinct things. This complexity was confessed, unwittingly perhaps, in the first humanist creed : ' I believe in one Blood, one Speech, one Cult, one congruous Way of Living.'[1] Modern ethnology, indeed, tends to subsume cult under way-of-living, as a peculiarly delicate test of conformity—and to regard language, alongside of both cult and way-of-living, as another manifestation of the same human reason ; distinguishing therefore two kinds of unity—one physical or morphological, as of one animal species in an animal kingdom, the other cultural or psychological, as of the sole incarnate occupant of a realm of mind ; and classifying the ' Science of Man ' accordingly. But, in essentials, that Athenian creed will serve: our latest ethnologists, and statesmen too, are faced with the same league of problems.

[1] Herodotus, viii. 144. After the battle of Salamis, when the Athenians are invited by Xerxes' envoy to desert the Greek cause, they say they cannot betray what ' is of one blood and of one speech, and has establishments of gods in common, and sacrifices, and habits of life of similar mode '.

The Unity of Mankind as an Animal Species

Whatever Greek statesmen thought about the gulf between Greek and Persian, or Greek and Barbarian generally, Greek ethnologists raised no fundamental barrier between the different sorts of Man. Good naturalists as they were, and experienced breeders of farm-stock, they accepted white, brown, and black men; and were prepared to accept any other breed that Nearchus or Pytheas might confront them with, as members of one brotherhood, just as they accepted white, brown, or black sheep, with horns of Ammon or with none. Eratosthenes, most philosophical, and therewith most *political* of them all, was bred in Cyrene, where some Greeks seem to have been black; and he worked in Alexandria, where the University was a human Zoo like that of London or Berlin. Their simple farmer's theory of natural selection attributed ' scorched-faced ' Aethiopians to sunburn, and other racial types to large factors of region and régime. The classical treatise is that of Hippocrates ' On Air, Water, and Places '.[1]

In the modern world, too, no serious doubt was cast on the specific unity of mankind, handed down from antiquity, until Linnaeus and Buffon had refined upon the biological notions of genus and species (for both of which there is only one word in Greek), and had defined species by the criterion of fertility. Now not only the great explorers, but every ship's captain, knew by this time that white men, at all events, would form fertile unions with all known kinds of humanity. But in the eighteenth century it became known also, and in the same empirical way, that the fertility of unions between white men and black was imperfect; and as this was the only human cross for which

---

[1] For details see the section on Herodotus in *Anthropology and the Classics*; and E. E. Sikes, *The Anthropology of the Greeks*.

there was any large quantity of evidence, the impression grew that the zoological distance between these races was greater than had been supposed. On the other hand, eighteenth-century formulators of the ' Rights of Man ' challenged reconsideration of the current practice of negro slavery ; and the upshot was a controversy. Abolitionists contended that the ' black brother ' was indeed a blood brother, and entitled to the ' Rights of Man ' ; their opponents replied that the negro, being (as they held) of another species, might justly be treated in all respects as one of white man's domestic animals, and be his property as well as his drudge. At the turn of the century, the adherence of Cuvier gave prestige to Polygenesis on its scientific side : and it took all the reasonableness of Prichard in the next generation to turn the tide even in England. But the issue of the American Civil War, to which reference has already been made, coincided so closely in time with the work of Darwin and Lyell on the real meaning of species and on the antiquity of man, that the controversy was closed without bitterness. The new phase of Polygenism which seems now to be opening, with successive discoveries of the quaternary stratification of races, and Keith's analysis of the family tree of the *Hominidae*, starts from wholly different data, unembarrassed by fears or hopes of a ' Neanderthal ' origin for the Negro, or for any living or recent *Homo*.

The ' human family ' then seems re-established as something more than a platform phrase ; and separatists (who are always with us) have had to fall back upon another criterion of disunity.

The Unity of Mankind as a Rational Animal

Omitting language for a moment (which since first telling of the ' Tower of Babel ' story has somewhat fallen from grace as a symptom of unity among mankind), or rather, subsuming it as one of the most essential exhibitions of rationality, and indeed its chief instrument, we come to Man's unity as a creature possessed of reason, and expressing this reasoning habit in specific modes of living, under whatever external surroundings. These being almost infinitely various, it is not always easy to compare examples of Man's reaction to them. For proof of the uniformity of human reasoning, indeed, we have to begin almost from an animal plane. ' Hath not a Jew eyes ? Hath not a Jew hands, organs, dimensions, senses, affections, passions ? Fed with the same food, subject to the same diseases, healed by the same means, warmed and cooled by the same summer and winter, as a Christian is ? ' And not only is men's hunger, and their sensitiveness to ' the same summer and winter ' similar : their ways of satisfying hunger, their conduct of the food-quest, their elementary organizations ' for the sake of maintaining life ', as Aristotle expressed it, exhibit one mental type throughout. In the domestication of nature's gifts it is the same : in the fashioning of implements and weapons, the improvisation of clothing and shelter, the almost instinctive impulse to ' play with fire ' which repels other animals. Style and finish may vary, and do vary widely from one province of culture to another ; but in their last mechanical analysis, a spade is a spade all the world over, and a celt a celt.

It was the service of the late General Pitt-Rivers in this country, and of Klemm more laboriously abroad, to establish this aspect of the ' Evolution of Culture ' beyond controversy : as it was the work of Boucher de Perthes, and of Sir John Evans and Sir John Lubbock to proceed in the reverse direction, from a criterion of utility to a hypothesis of design, and the conclusion that certain stones, of reputedly prehuman antiquity, must be the work of human hands, geared to human brains like ours. Tylor's

II UNITY IN PREHISTORIC TIMES

wider range of observation, conspicuously supplemented by other work of Lubbock, embraced all human activities in one formula of comparison, which is indeed as old as Thucydides.[1] We can infer, that is, something about early stages of an advanced culture from the present-day practices of savagery.

Yet, across this 'primitive culture', to use a phrase which has become classical, so reasonable, and therewith so full of uniformities, in its intimate interplay of hand and tongue with brain, patches of shadow fall; a chaos of such incredible absurdities and (in the widest sense) of 'barbarities', that the charitable hypothesis that here and there man has lost his way and just *stopped thinking* hardly seems adequate to account for things, and writers like Lévy-Bruhl are provoked to the pessimist guess that there can be a savage logic which is different from ours and yet is 'logical' in some coherent sense; which *stets verneint* the conclusions, and even the axioms, which are clear as day to us; and is a 'knowledge of evil' side by side with the knowledge of good.

But examples of this 'primitive thought', when we come to analyse them, all seem to resolve themselves into one or other of the ordinary sorts of fallacy, as our own logic-books expound them. If the study of them proves anything at all, it is the familiar aphorism that, while there is only one right way of doing and thinking, there are countless ways of going wrong. Among the most reasonable people (at their highest) that the world has yet seen, there were some of the worst miscarriages of reason and of morals; and throughout their great centuries there was no word either for the devil or for sin in their language. For the Greek all human wrongdoing came under the one simple category of ἁμαρτία, 'making a mistake', or better

[1] Thucydides i. 6 πολλὰ δ' ἂν καὶ ἄλλα τις ἀποδείξειε, τὸ παλαιὸν Ἑλληνικὸν ὁμοιότροπα τῷ νῦν βαρβαρικῷ διαιτώμενον.

'making a miss'. It is the slang of target-practice, for the correlative στοχάζειν, used of all happy guesses at truth, is likewise only the word for ' *aiming* straight '.

But why make mistakes ? Why these failures of co-ordination between design and execution, between nature's truth and man's theory and practice ? Why this declining from the best into sloppy or antiquated work, to name only two main sorts of technological fallacy ? Again the answer comes down, past Lucretius, from the Ionian physicist. It is only in superficial appearance that ' though reason is common to all, most men live as if they had a way of thinking of their own ',[1] Heraclitus' momentary despair anticipating Lévy-Bruhl almost verbally. Once penetrate, with Heraclitus himself, below the surface, and ' all men have it in them to understand themselves and to think straight '.[2] It is failure to think, not some distinct and illogical sort of thinking, that is the cause of the trouble: the lapse of that ' organized common sense ' which is the content of all ' science '.

Such disorganization of common sense, ' idiotic ' thinking, in the Heraclitan sense of an ἰδία φρόνησις, can be as cumulative, fallacy on fallacy, and as elaborately wrong, as the fabric of knowledge is cumulatively and elaborately right. ' Hath this man sinned, or his parents, that he was born blind ? ' That is the tragedy of primitive culture: for the brains are there and the eyes ; only they have never seen anything straight, because in the world they were bred up in there was nothing left straight to be seen.

Lucretius hit upon half the trouble when he referred the organized absurdities of his contemporaries to hereditary fear: which in the last analysis is a derangement of the

[1] τοῦ γὰρ λόγου ἐόντος ξυνοῦ, ζώουσιν οἱ πολλοὶ ὡς ἰδίαν ἔχοντες φρόνησιν.

[2] ἀνθρώποισι πᾶσι μέτεστι γινώσκειν ἑαυτοὺς καὶ σωφρονέειν.

II UNITY IN PREHISTORIC TIMES

higher activities extending to abdication. Its onset is an ataxy; and its culmination a paralysis. In its mental aspect it is failure of the Will-to-know; acceptance of an inferiority to which ignorance consigns us.

The other half of the trouble, less clearly diagnosed by Lucretius, but detected, as we have seen, by Heraclitus, is hereditary pride, based on ignorance no less than is Lucretian fear. It is the 'lie-in-the-soul', the conviction, assailed by Socrates and before his time as well as after, that we know how things stand, when in fact we do not. Like fear, in its mental aspect, it is a failure of the Will-to-know; once again, an acceptance of the inferior status of the ignorant.

Organized fears, then, lead to *tabu*, the systematic inhibition of experiment which might conflict with hypothesis; and organized pride, to *magic*, with its systematic disregard of the results of each experiment that is made, when it does so conflict with hypothesis. And it is these two superstructures of ignorance, inhibiting and insisting by turns, which add the glamour of irrationality to so much of the behaviour of mankind, and disguise its native rationalism and its morality too. Beset by fear and pride, craftsman and cultivator and explorer and reformer alike are in the same predicament. 'I could do this or that and do it thus, but may I?' and if such opinion as counts says 'Thou shalt not', the fallacious substitution of 'shalt not' for 'mayst' cannot fail to endanger advancement. It may be over the chipping of a flint axe, or a trade-union rule about a high-speed lathe; but if the craftsman conforms to opinion as such, and not through positive concurrence of his own judgement with it, he has accepted the fallacious conclusion as his own, and lets his work fall to second-hand and to second-best.

Wide uniformities of conduct and of material culture may therefore result from ignorance, no less than from knowledge, and unless we have very full acquaintance with the region and external conditions, it is not easy to decide whether any one of these uniformities is wisely uniform or not. The record of the dealings of quite well-meaning conquerors with the institutions and arts of their subjects is full of tragedies of this kind. I call to mind an example in Paraguay, where abstention from infanticide, after conversion to Christianity, nearly wrought the extinction of a native tribe, for the population at once began to exceed the means of subsistence ; and it was only when the committee in London was induced (just in time) to apply mission funds to the purchase of seeds and implements of agriculture that the danger was averted. It is not my purpose here to commend infanticide ; only to indicate that while man cannot live by bread alone, he cannot go on living, even a good life, if he really falls short of bread. So with devotion to an ideal unity of culture, we are to combine toleration of wide diversity, seeing how diverse are the surroundings which make up the Home of Man. Were Nature uniform, in a geographical sense, from pole to pole, civilization might be practically as well as ideally one, though it may fairly be doubted whether in such a world civilization, such as we know, would arise ; but with the present distribution of land and water, temperature and rainfall, and the complex of plants and animals which results from their interaction, unity among the phenomena of culture ceases to be practicable, and it has become hard for some (as we have seen) even to keep their faith in the unity of human reason.

It was not, in fact, till a rather later stage in the growth of science, either in the old world, or in our own, that anyone troubled himself about the existence of such unity at all. That men of alien blood should behave in alien and incomprehensible ways seemed to the Greek and to the navigators of the Renaissance equally natural. And

II UNITY IN PREHISTORIC TIMES   45

Herodotus and Bodin, to name only pioneers and masters, are agreed as to the cause. Variety in Man's behaviour is no impish trick of original sin : it is the response of his single reason to variety in Nature. Only when experience added intimacy with alien individuals to observations of their habits of life, did a common humanity in their behaviour begin to be so frequent and obvious as to cause surprise. Acquiescence in the discovery is implicit in Thucydides and Hobbes, and confessed in Aristotle and Locke. Had Europe broken into the Great East in Locke's day, as the Greeks broke into Persia in Aristotle's, we might have had completer analogy between the ethnology of Montesquieu and that of Eratosthenes than we can actually trace. The defect in the writer of the *Lettres Persanes* is in his knowledge of Persia, not of Paris and London : Eratosthenes, as we remember, was born in Cyrene and worked in Alexandria.

MAN IN CONFLICT WITH NATURE IN THE NORTH-WEST QUADRANT OF THE OLD WORLD

We come now, from this rather general survey of human faculty, to the more pertinent question, what sort of unity do we find in human achievement within that region, or rather within those regions, of the Old World where the stream-heads of our modern culture seem to take their rise ? The qualification which has slipped from my pen is half the answer already, for we are to deal not with one homogeneous region but with a cluster of regions in all climates from Arctic tundra to Sahara and the Nile, and in all altitudes from alpine to maritime. Unity of prehistoric culture, in such conditions, can at best be but a question of degree.

Modern ethnology, emancipated from a belief in an immediate consanguinity of mankind, by the spread of less infantile views about Noah's Ark, goes on to question the sufficiency of language as a bond of union, and forthwith stumbles over the Tower of Babel.

Two contemporary lines of discovery have tended to determine the result. Geology gives us a very long margin of time since the north-west quadrant began to be reinhabited by human beings after the Ice Age, and assumed approximately its present distribution of land and water. Archaeology, which in this aspect is the special stratigraphy of man, sanctions an extension of time, since not merely human beings but organized societies of men made their appearance in Europe, which far exceeds the period required, or commonly assumed, for the spread of any known Indo-European language, from any possible 'home' to any region where it was spoken at the beginning of historic time. And not only does archaeological evidence enable us to detect such societies sedentary for a while on this or that site over the face of Europe and its neighbourhood: it traces not merely one 'prehistoric culture', but a number of distinct types of such culture, each with its own geographical distribution, and with distributions which expand and contract at different times, superseding one type of culture here, and another there, and in turn superseded by others.

It is not easy to bring home the extent of this diversity to those who are not familiar with the physical condition of a Europe which was as yet largely in the 'backwood' stage of exploitation. But it will give some idea of the range of contrast, if we revert to the method of Thucydides,[1] and compare the unexploited Europe of the days before agriculture, with unexploited America at the time of its discovery by Europeans. Here, within the same geographical limits of the north temperate zone, and with the

[1] Thucydides, i. 5. He too, as it happens, is illustrating a primitive Old World, round the Aegean shores of Greece, by the contemporary West in the backwoods of Aetolia.

far simpler scheme of surface relief which characterizes the New World, we have civilizations as different as those of the Eskimo, the Algonkin peoples of the coniferous forests, the Huron and Iroquois of the deciduous hardwoods, horticultural Muscogeans in the south-east, buffalo-hunting Sioux on the prairie, predatory Apaches and Blackfeet in the foothills, and littoral and riparian fisherfolk on the Pacific slope: just as recognizable now, in their distributions and overlaps, by the fashions of their pipe-bowls and other débris, as are the representatives of the 'row-grave' culture or the makers of 'band-keramik' in Central Europe.

Keeping in mind this analogy of prehistoric Europe with pre-Columbian North America, let us classify the problems of subsistence which these Old World regions offered to prehistoric man; and consider, granting him all the reason in the world, and uniform physique (if you please) as well, how he is to formulate solutions which shall show any trace of uniformity, and yet be solutions for him of the one Protean problem, how to sustain life here and now?

Along the Arctic seaboard, homogeneous from Behring Strait nearly to the North Cape, we have the frozen tundra region, with a characteristic tundra culture; pushed now far north since Europe mellowed into a habitable world, but formerly widespread about the skirts of the shrinking ice-sheet. Here we hunt large animals and sea-shore beasts, and trap small-deer very ingeniously; we fish in the large northward-flowing rivers; and eventually (heaven knows after how long, or how far back from now) we borrowed a notion, probably from pastorals imprudently straying too far along those northward river-lanes through the forests, and domesticated our best of beasts, the reindeer; stealing a march here on our Alaskan cousins, who call them caribou and treat them so: *they* had no pastorals on the prairie southward to teach them otherwise, and when the Russians came and brought reindeer over from Asia, the silly fellows turned them loose and hunted them till they had eaten them all.

South of the tundra, the Great Northern Woodland encircles the planet, interrupted only by the treeless sea. Here too we hunt, and trap, and eat berries of the undergrowth, like Algonkins or Tacitean Germans, many of whom had no more skill in cattle than Algonkins. But we have not the place to ourselves, like the tundra folk and the Algonkins. Our forest world is in ever-present danger of disintegration, and our wood-craft with it. Fond folk with tame animals (poor sport, both of them, for sportsmen like us) come blundering in off the parkland away south, up the grassy glades, trampling undergrowth and scaring the game. People are saved from all that 'over there', because no one can tame the prairie buffalo and drive *him* over the hunting grounds ; some sport, too, the prairie buffalo ! And worse still, there are the people who come hacking and burning our great trees, and tearing up the turf and underwood, and all to plant their fancy grasses with the fat seeds, that the deer like to browse over ; and that is the only thing to make those people show fight, if we or the deer go among their fat-grass plots. Those people come up, too, from the south and the south-east, and have to go back thither for seed if their sowings fail. Of course they like their animals tame, like the other fellows ; but the grasses are their first string, as we bowmen say.

Southward, enveloping the Alpine ridges, except where the snow peaks perforate its carpet covering, the Woodland changes its character, rather than gives place to anything fresh along the shores of the Lake Region of the Old World. Here and there, in detached plateaux enfolded among the ranges (like the Salt Lake basin and the

II   .UNITY IN PREHISTORIC TIMES   49

Shoshonean plateaux in America), there are isolated grassy plains, repeating on a smaller scale the great grassland which skirts the Black Sea and the Caspian. Examples are the heart of Spain and of Asia Minor, and the miniature grasslands of the Balkan Peninsula, such as Thessaly and Eastern Thrace.

It is in the southern third, or thereabouts, of the continuous Woodland, where the deciduous forest trees begin to give place to evergreens, as they themselves replaced the conifers further north, that the minutely subdivided horticulture and arboriculture begins, which characterize the Mediterranean region. To call it agriculture would be to exaggerate its scale. It is more like a northerly extension of tropical *Hackbau*, as the Germans call those forms of plant-raising which dispense with plough and spade, and employ only mattocks or hoes, which are little more than earth-chopping celts. You have only to watch the unhandy way in which the Greek peasant and what Homer called his ' foot-trailing ' oxen work their Virgilian plough through the recesses of a field no bigger than a cabbage-patch, and well stocked with olive-trees besides, to realize how truly in this kind of farming ' the ox is in place of a house-slave to a poor man '. For the house-slave could handle a *zappa*, the spadelike Levantine hoe, where an ox would fail to turn round, yet where food-plants could be coaxed to grow, and an olive-tree would luxuriate.

This kind of garden-cultivation indeed repeats very closely the foodquest of the Muskogean cultivators in the South-eastern States, who make up the so-called 'civilized tribes ' and, almost alone among the Redskins, ' are all self-supporting and prosperous '.[1] In the Old World, as in the New, its distribution is closely defined by certain limits of rainfall and temperature, and most of all by the extent to which the rainfall is concentrated into a few

---

[1] Farrand, *The Basis of American History*, 1904, p. 270.

winter months, so that a dry warm summer is assured, which Man can mitigate and even exploit if he has access to perennial water. It extended, therefore, in quite early times, and still predominates, all round the mountainous shores of the Mediterranean, from Syria by Southern Europe to Algeria and Tunis, and penetrates inland and upland into the forests till summer clouds and rainfall check it. In this region of its distribution Greek and Roman legends betray the belief that grain-cultivation came late, and superseded a staple diet of tree produce, chestnut, walnut, filbert, and acorn.[1] And when the 'nobler grasses' came, it was barley and red wheat that predominated, as indeed they predominate still.

But this is only one part of the distribution of the garden-culture. Far north along the Atlantic seaboard, and as far inland as the mild Atlantic climate is perceptible, the same type prevails. Its ancient limit is traced meteorologically in Tacitus' complaints (for example) of the austerity of the lands beyond the Rhine. In this northern region grain crops pass from red to white wheat, from barley to oats, and from both to rye. The ease with which the Muskogean potato and tomato have been acclimatized, and their respective prevalence now in the Atlantic and Mediterranean sections, illustrate exactly the place which primitive hoe-culture held in the economy of the Old-World region. Early monuments of this culture, in which hoe and ox-plough are equally conspicuous, are the 'meraviglie' rock-carvings above Ventimiglia.[2] The fine flower of it is the Minoan civilization of the Crete and the

[1] The βαλανηφάγοι ἄνδρες, 'acorn-eating men', of Greek traditional ethnology.

[2] Bicknell, *The Prehistoric Rock Engravings in the Italian Maritime Alps*, Bordighera, 1902; *Further Explorations*, 1903. I begin to suspect that the stippled and shaded enclosures which accompany the drawings of oxen, ploughs, and men with hoes may represent the cultivation plots.

II UNITY IN PREHISTORIC TIMES 51

South Aegean. Egyptian agriculture is also in great part hoe-work.

South-eastward, outside the Carpathians, and within them also, in the great plain of Hungary, we meet a totally different régime; vast featureless and treeless grasslands, extending past the Black Sea and Caspian to the foot of the mountains of North Persia and the spurs of the Central Asian highlands. Here, if Man is to maintain himself at all, he must be master of tame animals which can eat the grass, and in turn sustain him. South of the eastward continuation of the woodland Mountain Zone, through Asia Minor into Persia, and also south of the Mediterranean lake-region and the ridges of Syria and the ' Africa Minor ' of Tunis, Algeria, and Morocco, which partly enclose it, lies another group of grasslands, Arabia and Sahara, desert-hearted, but capable of sustaining a considerable population of nomad pastoral folk round their margins and in oases, and of emitting them in volcanic emigrations now and then.

From the human point of view, the profound difference between the northern and the southern group of these grasslands, which collectively lie athwart the great east-and-west mountain zone of the Old World, is this. The southern grassland sustains sheep and goats almost exclusively; it acquired its domesticated horses recently (at earliest about 2000 B.C.) and from the north-east; and it relies, for transport, on camels and asses, not on wheeled vehicles. The northern, on the other hand, has sufficient perennial pasture to permit of oxen; it uses horses habitually; and it has utilized the timber of its parkland margin, where it passes over into the northern forest, to construct wheeled carts and ox-ploughs. Equipped with these fundamental implements of civilization, wheel-borne nomads have penetrated the Mountain Zone from the north again and again, introducing the cart into Egypt rather late, and perhaps even into Babylonia; though with these exceptions no secondary centre of cart-folk was ever established in the south. Obvious reasons for this failure lie in the scarcity of parkland and of perennial pasture for large cattle. At best, Assyria and Syria adopted the horsed chariot for war ; but these regions, like the Hittite chariot-users of Asia Minor, the Achaean conquerors of the Greek peninsula, and the Gauls in West-Central Europe, are rather within the parkland fringes of the Mountain Zone, and among those intermont plateaux which we have noted already, than borderers of the Grassland itself. In particular, they are all sedentary, and stand in this respect contrasted with the migratory Scythian cart-folk in the northern Grassland. The only nomad cart-folk within the Mountain Zone are the Gipsies,[1] and they seem mainly to have formed their habit of life in the largest intermont plateau of all, the vast table-land of Persia.

The plough is less easy to trace. All that can be safely said at present is that it is a device for applying the strength of large cattle to break up the soil for a grain crop, deeply and uniformly, and above all more rapidly than a man can dig it with a hoe. By his own effort a man can barely break up enough ground to supply his home with grain, except in irrigated land. With the simplest of ploughs he can do this and more, and yet have leisure for other pursuits within the ploughing season. But it is not yet clear in what region ploughing first began. Probably it was in the comparatively well-watered and well-wooded margin of one of the large grasslands ; but whether north or south of the Mountain Zone, or round the discontinuous plateaux within it, is not clear. The presumption of large cattle favours the north, yet Babylonia, and even Egypt, had large cattle from very early times. North Syria seems to

[1] I owe valuable information about the Gipsies to my friend Dr. John Sampson, of the University of Liverpool ; but he is in no way responsible for this interpretation of it.

dispute with Babylonia priority in the production of wheat. Somewhere in this region we may provisionally place the cradle of what I may perhaps describe as the Bread-and-Cheese culture, in which the staple foods are provided by grain-plants and cattle, the latter being valued for their strength and their milk products, but not primarily for their flesh.

Disseminated westward, the Bread-and-Cheese culture is found to suffer regional modification. Southward, among the Mediterranean evergreen flora and old hoe-cultivation, the dearth of summer grass makes the large cattle useless for milking, as well as for beef; they are bred exclusively for draught, as their gait and structure show, and while cheese is supplied by the sheep and goats, butter and animal-fats are replaced by the vegetable oils, of which the olive is the chief, a characteristic Mediterranean product, evergreen, deep-rooted against summer drought, and fleshy-fruited. A Bread-and-Olive culture results, familiar to all visitors to Mediterranean lands. In the deciduous forests of South-Central Europe there is grass in the clearings, and milk enough; but goats and sheep are restricted, as the undergrowth becomes deeper and denser, and the prime giver of fats is the forest-bred pig: in a land rolling with ham and sausages we reach the Bread-and-Bacon culture. Further afield still, and later, in proportion as the forest is opened out by semi-pastoral folk, the moister summer permits open meadow-land, with perennial grass, and the possibility of hay. Here too the grain crops may be so large that there is something over to fatten stock; and to Bread and Cheese the farmer of the north-western plains adds Beef. When there is coarse grain in plenty, of course, the large-boned horse of the north gradually replaces the ox at the plough, and permits him to be bred, as with ourselves, not for draught at all, but for milking and killing exclusively. It is in this final phase that the Bread-and-Beef culture passes over eventually into the New World, and into the South Temperate Zone.

It has been rather a long story to tell, and full of platitudes, but the gist of it is by this time clear. Whatever be the superstructure of social institutions, of arts and sciences, of religion and philosophy, that European men have built upon it, the régime which has made the Western World what it is, from before the dawn of metallurgy until now, has been generically a Bread culture ; based on that combination of pastoral and agricultural life in which large cattle co-operate with man in the laborious preparation of the soil which cereal crops require. But the Bread culture itself is always supplemented by some form of milk product, of which cheese is typical. It is almost always supplemented further by some special provision of fats; in Mediterranean conditions by olives and oil, involving extensive tree culture ; in the forest region by pig's meat ; and on the Atlantic seaboard by butter and beef.

The exhilarants show the same geographic control ; with the olive culture go the wines and brandies of the south ; with the forest culture, the ciders and the cherry brandies of Central Europe ; with the copious cereals and meadow-grass, the beers and whiskies of the North. In details, of course, the distribution of types is intricately confused ; but the main outline is clear ; and we reach a first glimpse of a coherent European culture, on the almost animal plane of regional foodquests.

RACE, LANGUAGE, AND CULTURE AS FACTORS OF UNITY

Precedence has been given in our inquiry to the mere animal struggle of man with nature for bare subsistence, for two distinct reasons. The first is economic, namely, that just because this struggle is without qualification that of a highly intelligent animal species to maintain itself under these or those conditions, it is one which befalls equally every breed or race of that species which is ever exposed to those conditions; and further, is no more mitigated by considerations of language than by considerations of race. The second reason is historical or archaeological. The spread of the Bread culture is dated so far back in the history of man in this region, as to make it certain that it preceded not merely the spread of the prevalent Indo-European group of languages, but even the present distribution of racial types. It certainly reached Italy, and the Atlantic seaboard as the British Isles, before the brachycephalic 'Alpine' men arrived there; and still more before the Boreal invasions of Britain and the opposite coasts. Indeed, it would be truer to say that in general each breed of man which has changed its distribution has had to adopt sooner or later the types of culture appropriate to the regions into which it has penetrated, than to associate the spread of any element of culture so fundamental as the food-quest with the migrations of any racial type.

Race, indeed, in Europe, as well as further afield, has been anything but a factor of unity. When we speak (on platforms) of Europeans as 'white men', we are in danger of forgetting, what every practical man in our audience knows, that we are dealing with at least three distinct breeds of mankind, which agree, indeed, rather imperfectly in the whiteness of their skin, but differ greatly in other points of structure and physique, including resistance to certain types of climate and regional diseases, and not least in temperament and the quality of their response to Nature's challenges of hardship or indulgence. Of these three breeds of man, only one, the blond Boreal giants (the only 'white men' in the strict sense of defect of pigment in skin, hair, and eyes) is exclusively European now, and has his habitat within the area of the 'Boreal' groups of animals and plants. His champions in ethnological propaganda seem to be of two minds about his earlier distribution; either his 'home' was round the Baltic, in which case it is difficult to see why he should be represented as a civilizing agency, in view of the cultural backwardness of that region; or else it was out on the Eurasian grassland, in which case he is as much an intruder into peninsular Europe as his brachycephalic 'Alpine' rival, and his claim to represent indigenous European man must go. The large part which he has played in European history seems to result partly from his great physical strength, surpassed (I believe) only by that of the Negro, partly from his reluctance, not so much to interbreed with more pigmented strains, but to admit the crossbred offspring to full partnership with himself. Even among his like, he has his own criteria by which one 'white man' knows another, and coheres with him politically.

Most strongly contrasted externally with the 'Boreal' type is the slight-built Mediterranean brunet. That his home is in the south, that he is closely related with the men of the African and Arabian grasslands, and that he was among the first post-glacial explorers of the Atlantic seaboard, is admitted. More doubt arises as to the extent to which he penetrated from these southern and western bases into the heart of peninsular Europe. Certainly as we trace him to the south-east he seems more and more restricted to the Mediterranean coastline, and at last has no early monopoly even of the islands. The contrast between Crete and Cyprus is instructive as to this. The 'Mediterranean' type, in fact, reaffirms to the anthropologist the close zoological affinity between South-west Europe and Northwest Africa.

But if Europe 'ends at the Pyrenees', it ends also anthropologically at the Balkans, or even at the Carpathians; for the whole Balkan Peninsula, and most of the highland core of peninsular Europe, is essentially continuous with

Asia Minor and the next eastward sections of the Mountain Zone, so far as its human population is concerned, no less than in its animals and plants. Biological continuity is as complete at the Bosphorus as it is at Gibraltar. Here, what remains in dispute is not so much whether ' Alpine ' types are ultimately of Anatolian origin, as whether their spread in Europe has been early or late, and whether their predecessors here were predominantly ' Boreal ' or ' Mediterranean '. It is difficult, and perhaps needless, to decide whether lack of evidence or political enthusiasm is more to blame for this ; for the Roundheads of prehistoric and of modern Europe are as contentious matter as their English namesakes in the seventeenth century.

To this broadly threefold analysis of European man, add only this, that ever since the old ' Sarmatian ' sea shrank to its present dimensions and left the grasslands open between Tienshan and the Carpathians, there has been a steady westward movement of Mongoloid folk until a strong enough Muscovy was interposed ; and that along the Northern Woodland also there has been westward movement, slower but no less persistent ; and it will be clear that it is not to race that we have to look for any uniform basis of our European culture.

Nor is such a basis to be found in Language. People often speak of Indo-European speech as though they really confused linguistic affinity with mutual intelligibility. But if you want to test the unifying influence of kindred languages, get a Welshman, a German, a Russian, and a Greek into a room together, and see what the 'concert of Europe ' amounts to. The odds are that if they confer at all, they will do so in French, which is in the strict sense of the word a ' modern ' language ; while if you allowed them to write and gave them time, there is just a chance that the Greek would impose his language on the other three.

There is no need to labour this point further than to recall the fateful bisection of the culture of the European peninsula which resulted from the linguistic alienation of Constantinople from Rome ; of the Mediterranean base which understood Latin, from that which thought in Greek. In this tragic respect, which the Turkish conquest, with its linguistic and religious sequel, has done little more than aggravate, Europe ends still at the Save ; whereas Rome's greatest daughters have reconquered more than all that Carthage ever held in Africa. And the re-incorporation of Britain, too, into the comity of nations is concurrent with the Latinization of its speech, on which the seal was set in 1611. Late as it was, then, in any case, in the prehistory of the region, the spread of a single type of linguistic structure over Europe has brought not peace, but a sword.

What then of Religion ? How far were the older ethnologists on the right lines, when (in spite of language, rather than aided by it) they co-ordinated their own Olympus with the confederate polytheisms of the North ? Here, too, we have to keep the dates in mind, and clear ourselves of enthusiasms. It is not from Tacitus or Caesar, nor even so near to the Olympians' dwelling-place as the Thrace of Herodotus' time, that we get our modern impression of the nearness of Olympus to Asgard. If northern genealogies are any guide,—and they are not likely to have reduced the real interval wittingly—Rome's empire reached its full extent while Asgard was in building, or before. And Olympus was in building, by Greek accounts, not many generations before the Trojan War. In both cases we are dealing with political and almost historical transactions ; it was not in finished societies like these that Great Gods (or their votaries either) set out from ' home ' over the face of Europe to unite it.

And when we pass behind Olympian structures, and look

into the cults which they served to federate, such uniformities as they present prove far too much. The open-air gods of Tacitus (*Germania*, chap. 9) are common to Semitic folk, and to many peoples further afield, who are either not sedentary or are themselves not easily 'confined within walls', but haunt 'forests and groves'.

Leaving, then, these high works of the mind, Language and Religion, which have proved but blind guides, and 'of a short stay' in this labyrinth, let us turn to the material evidence of industrial and aesthetic activity. Here we begin at least to get something like first-hand evidence, for we have the manufactured object itself, not Caesar's impression of a Celtic god, or Herodotus' transcript of a Scythian word. We can judge for ourselves of fabrics and styles, and though, of course, we have only objects of the least perishable sorts, stone, metal, pottery, we have, at all events, in the pottery the most imitative of arts, and therefore the widest basis for conclusions as to the principles of a style. Moreover, outside the sea-borne culture of the Mediterranean, pottery does not travel far: its uses are domestic, not commercial. John Gilpin's fate is typical of those who would carry things on horseback in bottles. Like words, however, potsherds enlighten us more about frontiers and contrasts than about uniformities. They are terribly provincial and tell their tale with a twang. We can trace our *Bandkeramik* and *Schnurkeramik* and *Urfirnissmalerei* and all that sort of technological idiom, across the map, as we can trace the *centum* and *satem* languages. But even if we could collate the 'Bandkeramiker' with the 'Satemvölker' as recent enthusiasts propose, we should be no nearer to a common technology for Europe than we were to a common language.

Metal, and even stone, implements do not help us much further, though they were traded more widely than pottery, and form larger provinces. In modern Europe, in the same way, pocket-knives are rather more uniform than milk-jugs ; and where they differ, are referable to fewer types. But there is no unity, nor for the present any prospect of it. For anything more, we are reduced to the great crises of material culture, such as the introduction of bronze, of iron, of glass and glazed earthenware ; and these we perceive increasingly not as turning points of the whole, but as processes within it, affecting now one region, now another, in a sequence which is clearly geographical and at very variable speed. Bronze, for example, took some thousands of years to permeate the continent of Europe ; iron perhaps as many hundreds ; platinum a little more than fifty years ; and radium less than five.

What we do get from this material evidence, however, is a quite indisputable sequence of styles in time in each locality where we can hit upon stratified remains. Dead men, they say, tell no tales ; potsherds are as truthful and eloquent as they are, for the very reason that, once broken, they are dead and done with, and are allowed to lie quiet in their rubbish heaps. Intervals indeed we cannot so easily measure ; but of sequences we can be sure, and by comparing the sequences on different sites we can go far towards tracing the spread and supersession of a style, sometimes over wide areas, and occasionally, with the help of the geography, we can be pretty sure of the routes by which innovations travelled. We can infer nothing, however, from this as to the movements of people : the vogue of the willow-pattern plate is no measure of our ' yellow-peril '. But where works of art can travel, ideas can travel too ; and can travel right across the frontiers of race and language and even of religion ; meaning at all events by these, the customary observance of each region, and of its endemic population. A few merchants, or craftsmen, or philosophers, work transformations in culture and bring about uniformities, of which language, or cult-edifices

II UNITY IN PREHISTORIC TIMES 61

give us no indication at all, or at best an aftermath of decadence.

It is not a merely ephemeral interest which draws attention at this point to the significance of engines of war, among this class of transferable inventions. Little has been done in a systematic way on this topic, but the rapidity with which a really important change in equipment and organization passes from camp to camp, and revolutionizes not only armies but states, when it is a question of survival or defeat, has its illustration in many phases of warfare, and ranks among the great levellers of national or regional pride.

The recorded movements of peoples in historic times, and the previous movements inferred from language, and other symptoms, indicate a long-established distribution of what might be described in meteorological phrase as *man-pressure*; certain regions being characterized either always or repeatedly by high man-pressure, and an outward flow of men into the cyclonic areas or vortexes of low man-pressure in the human covering (or biosphere) of the planet. Typical high-pressure regions are the Arabian peninsula with its repeated crises of Semitic eruption, and the great Eurasian grasslands. Typical regions of low man-pressure, and repeated irruption, are the South European peninsulas. Occasionally a region plays both parts, alternately accepting inhabitants, and unloading them on to other lands; examples are the Hungarian plain, Scandinavia, and Britain. Others again can hardly be said to have a population of their own at all, but are simple avenues of transmission, like Western Switzerland and the Hellespont Region. I am speaking now, of course, about ancient times. The causes of these recurrent movements are not clearly made out; but the movements themselves, and the fact that they are of regional recurrence, are matters of history.

Conspicuous among such movements are the westward

drift from Asia into peninsular Europe, in its three parallel
columns, through tundra, forest, and steppe ; and the
southward drifts, subsidiary to this, from East Central
Europe into the Balkan lands and round the head of the
Adriatic. The course of these drifts is laid out in detail, as
we have seen, by the physique of the regions ; and therewith is determined the kind of life which each set of folk
must be living if it is to survive the journey.

And here we come at once upon a new factor making
strongly for a more general uniformity of culture within
peninsular Europe than its physical character would at all
prepare us to expect. For although individual men often
respond very rapidly to fresh surroundings, and can change
their mode of life almost as they change their clothes,
societies react far more slowly ; at the pace, in fact, usually
of their most obstinate members. Confronted therefore
with the opportunity, or the need, for a change of habit,
in the course of a migration for example, they must either
refuse it, like a shy horse, or (if they accept it) enter on
their new career imperfectly trained, and extemporizing
adjustments here and there in very unworkmanlike fashion.
Only rarely does the statesman or ' lawgiver ' appear, just
when he is wanted, to bring Israel up out of Egypt into the
desert, and out of the desert into the good land beyond
Jordan, and to canonize a new code of behaviour suited to
a new set of needs. This social inertia, of which political
history is the sorry record, is of course least perceptible,
and most effective, when the region of transition is
graduated gently ; and we have already seen that this is
conspicuously so around the parkland margin of the
northern grassland, where it faces on peninsular Europe.
Let us follow this clue in detail.

We may safely assume, as we have seen, that for a long
while past, every group of newcomers into peninsular
Europe has come equipped with the particular type of

II UNITY IN PREHISTORIC TIMES 63

social organization which enabled it to make good, either on the tundra, or in the northern woodland, or on the steppe, or (if it came across the Bosphorus) on the enclosed plateaux of Asia Minor and beyond. The tundra does not greatly concern us, for the White Sea cuts through it, and deep into the woodland, and bars off the Lapps from the Samoyeds and their kin. Classical descriptions of the inhabitants of the North German plain make it clear that its culture, even so late as the first century B.C., was at its best a broken prolongation of the pastoral life of the steppe margin, and that less fortunate tribes either had never had cattle, like the hunting Redskins of the corresponding forest zone of North America, or had lost them since they entered the forest, and maintained themselves by hunting and robbery like the broken pastorals who infest the east edge of the Congo basin; the Chatti of Tacitus' day enjoying tyrannous hegemony not unlike that of the Five Nations.

It is probably to this westward drift from more purely pastoral condition to less, that we must attribute the only really large unity of European civilization in the later prehistoric ages, namely, its social organization in patriarchal households linked into clans and tribes. We may doubt whether this social type is permanently adaptable to a forest régime, any more than to industrial life. Certainly forest folk outside peninsular Europe only display it rarely and imperfectly. But it is characteristic of all pastoral folk; once established, it coheres and persists under great external stresses; and in early Europe its liability (strong though its structure is) to break up sooner or later into a more individualistic order, was counteracted by the recurrent drift of new grassland peoples westward from one of its principal homes. Grassland Arabia, let us note in passing, has been performing the same function, since history began, for its own marginal neighbours from Babylonia to Palestine and Egypt.

On the other hand, we now see why the feminism which recurs intermittently in our 'western' world culminates in those phases of its history when that world has been strong enough to close its avenues of intrusion for a while; in the far past which has left us the great goddesses and other matrilineal survivals; in industrial Babylonia; in the Minoan palaces; in fifth- and fourth-century Greece, as Aristophanes joins with Euripides to admit, and Euripides with Plato to advocate; in the *Femmes savantes* of renascent Europe; in eighteenth-century France, which seemed to itself so impregnable; and in the *fin-de-siècle* Europe of yesterday, pulling down its barns to build greater.

No one would suggest that this patriarchal and tribal structure favoured political unity or large enterprises of any kind. In fact, throughout the early history of Europe these coherent kinship groups, with their inner insulation and their inability to offer anything but passive resistance to the forces which were to dissolve them, were an insuperable bar to anything politically larger. 'If only these could hold together, they would rule the world' is the judgement of Herodotus on Scythia, of Thucydides on Thrace, of Polybius and Caesar upon Gaul, of Tacitus on Germany: each with the unspoken afterthought 'but thank goodness that they cannot!'

But while it hindered larger growths of political structure, so long as it remained intact, and furnished a strong social skeleton upon which to frame manners and ideals which are among man's highest achievements, patriarchal society had its own dangers, and has now so nearly succumbed to them, that to see its institutions in working order we have to penetrate into Albania or amongst the least modern backwoods of the Slav-speaking east. To take only the leading instance, Greek tribal society dissolved within historic times under the double attack of individualism, industrial and commercial, at the one end, and of the federalism of the city state, at the other. For Aristotle the village-community was the 'colony' (ἀποικία) or direct offspring of the patriarchal household, but he nowhere admits the city-state to be the 'colony' of the village-community. On the contrary, at the risk of upsetting his own theory of the state as a natural outgrowth of man's political nature, he lays stress on 'the man who first introduced them to each other' as the 'author of the greatest advantages'. And it was precisely this process of 'introducing them to one another', so that the members of hitherto autonomous clans became friends instead of enemies, and were thenceforth citizens all, in one and the same city-state, that terminated that period of migrations and political chaos which separates the Minoan from the Hellenic Age in Greek lands. Rome's mission among the tribal societies of Italy is essentially the same; and it is the lack of any such missionary of political enlightenment beyond the frontier of the Roman State in its imperial fullness, that makes early mediaeval problems, which were essentially the same, so slow to be solved.

We are now hard upon the borderland of history, and we take leave of a peninsular Europe—for the grassland stands still outside, as a distinct geographic entity—in which the diverse races, and languages, and religious schemes, and material cultures, are almost wholly propagated under the forms of societies of one homogeneous type, autonomous, indeed, like the states in the loosest of federations, and involved annually, somewhere or other, in intertribal feuds and war; but sufficiently acquainted with each other's customs to know that they were based on the same large needs, not merely of 'living' somehow but of 'living well', and to respect this common heritage of intertribal customs, so far that in their uttermost dealings with admitted aliens they were wont to 'make war like gentlemen '. To Homer's audience it was sure proof that Odysseus was really ' at the back of nowhere ', when the Cyclops was unable to behave when a stranger came to his cave : he was a monster, of knowledge not according to the rules '.[1] It was a criticism of despair, like that of M. Lévy-Bruhl: for the Cyclops had the ' will to power '.[2]

Here, then, was a social structure and a political world, an *oikoumené* where *men* could *live*, tolerant of fairly wide variations in detail, within a general uniformity : for tribal society in Middle Italy or even in Western Greece, as we first catch sight of it, was by no means homogeneous with tribal society beyond the Alps in the times of Caesar and Tacitus. But apart from these variations, tribal Europe was a coherent whole ; and it was so because, and as long as, no new problems of adjustment between Man and Nature arose to upset the balance struck by that Bread-culture with which we were concerned just now. For the patriarchal tribal societies, as we watch them still in Albania for example, are neither more nor less than the political aspect of that culture, and their varieties and deviations stand in close correlation with the varieties which we have seen the Bread-culture assume.

In the same way, the break-down of this social structure proceeds, step by step, in relation with the two great changes to which normal Bread-culture is exposed. On the one hand, primitive self-sufficiency (the retrospective ideal of Greek political thought) was infringed irrevocably as soon as contact was made with a region, like ancient Scythia, where, as Herodotus puts it, ' there are no earthquakes and they grow wheat to sell ' ; for in the Mountain Zone you are never secure against shocks, and almost never

[1] *Odyssey* ix. 428 πέλωρ, ἀθεμίστια εἰδώς.
[2] *Odyssey* ix. 214-15:
ἄνδρ' ἐπελεύσεσθαι μεγάλην ἐπιειμένον ἀλκήν,
ἄγριον, οὔτε δίκας εὖ εἰδότα οὔτε θέμιστας.

have any surplus of grain. Once in oversea contact with lands like these, it became more economical to buy grain thence, and to pay for it by increasing the production of oil and wine, than to grow everything at home ; and a new and ' limitlesss ' source of wealth emerged in the process of exchange.

On the other hand, oil and wine needing far less labour than grain-crops and offering longer leisure (which for Greeks meant the chance to start doing something else), the contemporary revelation of mineral wealth, and of many forms of craftsmanship, again largely (though not wholly) introduced from oversea, created another source of wealth, no less ' limitless ' and dangerously unmanageable, in a world where wealth of any kind was literally ' so little good '. And this industrial wealth, like its commercial counterpart, was personal wealth, owed wholly to skill and push, and in no way due to your clansmen or your clan. When the poet cursed the discovery of metals, he put his finger on the ' key-industry ' of the whole industrial development ; and when he cursed the invention of shipping, he struck at the root-trouble of all, which had revealed to autonomous Bread-cultured tribes in peninsular Europe lands otherwise constituted and endowed by Nature, the exploitation of which seemed in the beginning so easy and obvious, but is, in fact, so profound a revolution for the societies whose members have attempted it. The tree of the knowledge of good and evil was for him the shipbuilding pine.[1]

---

[1] Horace, *Epode* xvi. In his ' better land '—
   Non huc Argoo contendit remige pinus,
      Neque impudica Colchis intulit pedem. . . .
   Iuppiter illa piæ *secrevit* litora genti,
      Ut inquinavit ære tempus aureum ;
   Ære, dehinc ferro duravit sæcula ; quorum
      Piis secunda, vate me, datur fuga.

But the dissolution of early European society and culture under the stress of contact with regions outside Europe is no matter of prehistoric times. The task of this essay is over when it has presented that society and culture as Man's reasoned attempt to 'live well' in an exclusively European world.

Books for Reference

Marett, *Anthropology*. Home University Library.
J. L. Myres, *The Dawn of History*. Home University Library.

III

THE CONTRIBUTION OF GREECE AND ROME

It might appear the height of paradox to preface a discourse on the Ancient World by asserting the conviction that the only genuine and important history is contemporary history. Yet reflection on this doctrine will show that it is not only consistent with a serious and steady interest in what is called Antiquity (and indeed in the past in general), but its only rational basis and justification. Were the past really past it were dead—dead and done with, and it were wisdom for us who are alive to let the dead bury their dead. Much of what has been done and suffered under the sun is indeed gone beyond recall, and is well buried in forgetfulness. In such forgetfulness lies the fact and evidence of progress. ' Vex not its ghost '; no necromancy will or should evoke the departed spirits or avail to make them utter significant speech to living men. The chain of links which once bound stage to stage of human history is somewhere for ever broken; and as we retrace, in the memory of the race or in that of individual, the Ariadne-clue which we here call ' the unity of History ' it vanishes somewhere beyond our vision into the dark backward and abysm of time. True, of late Archaeology and Anthropology have cast their search-lights into the darkness, piercing a little deeper than of old into the mists that surround the origins of our civilization; but before that dimly illuminated region of pre-history there still lies, and will always lie, an impenetrable pall. As again in thought we move forward down the stream of time, the light available to us for a while increases, increases till we reach the present where it threatens to blind us with its dazzling excess, and then suddenly fades and is quenched in the twilight and final darkness by which the future is hidden from us. Of the whole stream of history our best or utmost intelligence illuminates but a short reach, and that imperfectly.

'Our ignorance is infinitely greater than our knowledge,' and the wise historian is sobered but not discouraged by this reminder of the limits of his possible understanding. Neither the remote past nor the distant future can be the objects of knowledge nor, properly speaking, the subjects of judgement. If our insatiate curiosity has bounds thus eternally set to its satisfaction, we remember also that it is not either in the past or the future that we live, that we act and are acted upon, determine or have determined for us what we do or are to do, what we suffer or are to suffer. The present alone is real, and of the real alone is genuine knowledge possible. But if this is so, it is also so that of this alone does it import us to ascertain the true nature. What we have to discover (or perish in our blindness) is what we now are and where we now stand. All other so-called knowledge or understanding, save as it ministers to the framing of a true judgement concerning our present selves and our present situation and world, is but vanity or lumber, at best a rhetorical device for bringing before ourselves or others what we so judge concerning the one and the other. Genuine understanding, however it disguise itself as chronicle or prophecy, is always of the present or nothing.

But this present is not the momentary meeting-place of two eternities or the brief span of time which psychologists have named 'the specious present'. Its content is whatsoever is not the dead past or the unborn future; it is whatever is still or already alive, whatever is yet or already operative and formative in our inward selves

III GREECE AND ROME

or our outward environment—in a word what is contemporary, contemporary with our present doings and sufferings. To such a present it is idle to attempt to fix limits of date before or behind. A new conception of the unity of History rises before us as we realize that the Past and the Future are not *severed* by the Present, but that these meet and are made one in its living and concrete actuality. This is the fact, the centre to which all radii converge and from which they diverge again; and in the Present the Past and the Future live and are, together and all at once.

Bearing this in mind, we approach the records of history in a new spirit and with a new hope. We desire to know neither origins nor ends, we expect no cosmogony and we look for no apocalyptic vision. What we aim at understanding is what we now are and where we now stand, and we realize that to understand this we must not restrict our study to what is merely of recent acquisition or growth. Neither ourselves nor our environment are bounded by chronological limits; both are contemporary with the Pyramids just as much as with the Eiffel Tower. We are not merely the heirs but the epitomes of the ages. As our bodies are but the present forms on which the secular forces of the earth continue their dateless activities, so our spirits, our minds, our very selves are the forms in which other spirits now forgotten or dimly remembered still live and move and have their being, fulfilling the work which, while still their names were named, they initiated or advanced. Not in pious gratitude only must we labour to rescue their memory from fast-coming oblivion, but because only so can we reach that knowledge of ourselves and our world which is to us as living men all and alone important. Nor will such study deny to us the reward we seek. So approaching the labours of the historian, we shall not be jealous because

he comes before us with a tale, or as we call it, with a
'story'—a narrative of 'old unhappy things and battles
long ago'. For though he so puts it, spacing it out in
sections, half-concealing, half-revealing its logical connexions and ultimate unity, its real meaning, its ultimate
—which is also its present—import is an account of what
we now are and the situation in which we now stand;
and unless somehow for each of us its message comes into
such an account, distils and sublimates into such a
quintessential judgement on the present, History remains
but 'a tale of sound and fury, signifying nothing'. It
is in the profoundest sense useless to us unless in the end
we can say '*De nobis fabula narratur*'—it is *our* history
to which we have been listening.

This is especially true of the history of the Ancient
World—the world of classical antiquity. It is not a dead
world; its deeds and thoughts are not past but still live,
still 'breathe and burn' in us. They are largely the stuff
of which our present selves and our present world are
made. Not merely, I repeat, in the sense that then were
the foundations of both laid, not merely in the sense that
we are heirs to the labours of our ancestors. We *are* the
Greeks and the Romans, made what we now are by
their deeds and thoughts and experiences, our world their
world, at a later stage of an evolution never interrupted
but always one and single. Our births and deaths are
but a sleep and a forgetting in the unbroken biography
of a spirit, not above but in us all, which is the hero of
the history of European civilization, itself a part of the
history of Humanity. Thus the history of Antiquity, and
especially of Classical Antiquity, is the record of the
thoughts and deeds of our own youth.

> Our deeds (and also our thoughts) still travel with us
>   from afar,
> And what we have been makes us what we are.

This is the spirit and the conviction in which I would invite you to approach the study of Classical Antiquity —not merely in that of gratitude and reverence, not certainly in that of idle and futile curiosity, but as seekers for knowledge of yourselves and your world. For what other knowledge matters?

This quest is but the beginning of a search which is and must be lifelong. Perhaps I am wrong in calling it the beginning, and there are others who would and do bid you begin earlier. I can only ask you to begin where I began or begin myself. At any rate if you begin later or elsewhere I am confident that you will lose much light on your present selves and your present world. My own temptation has been rather to stop too soon and so to overleap the intervening period—the 'Middle Ages'— between such Antiquity and the Present. Fortunately for you, you have guides who will point out to you the way of a profitable and instructive journey across the— to me—unknown or imperfectly explored land. I must, however, in no controversy with any of my fellow lecturers here, say a word on the contention that the true beginning of the modern mind and its world—our mind and our world—lies later and elsewhere than in Classical Antiquity. The birthday and birthplace of that mind and its world have been variously fixed. We have been bidden to find the one, say, as late as the sixteenth century and the other—not from the same point of view—in the plains and woods of Northern Europe or in the deserts of Arabia or in some still more vaguely indicated region of the East. But I must avow my conviction that our civilization—and I specially remember that we are Englishmen—is not only in origin but in essence, Greco-Roman, modified no doubt by influences unknown to that in its earlier stages, but still Greco-Roman grown to a larger stature and a clearer self-consciousness, self-shaped to its present form, the same vital and vitalizing force, constantly reinvigorated and re-enlightened by reflection upon its own past. It is a true instinct that in this country still bases our system of higher education upon a study of the languages and literature of Classical Antiquity. We are, as Englishmen, co-heirs, because co-descendants of Classical Antiquity, with France and Italy and Greece, yes also with Germany, for European civilization—and not European civilization only—is, I reiterate, in essence still Greco-Roman, not Teutonic or Semitic. At least, if this inheritance is not ours by descent it is ours by adoption, and we are equally legitimate members of the household. And the bonds of such spiritual kinship are closer and more durable than those of blood, if indeed those of blood provably exist at all.

The works and thoughts of which I am to speak—the dreams, the plans, the hopes and aspirations—are assuredly ours also, the stuff and substance of our being, our inner *genius*, our guiding and controlling selves, what we in our first youth imagined and conceived, what we believed, what we, in our later maturity, designed and in part executed. If we turn inward we cannot read them there, for the characters are small and faded; but as we hear their history recounted as it is by professional historians, we recognize it as the record of a past which is our very own, while at the same time it is a past which we share with other nations who are our co-partners in the work of conserving, deepening, extending, enriching the present-day civilization of Europe and the world.

In most of us at all times, and in all of us at most times, these influences and their operations lie deep below the threshold of consciousness, some of them deeper than any plummet of self-analysis can sound. They are also the unseen foundations of the social and political superstructure in which we live. Or, to use another figure, they form the fertile soil in which we, with all our activities and institutions, are rooted and from which we draw no small part of our spiritual sustenance. Hence it is highly pertinent here and now to examine them, for in this identity of foundation is to be found the primary unity of the now diffused life of Europe which has parted into so many and so widely divergent currents of national life. We all come spiritually from the same ancient home, and it is well and wise to recall its memories. So we and others shall be the more disposed to re-knit the old bonds and to weave new ones which may one day restore on a grander scale, in more organized fullness and more efficacious potency, the primordial unity which interests and passions have with rude violence, at least in appearance, disrupted and dissolved and so for a time arrested or enfeebled.

I have many predecessors in the task of answering the question, What do we owe to the Greeks? Any answer which I have to offer, must, in the compass at my disposal, be imperfect; it must also be abstract; and lastly it cannot but be in form dogmatic. But I think it is not too much to say that it is to the Greeks that we owe the very conception of civilization and through that in large measure its very existence. The truth of this is more evident if we put the truth in another way, saying that the Greeks first explicitly recognized the contrast between the barbarous and the civilized state of mankind, and delivered themselves and us from the former by defining the latter and attempting, not without success, to establish it in actual reality. No doubt before them men had felt the pressure of barbarism within and without, and had framed dreams of something better, but it was the Greeks who first defined and conceived the ideal and so made it possible to realize it. Their distinctive peculiarity lay in their setting themselves not merely to imagine but to think out an ideal of civilized life, and narrowly and abstractly as to the end they conceived this ideal, they discerned the main essential lines of its structure, the permanent laws of its development and well-being. In doing this they discovered the need and efficacy of knowledge for the conduct of human life, individual and collective; and found in knowledge no mere means to living but a new and heightened form of life itself, lifted above the trammelling conditions, the disillusionments and disappointments of the merely practical life. Thus they created Science and Philosophy, bequeathing to us the ideals and the results of the one and the other. We may so far define their contribution as consisting in the thought of Civilization-through-knowledge, a thought which was not a thought only but a potent and effective instrument of action, not a mere ideal but an ideal governing, directing, and realized, in action and life.

We have also to recognize another most powerful influence of which they were the vehicles—closely related to the other. The Greeks first articulately conceived and deliberately pursued the ideal of Freedom. It was, I say, closely related to the other, for they meant by it not merely freedom from physical or political constraint but also inward freedom from prejudice and passion, and they held that knowledge and freedom rendered one another possible. We may amend our formula and re-state their contribution as the idea and fact of civilization regarded as a process in and to Freedom under the control of Knowledge or Reason, each inspiring, guiding, and fertilizing the other. Theory and practice thus co-operate and help one another forward; each in its advance liberates the other for a further effort. The several faculties of the human spirit work harmoniously together in mutual respect and reciprocal alliance. Hence arises another distinctive feature of the Greek ideal, namely, that of wholeness or all-round completeness; there is in it no one-sided insistence on this or that element in human nature, no tendency to ascetic mutilation, no fear or jealousy of what is merely human, tainted by its animal origin or its secular associations.

But we must not exaggerate. This ideal was imperfectly defined, still more imperfectly executed or realized. It would be absurd to suppose that it was held by all Greeks; it was indeed advocated by and for a minority only. Those who now find in it the impulse and guide of Greek history might be hard put to it if they were obliged to produce evidence of their faith, and they would be forced to confess that there was much to be said against their interpretation. There is to be acknowledged first the apparent want of internal unity in the Greek world, split up as it was into small and mutually hostile civic groups; and secondly, the loose coherence of each of these groups within itself (for each, we might almost say normally, was torn by intestine faction). It is a commonplace also that Greek civilization rested upon slavery, so that barbarism was not expelled but remained as a domestic and ever-present evil. Freedom and enlightenment was not in thought or practice designed for all men, but only for Greeks, and among them only in reality for a privileged minority. The notion of a civilized world or even a civilized Greece was, if present at all, present only in feeling or imagination, not in clear vision or distinct thought, still less as an ideal of practical politics. On the other hand the ideal so narrowly conceived was not *in principle* confined to a ' chosen people ', or to one strain of blood. It supplied a programme extensible to all who could show their title to be regarded as members of the common race of humanity. As the special features of Greek civilization faded, the lineaments of this common humanity emerged more clearly into view, and the Greek, when he was compelled to give up his parochialism and provincialism, found himself already in spirit prepared to take his place as a citizen of the world. He had learned his lesson, and to him the whole world went to school, first to learn of him what civilization meant and then to better his instructions.

This the world did, but not once for all; for every time since that mankind, or at least European mankind, has begun to lose faith in its dream of civilization or has again to shake itself free from the menace of outward or inward barbarism, it has always reverted to the thought and life of Greece and drawn inexhaustibly from it new light and new fruit, for it is its own thought and its own life, while still there ran in its veins the freshness and the vigour, the blitheness and hopefulness of its immortal youth. In meditating upon the unforgotten debt which we owe to Greece, we revive in memory what the spirit which now lives and moves in us not only once accomplished but still in each new generation accomplishes, accomplishing ever the better if it repeats its former achievements with increased consciousness and more deliberate care. We too here and now have to define what we mean by civilization, by knowledge, by freedom. Otherwise our future will be determined for us, and not by us. ' What is to come out of this struggle ? Just anything that may come out of it, or something we mean *shall* come out of it ? ' Assuredly, if we are not to stand bankrupt before our present problem, we must go to school with Greece, with Rome, with Classical Antiquity, and in the end with all History, that is to say, with our own experience as a whole ; or out of the spreading chaos no civilized cosmos will be re-born. Our civilization has been shaken to its foundations, the task before us and our descendants is to rebuild once more in Europe a habitable city for the mind of man; and in designing and reconstructing it we must take counsel with our predecessors who first found the way of escape from outward and inward barbarism, doing for and in us what we would do for and in our successors.

The first and most obvious achievement of the Greek mind was the deliverance of itself in the sphere of the imagination. Behind the fair creations of Greek art lies a dark and ugly background, but it does lie behind them. That was its first conquest. Under the magic spell of Art the hateful and terrifying shapes of barbarous religion retreated and the world of imagination was peopled with gracious and attractive figures. The Greek Pantheon is, for all its defects, a world of dignified and beautiful humanity. ' No thorn or threat stains its beauty bright.' On the whole the gods which are its denizens are humanized and humane, the friends and allies of men, who therefore feel themselves not abased or helpless in their relations with them. ' Of one kind are gods and men,' and their common world is one in which men feel themselves at home. Dark shadows there are, but they hide no mysteries to appal and unman. The imagination is free to follow its own laws, and so to create what is lovely and lovable. Language is no longer a tyrant but a willing and dexterous servant, and the Greek language reflecting, as all language does, the spirit of its users, is the most perfect instrument that the human mind has ever devised for the expression of its dreams. The works which were then created have ever since haunted the mind of Europe like a passion, and we are right in speaking of them as immortal, ' a joy for ever '.

In such a manner the Greek mind humanized its world, and in doing so humanized itself, or rather divinized itself, without stretching to the breaking-point the strands which bound itself to its world. But it did not stop there, and we do it wrong if we dwell too exclusively on its triumphant achievements in literature and art. For 'speech created thought, which is the measure of the universe'. The Greeks were not only supreme artists but also the pioneers of thought. They first took the measure of the Universe in which they lived, asserting the mind of man to be its measure, and it amenable and subject to reason. The world they lived in was not only beautiful to the imagination, it was also reasonable, penetrable, and governable by the intellect. The ways of it and everything in it were regular and orderly, predictable, explicable not eccentric, erratic, baffling and inscrutable. Not only was Nature knowable; it was also through knowledge of it manageable, a realm over which man could extend his sway, making it ever a more and more habitable home. In it and availing himself of its offered aid he built his households and his cities, dwelling comfortably in his habitations. But the thought which enabled him to lay a secure basis, economic and social or political, for his life had other issues and promised other fruit. The Greek mind became interested in knowledge for its own sake and in itself as the knower of its world.

The second and more important creation of the Greek mind was Science or the Sciences. In no earlier civilization can we trace anything but the faintest germs of this, while in Greek civilization it comes almost at once to flower and fruit. First and foremost we have to think of Mathematics, of Arithmetic and Geometry and Optics and Acoustics and Astronomy, but we must not forget also their later and perhaps not wholly so successful advances in Physics and Chemistry, in Botany and Zoology, in Anatomy and Physiology. Doubtless, especially in the case of the Sciences where experiments are required and have proved so fertile in the extension of our knowledge, there were grave defects, and too much trust was placed in mere observation and hasty speculation; but what they accomplished in Science is no less but more marvellous than what they accomplished in Art. The idea of Science was there, disengaged from the limiting restrictions of practical necessities, the idea of free and therefore all the more potent Science. The whole physical—and much more than the physical—environment of human life was proclaimed permeable to human thought and therefore governable by human will or at any rate already amicable and amenable to human purposes.

But yet a third advance was made. The Greek mind became conscious of itself as the knower and therefore the lord and master of its world. Turning inward upon itself it discovered itself as the centre of its universe and set itself to explore this new inner realm of being. In the consciousness of itself it found inexhaustible interest and strength. Thus it created Philosophy, its last and greatest gift to humanity. In so doing it freed itself from the trammels even of Science, which thus became its servant and not its master—at the same time finally liberating itself from the narrowing and blinding influences of passion and imagination and all the shackles of merely practical needs and disabilities. Here too it fixed the idea or the ideal. 'Life without reflection upon life, without self-examination and self-study and self-knowledge, is a life not worth living by man.' In doing so it revealed a self deeper than the physical being of man and an environment wider and more real—more stable and permanent—than the physical cosmos, finding in the one and the other something more enduring, substantial, and precious than shows itself either to Science or the economic and political prudence, yet which alone gives meaning and worth to the one and the other. Thus for the first time arose before the mind of man the conception of a life not sunk in nature and practice, but superior to them and the end or meaning of their existence—a life of intense activity, of unfailing interest, of inexhaustible and eternal value.

This life was throughout the duration of Greek thought too narrowly conceived. It was frequently thought and spoken of as the life of a spectator or bystander or onlooker, as a life withdrawn or isolated, cut off from what we should call ordinary human business and concerns, a life into which we, or at least a few of us, could escape or be transported at rare intervals and under exceptionally favourable circumstances. Yet in principle it was open to all, and certainly not confined to those privileged by birth or wealth or social position. It was not the reward of magical favour or ascetic exercises, it was reached by the beaten path of the loyal citizen and the resolute student. There was about it no esoteric mystery or other-worldliness. And if to reach it was a high privilege its attainment brought with it the imperative duty of a descent into the ordinary world to instruct, to enlighten, to comfort and help and console, to play a part in the great business and work of human civilization. In a sense this was, and is, the most permanent and fruitful gift of Greece to the European world.

These then were the three ideas or ideals which the Greeks wrought into the very texture and substance of the modern mind, the idea of Art, the idea of Science, the idea of Philosophy; in all three introducing and still more deeply implanting the ideas of Freedom as the motive and end of civilized life and of Knowledge as its guide and ally. It may be thought that I have dwelt too much on theory, and have not said enough of the specific contribution of Greece as working out in practice a certain type or types of corporate life such as the City State; but the fact is that in Greek civilization theory continually outran practice and that it endowed mankind much more with ideas or ideals than with practical illustrations or models for our imitation. Yet again we must not exaggerate or imagine these ideas as merely Utopian or such stuff as dreams are made of. The ferment which they set up burst the fabric of Greek social and political institutions, but it clarified and steadied down, as the enthusiasms of youth may do, into the sober designs of grave and energetic manhood.

The spectacle of the dissolution of the Greek civilization is not a pleasant one. ' The glory that was Greece ' fades out of the world and leaves it grey and dull, and there was worse than this ; there was also decay and degeneracy and corruption. To dwell upon it is as the sin of Ham. Nevertheless what took place was not a mere relapse towards barbarism, but on the contrary the supersession of a form of civilization which had done its work by another form less attractive, but more sound and solid. The Romans have the airs of grown and grave men beside the perpetual youth of Greece, (the Greeks were ' always children ') but they are well aware of how much they learned and had to learn from their predecessors in the task of civilizing the world. So much is this so that in many departments of civilized life they look upon themselves as imitating the Greeks and carrying out their ideas. In this they were less than just to themselves, for even in the world of art they continued to create ; and certainly in literature they produced works not unworthy to stand beside their chosen models. Especially they created a prose style, which without ceasing to be artistic served the sober and serious purposes of political oratory and historic record. But their peculiar genius showed itself most in the applied arts which pressed Greek science into the ministry of life in architecture and engineering. Their roads and bridges and aqueducts still stand to bear witness of them. It would be a great error to deny to them fertile advance in the sciences, because their discoveries are so immediately put to the proof in practice and so little disengage themselves into express theory from their applications.

But before we proceed to reckon up their contributions to European civilization it is well to correct a misconception which arises only too easily from an accident of our education. It is the custom in England to concentrate attention upon a brief period in the history of Rome, ignoring on the one hand the early Republican period and on the other the later Imperial. There is thus lost to our imaginations those figures and their deeds which seemed for example to Shakespeare most characteristically Roman and to our more thoughtful consideration those achievements which most deeply moulded the fabric of Europe. The latter is the greater loss, and here we must remember that it is the history of *Imperial* Rome that is most relevant to our purpose and most informative. Under the Empire Rome worked as a master, no longer as an apprentice or a journeyman. The theatre of her civilizing activities was here little less than the whole world then known, and the boast is not unjustified that she made into a city what had formerly been but a world, as we might say, merely a geographical expression. The record of that progress reads to us too much as a narrative of incessant warfare, and we are accustomed to think of her empire as a gigantic military power, but in reality it was in aim and result essentially pacific, and so appeared to those who lived under her sway. To them the name of her empire was the ' Roman peace '. It was as such that the memory of it haunted the minds of men when it too broke down from internal economic disorders and external pressure, and a distracted and divided Europe looked back to it as the pattern for a restored civilization.

The aim and result of the Roman Empire was peace,

a world-wide peace. It is true that this end was not very articulately defined by those who pursued it, but (perhaps just because of that) the means to it were more practically designed and more effectively executed. The civilized world was one and to be treated as one ; it was still Rome under a single government and a single head. There arose then the idea of a supreme sovereignty one and indivisible, that was the absolutely indispensable condition of a world peace. But the necessity of organization was equally grasped, insisted upon, realized. The civilized world was covered with a network of institutions through which the will of the Emperor flowed and circulated throughout the Empire. Peace through system and order—that was the secret of the Roman success. But two other ideas must be added to complete the explanation. The one was the idea or ideal of Justice ; no system and no order could work unless it was, and commended itself to its subjects as being, scrupulously and exactly just. The second idea was that in order to be this it must be a legal system, based upon a known body of legal rights and duties, determining and controlling the whole conduct of the subjects to the sovereign and to one another. The notion which the Romans, not so much by their thought or speech, but by their acts, added to the world's stock was that of a peace secured and maintained by the just operation throughout the civilized world of a system of law the same for all, issuing from and enforced by a single central power.

The notion is at least grandiose, and so stated seems almost too high and difficult for human nature to realize. Yet for centuries it was applied, and applied with marvellous success. Nor in spite of its apparent failure in the end has the idea of it ceased to dominate men's minds. I do not speak here of the transitory imitation of it by the Carolingians or of the attempt at the restitution or copy of it in the spiritual sphere of the Church, or again of its phantom survival in the ghostly form of the Holy Roman Empire. But I would point to the way in which it still—in thought—controls us when without essential alteration of the idea we transfer its application to the nation and still look for the secret of *its* peace and strength in an organization of all its activities under a law proceeding from and enforced by a sovereign will resident somewhere within its structure, a law demanding and receiving obedience from all loyal subjects. Nor is the hope extinct that the way to a wider or world-wide peace lies through the restoration of a similar system in its application to international relations. Though I am unable to share this hope (or indeed the desire that its realization should be endeavoured after), I find it impossible to judge that it has yet lost its hold on men's minds or is without elements of importance in view of our present problem and perplexity.

It is perhaps more profitable to ask what we have to learn from the history both of its success and its failure. Of its success for a time and long time in the history of Europe there can be no doubt, and on its permanent effects rests much of what is most sound and stable in the civilization of modern Europe. Peace there was because of it, and again because of it and what it accomplished Europe resisted and survived internal disorder and barbarian invasion so that, as I said above, what still exists as a united or allied Europe is the Roman or Romanized world. Roman ideas and ideals still hold it together, although the Roman Empire has declined and fallen, and no other Empire has risen or, I trust, may rise, upon its ruins. It is not my business to analyse the causes of that decline and fall, though a few words on them may not be out of place. In the first place it declined and fell because those who administered ignored its economic substructure, paying no attention to the causes which were undermining its very material basis, or the enormous suffering which the neglect and consequent disorganization of that entailed. In the second, and partly because of that neglect, they did not sufficiently strengthen its defences against external attack; I do not so much mean in the way of remissness in military preparation as by a surcease of the former policy of bringing their barbarous or semi-civilized neighbours into the higher system, and so extending the range of civilization. It is perhaps fanciful to suggest that we are now suffering the penalty of the failure of Rome to Romanize, that is to say, to civilize their Teutonic neighbours. In the third place, they erred by not recognizing and taking account of new forces which in the way of ideas were entering into the conception of civilized life, the ideas which we mass together under the head of feudalism, the idea of nationality. Under the influence of the one and the other the ideal of a single world State, with a uniform or rigid system of laws resting upon a sovereign will, one and indivisible, dissolved, or at least entered upon dissolution, approving itself unadapted or unadaptable to the needs of a novel and immensely more complex situation of the world. No mere tinkering at it did or could suffice to save it; and the organization of Europe based upon it collapsed.

The Revolution of the end of the eighteenth and the beginning of the nineteenth centuries was in many ways the last attempt to reinstate it, and failure to do so pronounced its doom. We cannot now look forward to the reorganization of civilized Europe on the model of the Roman Empire or of an Empire at all, and the more definitely formulated hope of salvation by the erection or re-erection of an international system of law in any real sense seems to me an unsubstantial dream—the administration of a belated nostrum for our disease, not a panacea. Not that way do the lessons of history point. The Roman ideal must be transformed, must be reborn, if it is not to lead our anticipations and our actions wholly astray. No more in the political or secular sphere than in the spiritual or ecclesiastical is ' Romanism ' a possible guide to the reconstruction of modern European civilization. For that far too much water (and blood) has run under the bridge. Yet the spirit which gave it life and efficacy is immortal, and the study of the secret of its vitality and power is a necessity for us. In the work of reconstruction we must learn from the Romans the value of System and Order, of Justice and Law, as from Greece we have ever afresh to learn the love of Freedom and Truth.

The Greeks have given us the idea of a life worth living which civilization renders possible, but does not directly produce. This life in its essential features they rightly conceived, but its content they failed to articulate, and whether because of that or not, they failed to realize its indispensable conditions, material, economic, political, &c. The Romans did more effectively realize this, but they lost sight of the ends in the means, securing a peace, a comfort, an ease, a leisure of which they made no particularly valuable use. It has been said that at no time in the world's history were civilized men so happy as under the Roman Empire. It might be said with greater truth that at no time were civilized men so unhappy, for the happiness that was theirs was empty, mere dead-sea fruit, dust and ashes in the mouth ; a very Death in Life. Life was without savour, and they turned away from it in weariness and disgust and despair, seeking and finding in Philosophy—the fruits of reflection upon life—nothing better than consolation for the wounds and disillusions of life. Thus those who gave their lives to Rome lost heart, and retreating into themselves found nothing there but solitude and emptiness. Civilization was but the husk of a life that had fled.

Nevertheless, as it is necessary for the living body to deposit a bony skeleton and for the living soul to harden its impulses into habits and stiffen its aspirations into rules and plans of action, so civilization as a whole must create within and around it a structure of ordered and systematic thought and action within which the higher forces now recognized and disengaged may be all the more free to do their work. Without such a mechanical or apparently unspiritual basis these forces can only work fugitively, erratically, and so ineffectively, as they did in the Greek world. To the prosaic business of creating or recreating and maintaining in being such a structure a large part of our energies must be devoted, and in all this from the Romans we have still much to learn. If we decline to learn and digest this lesson, turning from such concernment in disgust or disdain, our lives will be lost in vain dreams, in idle longings and empty regrets ; and the kingdom of Freedom and Truth will be taken from us and given to others who have known how to grow up and to face like men the hardships and hazards without which it cannot be won or held. From the inspiring visions of these ideals we must turn as we did when we and our world were Roman, to the serious and sober task of creating a political and legal structure on which the eternal spirit of European civilization can resume its work of extending, deepening, enriching, the common life of Humanity.

It seems as if we—the heirs of their experience—bound to face a more appalling problem, are bankrupt, even of hopes, having lost both the ideal of a life worth living on this earth and that of some large and complex organization rendering this life possible. But this is not so, for the forces which in Antiquity created and for long maintained a civilization at first desirable and then strong, are not spent. Still they make the Greco-Roman civilization which is ours a thing worth living and dying for ; still they hold us together in a unity and concord deeper than ever plummet can sound, obscured but not destroyed by the present noise and confusion of battle. Still at heart we care—and not we only but also our enemies and all neutrals benevolent or malevolent—for the ends for which civilization exists, for the peace and order and justice which are their necessary conditions : we still have minds to devise and wills to execute whatever is necessary to its progress. Still we are willing to learn of history and resolved to better its instruction, to know ourselves and our world and adjust our ideas and our acts to the situation in which we find ourselves. The civilized world has not lost heart or hope ; and will not, so long as the dreams of its immortal youth and the plans of its immortal manhood are not lost to its memory or passed beyond its retrospective reflection.

Note. The doctrine that all History is contemporary History has been best set forth by Benedetto Croce, of Naples, from whose works several expressions have here been borrowed, with a profound acknowledgement of indebtedness to him.

BOOKS FOR REFERENCE

Hegel, *Philosophy of History*, Parts II and III (to be read not as philosophy, but as history guided and enlightened by philosophy). Translation in Bohn's Library.

Marvin, *The Living Past*. Clarendon Press.

Adamson, *The Development of Greek Philosophy*. W. Blackwood. (For a brief but pregnant account consult Webb's *History of Philosophy*. Home University Library.)

Butcher's *Some Aspects of the Greek Genius* (' What we owe to Greece '). Macmillan.

Murray's *Rise of the Greek Epic*. Clarendon Press.

Warde Fowler's *Rome*. Home University Library.

Bryce's *Holy Roman Empire*. Macmillan.

IV

UNITY IN THE MIDDLE AGES[1]

Ergo humanum genus bene se habet et optime, quando secundum quod potest Deo adsimilatur. Sed genus humanum maxime Deo adsimilatur quando maxime est unum ; vera enim ratio unius in solo illo est. Propter quod scriptum est : ' Audi, Israel, Dominus Deus tuus unus est '. DANTE, *De Monarchia*, I. viii.

I

HE who shuts his eyes to-day to make a mental picture of the world sees a globe in which the mass of Asia, the bulk of Africa, and the length of America vastly outweigh in the balance the straggling and sea-sown continent of Europe. He sees all manner of races, white and yellow, brown and black, toiling, like infinitesimal specks, in every manner of way over many thousands of miles ; and he knows that an infinite variety of creeds and civilizations, of practices and beliefs—some immemorially old, some crudely new ; some starkly savage, and some softly humane—diversify the hearts of a thousand million living beings. But if we would enter the Middle Ages, in that height and glory of their achievement which extended from the middle of the eleventh to the end of the thirteenth century, we must contract our view abruptly. The known world of the twelfth century is a very much smaller world than ours, and it is a world of a vastly greater unity. It is a Mediterranean world ; and ' Rome,

[1] I should like to dedicate this essay to my friend and old pupil, the Rev. Bede Jarrett, O.P., to whom I owe much, and to whose book on *Mediaeval Socialism* I should like to refer my readers.

the head of the world, rules the reins of the round globe '. From Rome the view may travel to the Sahara in the south; in the east to the Euphrates, the Dniester, and the Vistula ; in the north to the Sound and the Cattegat (though some, indeed, may have heard of Iceland), and in the west to the farther shores of Ireland and of Spain. Outside these bounds there is something, at any rate to the east, but it is something shadowy and wavering, full of myth and fable. Inside these bounds there is the clear light of a Christian Church, and the definite outline of a single society, of which all are baptized members, and by which all are knit together in a single fellowship.

Economically the world was as different from our own as it was geographically. Money, if not unknown, was for the most part unused. It had drifted eastwards, in the latter days of the Roman Empire, to purchase silks and spices ; and it had never returned. From the days of Diocletian, society had been thrown back on an economy in kind. Taxes took the form either of payments of personal service or of quotas of produce : rents were paid either in labour or in food. The presence of money means a richly articulated society, infinitely differentiated by division of labour, and infinitely connected by a consequent nexus of exchange. The society of the Middle Ages was not richly articulated. There were merchants and artisans in the towns ; but the great bulk of the population lived in country villages, and gained subsistence directly from the soil. Each village was practically self-sufficing ; at the most it imported commodities like iron and salt ; for the rest, it drew on itself and its own resources. This produced at once a great uniformity and a great isolation. There was a great uniformity, because most men lived the same grey, quiet life of agriculture. The peasantry of Europe, in these days when most men were peasants, lived in the same way, under the same custom of the manor, from Berwick to Carcassonne, and from Carcassonne to Magdeburg. But there was also a great isolation. Men were tied to their manors; and the men of King's Ripton could even talk of the ' nation ' of their village. If they were not tied by conditions of status and the legal rights of their lord, they were still tied, none the less, by the want of any alternative life. There were towns indeed ; but towns were themselves very largely agricultural—the homes of *summa rusticitas*—and what industry and commerce they practised was the perquisite and prerogative of local guilds. Custom was king of all things, and custom had assorted men in compartments in which they generally stayed. The kaleidoscopic coming and going of a society based on monetary exchanges—its speedy riches and speedy bankruptcies, its embarrassment of alternative careers all open to talents—these were unthought and undreamed of. The same uniformity and the same isolation marked also, if in a less degree, the knightly class which followed the profession of arms. A common feudal system, if we can call that a system which was essentially unsystematic,.reigned over the whole of Western Europe, and, when Western Europe went crusading into Syria, established itself in Syria. Historians have tried to establish distinctions between the feudalism of one country and that of another—between the feudalism of England, for instance, and that of France. It is generally held nowadays that they have failed to establish the distinction. A fief in England was uniform with a fief in France, as a manor in one country was uniform with manors in other countries, and a town in one country with towns in others. ' One cannot establish a line of demarcation between German and French towns,' says a famous Belgian historian, ' just as one cannot distinguish between French and German feudalism.'[1] The

[1] Pirenne, *Revue Historique*, liii. p. 82.

historian of the economic and institutional life of the Middle Ages will err unless he proceeds on the assumption of its general uniformity. But the uniformity of the fief, like that of the manor and the town, was compatible with much isolation. Each fief was a centre of local life and a home of local custom. The members of the feudal class lived, for the most part, local and isolated lives. Fighting, indeed, would bring them together; but when the 'season' was over, and the forty days of service were done, life ran back to its old ruts in the manor-hall, and if some of the summer was spent in company, much of the winter was spent in isolation. On a society of this order—stable, customary, uniform, with its thousands of isolated centres —the Church descended with a quickening inspiration and a permeating unity. Most of us find a large play for our minds to-day in the competition of economics or the struggles of politics. The life of the mind was opened to the Middle Ages by the hands of the Church. We may almost say that there was an exact antithesis between those days and these latter days, if it were not that exact antitheses never occur outside the world of logic. But it is as nearly true as are most antitheses that while our modern world is curiously knit together by the economic bonds of international finance, and yet sadly divided (and never more sadly than to-day) by the clash of different national cultures and different creeds, the mediaeval world, sundered as it was economically into separate manors and separate towns, each leading a self-sufficing life on its own account, was yet linked together by unity of culture and unity of faith. It had a single mind, and many pockets. We have a single pocket, and many minds. That is why the wits of many nowadays will persist in going woolgathering into the Middle Ages, to find a comfort which they cannot draw from the golden age of international finance.

But retrogression was never yet the way of progress. It is probable, for instance, that the sanitation of the Middle Ages was very inadequate, and their meals sadly indigestible; and it would be useless to provoke a revolt of the nose and the stomach in order to satisfy a craving of the mind. An uncritical mediaevalism is the child of ignorance of the Middle Ages. Sick of vaunting national cultures, we may recur to an age in which they had not yet been born—the age of a single and international culture; but we must remember, all the same, that the strength of the Middle Ages was rooted in weakness. They were on a low stage of economic development; and it was precisely because they were on a low stage of economic development that they found it so easy to believe in the unity of civilization. Unity of a sort is easy when there are few factors to be united; it is more difficult, and it is a higher thing, when it is a synthesis of many different elements. The Middle Ages had not attained a national economy: their economy was at the best municipal, and for the most part only parochial. A national economy has a higher economic value than a municipal or parochial economy, because it means the production of a greater number of utilities at a less cost, and a richer and fuller life of the mind, with more varied activities and more intricate connexions. A national economy could only develop along with—perhaps we may say it could only develop through—a national system of politics; and the national State, which is with us to-day, and with some of whose works we are discontented, was a necessary condition of economic progress. With the coming of the national State the facile internationalism of the Middle Ages had to disappear; and as economics and politics ran into national channels, the life of the spirit, hitherto an international life, suffered the same change, and national religions, if such a thing be not a contradiction in terms, were duly born. But a national economy, a national State, a national Church were all things unknown to the Middle Ages. Its economy was a village economy: its mental culture was an international culture bestowed by a universal Church (a village culture there could not be, and with a universal Church the only possible culture was necessarily international); while, as for its politics, they were something betwixt and between—sometimes parochial, when a local feudal lord drew to himself sovereignty; sometimes national, when a strong king arose in Israel; and sometimes, under a Charlemagne, almost international.

A consideration of the linguistic factor may help to throw light on the point in question. Here again we may trace the same isolation and the same uniformity which we have also seen in the world of economics. There was an infinity of dialects, but a paucity of languages, in the Middle Ages. One is told that to-day there are dialects in the Bight of Heligoland and among the Faroes which are peculiar to a single family. Something of the same sort must have existed in the Middle Ages. Just as there were local customs of the manor, the town, and the fief, there must have been local dialects of villages and even of hamlets. But here again isolation was compatible with uniformity. There were perhaps only two languages of any general vogue in the central epoch of the Middle Ages, and they were confined by no national frontiers. First there was Latin, the language of the Church, and since learning belonged to the Church, the language of learning. Scholars used the same language in Oxford and Prague, in Paris and Bologna; and within the confines of Latin Christianity scholarship was an undivided unity. Besides Latin the only other language of any general vogue in the middle of the Middle Ages was vulgar Latin, or Romance. To Dante, writing at the close of the thirteenth century, Romance was still one *idioma*—even if it were *trifarium*, according as its ' yes ' was *oïl*, or *oc*, or *si*.[1] Of the three branches of this *idioma*, that of *oïl*, or Northern France, was easily predominant. The Norman conquest of England carried it to London : the Norman conquest of Sicily carried it to Palermo : the Crusades carried it to Jerusalem. With it you might have travelled most of the mediaeval world from end to end. It was the language of courts ; it was the language of chansons ; it was the language of all lay culture. It was the language of England, France, and Italy ; and St. Francis himself had delighted in his youth in the literature which it enshrined.

The linguistic basis of mediaeval civilization was thus Latin, either in its classical or in its vulgar form. There were of course other languages, and some of these had no small vogue. Just before the period of which we are treating—the period which extends from 1050 to 1300—Icelandic had a wide scope. It might have been heard not only in Scandinavia and the Northern Isles, but in a great part of the British Islands, in Normandy, in Russia— along the river-road that ran to Constantinople—and in Constantinople itself. But the fact remains that the linguistic basis of mediaeval thought and literature was a Latin basis. The Romance University of Paris was the capital of learning : the Romance tongue of Northern France was the tongue of society. And as the linguistic basis of mediaeval civilization was Romance, so, too, was mediaeval civilization itself. The genius of Latin Christianity was the source of its inspiration : the spirit of the Romance peoples was the breath of its being. The souvenir of the old Roman Empire provided the scheme of its political ideas ; and the Holy Roman Empire, if a religious consecration had given it a new sanctity, was Roman still.

[1] *De Vulgari Eloquio*, I. viii.

Yet the irruption of the Teutons into the Empire had left its mark; and the emperor of the Middle Ages was always of Teutonic stock. It was perhaps at this point that the unity of the mediaeval scheme betrayed a fatal flaw. It would be futile to urge that the dualism which showed itself in the struggles of papacy and empire had primarily, or even to any considerable extent, a racial basis. Those struggles are struggles of principles rather than of races; they are contentions between a secular and a clerical view of life, rather than between the genius of Rome and the genius of Germany. Hildebrand stood for a free Church— a Church free from secular power because it was controlled by the papacy. Henry IV stood for the right of the secular power to use the clergy for purposes of secular government, and to control the episcopacy as one of the organs of secular administration. But the fact remains that a scheme which rested on a Teutonic emperor and a Roman pontiff was already a thing internally discordant, before these other and deeper dissensions appeared to increase the discord.

Such were the bases on which the unity of mediaeval civilization had to depend. There was a contracted world, which men could regard as a unity, with a single centre of coherence. There was a low stage of economic development, which on the one hand meant a general uniformity of life, in fief and manor and town, and on the other hand meant a local isolation, that needed, and in the unity of the Church found, some method of unification. With many varieties of dialect, there was yet a general identity of language, which made possible the development, and fostered the dissemination, of a single and identical culture. Nationalism, whether as an economic development, or as a way of life and a mode of the human spirit, was as yet practically unknown. Races might disagree; classes might quarrel; kings might fight; there was hardly ever a national conflict in the proper sense of the word. The mediaeval lines of division, it is often said, were horizontal rather than vertical. There were different estates rather than different states. The feudal class was homogeneous throughout Western Europe; the clerical class was a single corporation through all the extent of Latin Christianity; and the peasantry and the townsfolk of England were very little different from the peasantry and the townsfolk of France. We have to think of a general European system of estates rather than of any balance of rival powers.

II

The unity which rested on these bases begins to appear, as a reality and not only an idea, about the middle of the eleventh century, and lasts till the end of the thirteenth. That unity, as we have seen, was essentially ecclesiastical. It was the product of the Church: we may almost say that it was the Church. Before 1050 the Catholic Church, however universal in theory, had hardly been universal in fact. The period of the Frankish, the Saxon, and the early Salian emperors had been a period of what German writers call the *Landeskirche*. The power of the Bishop of Rome had not yet been fully established; and the great churches of Reims and Mainz and Milan were practically independent centres. Independent of the papacy, they were not independent of the lay rulers within whose dominions they lay. On the contrary, their members were deeply engaged in lay activities; they were landlords, feudatories, and officials in their various countries. In the face of these facts, the Gregorian movement of the eleventh century pursues two closely interconnected objects. It aims at asserting the universal primacy of the papacy; it aims at vindicating the freedom of the clergy from all secular power. The one aim is a means to the other: the pope cannot be universal primate, unless the clergy he controls are free from secular control; and the clergy cannot be free from secular control, unless the universal primacy of the papacy effects their liberation. Gregorianism wins a great if not a thorough triumph. It establishes the theory, and in a very large measure the practice, of ecclesiastical unity. The days of the *Landeskirche* are numbered: the days of the Church Universal under the universal primacy of Rome are begun. But when the universality of the Church has once been established in point of extension, it begins to be also asserted in point of intensity. Once ubiquitous, the papacy seeks to be omnicompetent. Depositary of the truth, and only depositary of the truth, by divine revelation, the Church, under the guidance of the papacy, seeks to realize the truth in every reach of life, and to control, in the light of Christian principle, every play of human activity. Learning and education, trade and commerce, war and peace, are all to be drawn into her orbit. By the application of Christian principle a great synthesis of human life is to be achieved, and the *lex Christi* is to be made a *lex animata in terris*.

This was the greatest ambition that has ever been cherished. It meant nothing less than the establishment of a *civitas Dei* on earth. And this kingdom of God was to be very different from that of which St. Augustine had written. His city of God was neither the actual Church nor the actual State, nor a fusion of both. It was a spiritual society of the predestined faithful, and, as such, thoroughly distinct from the State and secular society. The city of God which the great mediaeval popes were seeking to establish was a city of this world, if not of this world only. It was a fusion of the actual Church, reformed by papal direction and governed by papal control, with actual lay society, similarly reformed and similarly governed. Logically this meant a theocracy, and the bull of Boniface VIII, by which he claimed that every human creature was subject to the Roman pontiff, was its necessary outcome. But a theocracy was only a means, and a means that was never greatly emphasized in the best days of the papacy. It was the end that mattered; and the end was the moulding of human life into conformity with divine truth. The end may appear fantastic, unless one remembers the plenitude of means which stood at the command of the mediaeval Church. The seven sacraments had become the core of her organization. Central among the seven stood the sacrament of the Mass, in which bread and wine were transubstantiated into the divine body and blood of our Lord. By that sacrament men could touch God; and by its mediation the believer met the supreme object of his belief. Only the priest could celebrate the great mystery; and only those who were fit could be admitted by him to participation. The sacrament of penance, which became the antechamber, as it were, to the Mass, enabled the priest to determine the terms of admission. Outside the sacraments stood the Church courts, exercising a large measure of ethical and religious discipline over all Christians; and in reserve, most terrible of all weapons, were the powers of excommunication and interdict, which could shut men and cities from the rites of the Church and the presence of the Lord. Who shall say, remembering these things, that the aims of the mediaeval Church were visionary or impracticable?

For a time, and in some measure, they were actually accomplished. Let us look at each estate in turn, and measure the accomplishment—speaking first of the knightly world, and the Church's control of war and peace; then of the world of the commons, and the Church's control of trade and commerce; and last of the clerical world, and the Church's control of learning and education.

The control of war and peace was a steady aim of the Church from the beginning of the eleventh century. The evil of feudalism was its propensity to private war. To cure that evil the Church invented the Truce of God. The Truce was a diocesan matter. The ' form ' of Truce was enacted in a diocesan assembly, and the people of the diocese formed a *communitas pacis* for its enforcement. There was no attempt to put an absolute stop to private war ; the Truce was only directed to a limitation of the times and seasons in which feuds could be waged, and a definition of the persons who were to be exempted from their menace. But from seeking to limit the fighting instinct of a feudal society, the Church soon rose to the idea of enlisting that instinct under her own banner and directing it to her own ends. So arose chivalry, which, like most of the institutions of the Middle Ages, was the invention of the Church. Chivalry was the consecration of the fighting instinct to the defence of the widow, the fatherless, and the oppressed ; and by the beginning of the eleventh century liturgies already contain the form of religious service by which neophytes were initiated into knighthood. This early and religious form of chivalry (there was a later and lay form, invented by troubadour and trouvère, which was chiefly concerned with the rules for the loves of knights and ladies) culminated in the Crusades. In the Crusades we touch perhaps the most typical expression of the mediaeval spirit. Here we may see the clergy moulding into conformity with Christian principle the apparently unpromising and intractable stuff of feudal pugnacity : here we may see the papacy asserting its primacy of a united Europe by gathering Christian men together for the common purpose of carrying the flag of their faith to the grave of their Redeemer. Here the permeating influence of Christian revelation may be seen attempting to permeate even foreign policy (for what are the Crusades but the foreign policy of a Christian commonwealth controlled and directed by the papacy?); and here again even the instinct for colonial expansion, so often the root of desperate wars, was brought into line with the unity of all nations in Christ, and made to serve the cause of Him ' in whom alone is to be found the true nature of the One '.

There is another aspect of the clerical control of peace and war in the interest of Christian unity which must not be forgotten. The papacy sought to become an international tribunal. The need for such a tribunal was as much a mediaeval as it is a modern commonplace. Dante, who sought to vindicate for the emperor, rather than for the pope, the position and power of an international judge, has started the argument in famous words. ' Between any two princes, of whom the one is in no way subject to the other, disputes may arise, either by their own fault, or by that of their subjects. Judgement must therefore be given between them. And since neither can have cognizance of the other, because neither is subject to the other, there must be a third of ampler jurisdiction, to control both by the ambit of his power.'[1] Such ampler jurisdiction, which might indeed be claimed for the emperor, but which he had never the power to exercise, was both claimed and exercised by the papacy. The papacy, which sought to enforce the Christian canon of conduct in every reach of life and every sphere of activity, would never admit that disputes between sovereign princes lay outside the rule of that canon. Innocent III, in a letter to the French bishops defending his claim to arbitrate between France and England, stands very far from any such admission. ' It belongs to our office ', he argues, ' to correct all Christian men for every mortal sin, and if they despise correction, to coerce them by ecclesiastical

[1] *De Monarchia*, I. x.

censure. And if any shall say, that kings must be treated in one way, and other men in another, we appeal in answer to the law of God, wherein it is written, " Ye shall judge the great as the small, and there shall be no acceptance of persons among you." But if it is ours to proceed against criminal sin, we are especially bound so to do when we find a sin against peace.'[1] Here, in these words of Innocent, the clerical claim to control of peace and war touches its highest point. In the name of a Christian principle, permeating all things, and reducing all things to unity, the dread arbitrament of war is itself to be submitted to a higher and finer arbitration. The claim was too high to be sustained or translated into effect. It is not too high to be admired.

Nor was it altogether remote from the actual life of the day. Even to the laity of the Middle Ages, war was not a mere conflict of powers, in which the strongest power must necessarily prevail. It was a conflict of rights before a watching God of battles, in which the greatest right could be trusted to emerge victorious. War between States was analogous to the ordeal of battle between individuals: it was a legal way of testing rights. Now ordeal by battle was a mode of procedure in courts of law, and a mode of procedure whose conduct and control belonged to the clergy. If, therefore, war between States is analogous to ordeal, it follows, first, that it is a legal procedure which needs a high court for its interpretation (and what court could be more competent than the papal curia ?), and, next, that it is a matter which in its nature touches the clergy. Such ideas were a natural basis for the Church's attempt to control the issues of war and peace; and if we remember these ideas, we shall acquit the Church of any impracticable quixotism.

The attempt to control trade and commerce was no less

[1] Cf. Carlyle, *Mediaeval Political Theory in the West*, ii. 219-22.

lofty and no less arduous. It is perhaps still easier to stop war than to stop competition; and yet the Church made the attempt. The Christian law of love was set against the economic law of demand and supply. It was canonical doctrine that the buyer should take no more, and the seller offer no less, than the just price of a commodity—a price which would in practice depend on the cost of production. The rule for prices was also the rule for wages: the just wage was the natural complement of the just price. The prohibition of usury and of the taking of interest was another factor in the same circle of ideas. If prices and wages are both to be returns for work done, and returns of an exact equivalence, then, on the assumptions which the canonists made—that the usurer does no work, and that his loan is unproductive of any new value—it necessarily follows that no return is due, or can be justly paid, for the use of borrowed money. Work is the one title of all acquisition, and all acquisition should be in exact proportion to the amount of work done. This is the basic principle, and it is the principle of the Divine Law: *In sudore frontis tuae comedes panem tuum.* Once more, therefore, and once more in an unpromising and intractable material, we find the Church seeking to enforce the unity of the Christian principle and to reduce the Many to the One. In the same way, and from the same motive, that private war was to be banished from the feudal class in the country, competition—the private war of commerce—was to be eliminated from the trading classes in the towns. Nor was the attack on competition, any more than the attack on war, so much of a forlorn hope as it may seem to a modern age. Even to-day, custom is still a force which checks the operation of competition, and custom covered a far greater area in the Middle Ages than it does to-day. The rent of land, whether paid in labour or in kind, was a customary rent; and in every mediaeval

community the landed class was the majority. It was
an easy transition from fixed and customary rents to the
fixing of just prices for commodities and services. Lay
sentiment supported clerical principle. Guilds compelled
their members to sell commodities at a level price, and in
a spirit of collectivism endeavoured to prevent the making
of corners and the practice of undercutting. Governments
refused to recognize the 'laws' of demand and supply, and
sought, by Statutes of Labourers, to force masters to give,
and workman to receive, no more and no less than a ' just '
and proper wage.

It was not only by the regulation of trade and commerce
that the Church sought to penetrate the life of the towns.
The friars made their homes in the towns in the thirteenth
century; and the activity of the friars—Franciscan and
Dominican, Austin and Carmelite—enabled the Church to
exercise an influence on municipal life no less far-reaching
than that which she sought to exert on the feudal classes.
Towns became trustees of property for the use of the
mendicant orders; and the orders of Tertiaries, which
flourished among them, enabled the townsfolk to attach
themselves to religious societies without quitting the
pursuits of lay life. A mediaeval town—with its trade and
commerce regulated, however imperfectly, by Christian
principle; with its town council acting as trustee for
religious orders; and with its members attached as
Tertiaries to those orders—might be regarded as something
of a type of Christian society; and St. Thomas, partly
under the influence of these conditions, if partly also
under the influence of the Aristotelian philosophy of the
πόλις, is led to find in the life of the town the closest
approach to the ethics of Christianity.

The control of learning and education by the Church is
the most peculiar and essential aspect of her activity.
The control of war and peace was a matter of guiding the

estate of the baronage; the control of trade and commerce was a way of directing the estate of the commons; but the control of learning and education was nothing more nor less than the Church's guidance of herself and her direction of her own estate. *Studium* may be distinguished from *sacerdotium* by mediaeval writers; but the students of a mediaeval university are all 'clergy', and the curricula of mediaeval universities are essentially clerical. All knowledge, it is true, falls within their scope; but every branch of knowledge, from dialectic to astronomy, is studied from the same angle, and for the same object—*ad maiorem Dei gloriam*. Here, as elsewhere, the penetrating and assimilative genius of the Church moulded and informed a matter which was not, in its nature, easily receptive of a clerical impression. The whole accumulated store of the lay learning of the ages—geometry, astronomy, and natural science; grammar and rhetoric; logic and metaphysics—this was the matter to be moulded and the stuff to be permeated; and on this stuff St. Thomas wrought the greatest miracle of genuine alchemy which is anywhere to be found in the annals of learning.

The learning which the Church had to transform was essentially the learning of the Hellenic world. Created by the centuries of nimble and inventive thought which lie between the time of Thales and that of Hipparchus, this learning had been systematized into a *corpus scientiae* during that age of Greek scholasticism which generally goes by the name of Hellenistic. In its systematized Hellenistic form, it had been received by the Roman world, and had become the culture of the Roman Empire. By writers ranging from Ptolemy to Boethius the body of all known knowledge had been arranged in a digest or series of pandects; and along with the legal codification of Justinian it had been handed to the Christian Church

as the heritage of the ancient world. The attitude of the
Church to that heritage was for long unfixed and uncertain.
The logic, and still more the metaphysics, of Aristotle
were not the most comfortable of neighbours to the new
body of Christian revelation committed to the Church's
keeping. In the hand of Berengar of Tours the methods
of Greek logic proved a corrosive to the received doctrine
of the Mass. In the hands of Abelard, in the *Sic et Non*,
they served to suggest the need of criticism of the text of
Christian tradition. If unity was to be preserved, a bridge
must be built between the secular science of the Greeks
and the religious faith of the Church. In the thirteenth
century that bridge was built. Aristotle was reconciled
with St. Augustine; the *Organon*, the *Ethics*, and the
Politics were incorporated in the body of Christian culture;
and the mediaeval instinct for unification celebrated its
greatest and perhaps its most arduous triumph.

The thirteenth century thus witnessed a unity of
civilization alike as a structure of life and as a content of
the human mind. On the one hand, there rose a single
governing scheme of society, which culminated in the
universal primacy of Rome and the Roman pontiff. On
the other hand, set in this scheme, and contained in this
structure, there was a single stuff of thought, directed to
the manifestation of the eternal glory of God. The
framework we may chiefly ascribe to Gregory VII; the
content to St. Thomas Aquinas. But the whole resultant
unity is less the product of great personalities than of
a common instinct and a common conviction. Men saw
the world *sub specie unitatis*; and its kaleidoscopic
variety was insensibly focused into a single scheme under
the stress of their vision. The heavens showed forth the
glory of God, and the firmament declared His handiwork.
Zoology became, like everything else, a willing servant
of Christianity; and *bestiaria moralizata* were written to

show how all beasts were made for an ensample, and served for a type, of the one and only truth. All things, indeed, were types and allegories to this way of thinking; and just as every text in the Bible was an allegory to mediaeval interpretation, so all things in the world of creation, animate and inanimate, the jewel with its 'virtue' as well as the beast with its 'moral', became allegories and parables of heavenly meanings. Thus the world of perception became unreal, that it might be transmuted into the real world of faith; and symbolism like that of Hugh of St. Victor dominated men's thought, making all things (like the Mass itself, if in a less degree) into *signa rei sacrae*.

The unity of knowledge was thus purchased at a price. Things must cease to be studied in themselves, and must be allegorized into types, in order that they might be reduced to a unity. Perhaps the purchase of unity on terms such as these is a bad bargain; and it is at any rate obvious that in such an atmosphere scientific thought will not flourish, or man learn to adjust himself readily to the laws of his environment. From the standpoint of natural science we may readily condemn the Middle Ages and all their works; and we may prefer a single *Opus* of Roger Bacon to the whole of the *Summa* of St. Thomas. But it is necessary to judge an age which was destitute of natural science by some other criterion than that of science; nor must we hasten to say that the Middle Ages found the Universal so easily, because they ignored the Particular so absolutely. The truth is, that though mediaeval thinkers knew far more of the writings of Aristotle than they did of those of Plato, they were none the less far better Platonists than they were Aristotelians. If they had been better Aristotelians, they would have been better biologists; but as they were good Platonists, they had a conception of the purpose and system of human life in society, which perhaps excuses all, and more than all, the defects of their biology. Any survey, however brief, of the political theory of the Middle Ages will show at once its Platonic character and its incessant impulse towards the achievement of unity.

III

To mediaeval thought, as to Plato, the unity of society is an organic unity, in the sense that each member of society is an organ of the whole to which he belongs, and discharges a function at once peculiar to himself and necessary to the full life of the whole. Monasticism, so often misrepresented, attains its true meaning in the light of this conception. The monk is a necessary organ of Christian society, discharging his function of prayer and devotion for the benefit not of himself solely, or primarily, but rather of every member of that society. He prays for the sins of the whole world, and by his prayer he contributes to the realization of the end of the world, which is the attainment of salvation. In the same way the conception of a treasury of merits, afterwards perverted in the system of indulgences, belongs to an organic theory and practice of society. The merits which Christ and the saints have accumulated are a fund for the use of the whole of Christian society, a fund on which any member can draw for his own salvation, just because each is fitly joined and knit together with all the rest in a single body for the attainment of a single purpose. But we need not take isolated instances of the Platonism of mediaeval thought. The whole basic conception of a system of estates, which recurs everywhere in mediaeval life, is a Platonic conception. The estates of clergy, baronage, and commons are the Platonic classes of guardians, auxiliaries, and farmers. The Platonic creed of τὸ αὑτοῦ πράττειν (' Do thine own duty ') is the Christian creed of 'doing my duty in that state of life to which it shall please God to call me'. The Middle Ages are full of a spontaneous Platonism, and inspired by an *anima naturaliter Platonica*. The control which the mediaeval clergy exercised over Christian society in the light of divine revelation repeats the control which the guardians of Plato were to exercise over civic society in the light of the Idea of the Good. The communism of the mediaeval monastery is reminiscent of the communism of the Platonic barracks. And if there are differences between the society imagined by Plato and the society envisaged by the mediaeval Church, these differences only show that the mediaeval Church was trying to raise Platonism to a higher power, and to do so in the light of conceptions which were themselves Greek, though they belonged to a Greece posterior to the days of Plato. These conceptions—which were cherished by Stoic thinkers; which penetrated into Roman Law; and which from Roman Law flowed into the teaching and theory of the early fathers of the Church —are mainly two. One is the conception of human equality; the other, and correlative, conception is that of a single society of all the human race. The equality of men, and the universality of the city of God in which they are all contained, are conceptions which were no less present to Marcus Aurelius than they were to St. Augustine. They are conceptions which made the instinctive Platonism of the mediaeval Church even more soaring than that of Plato. While the Republic of Plato had halted at the stage of a civic society, the *respublica Christiana* of the Middle Ages rose to the height of a single *humana civilitas*. While Plato had divided the men of his Republic into classes of gold and silver and bronze, and had reserved the ecstasy of the aspect of the divine Idea for a single class, the mediaeval Church opened the mystery of the Mass and the glory of the fruition of God to all believers,

and, if she believed in three estates, nevertheless gathered
the three in one around the common altar of the Redeemer.
Serfdom might still remain, and find tolerance, in the
economic working of society; but in the Church herself,
assembled together for the intimate purposes of her own
life, there was 'neither bond nor free'.

The prevalence of Realism, which marks mediaeval
metaphysics down to the end of the thirteenth century,
is another Platonic inheritance, and another impulse to
unity. The Universal *is*, and is a veritable thing, in
which the Particular shares, and acquires its substance by
its degree of sharing. The One transcends the Many ; the
unity of mankind is greater than the differences between
men ; and the university of mortal men, as Ockham
writes, is one community. If there be thus one community,
and one only, some negative results follow, which have
their importance. In the first place, we can hardly say
that the Middle Ages have any conception of the State.
The notion of the State involves plurality ; but plurality
is *ex hypothesi* not to be found. The notion of the State
further involves sovereignty, in the sense of final and
complete control of its members by each of a number of
societies. But this, again, is *ex hypothesi* not to be found.
There is one final control, and one only, in the mediaeval
system—the control of Christian principle, exerted in the
last resort, and exerted everywhere, without respect of
persons, by the ruling vicar of Christ. But if plurality
and sovereignty thus disappear from our political philosophy, we need a new orientation of all our theory. We
must forget to speak of nations. We must forget, as
probably many of us would be very glad to forget, the
claims of national cultures, each pretending to be a complete satisfaction and fulfilment of the national mind ; and
we must remember, with Dante, that culture (which he
called ' civility) is the common possession of Christian

humanity. We must even forget, to some extent, the existence of different national laws. It is true that mediaeval theory admitted the fact of customary law, which varied from place to place. But this customary law was hardly national: it varied not only from country to country, but also from fief to fief, and even from manor to manor. It was too multiform to be national, and too infinitely various to square with political boundaries. Nor was customary law, in mediaeval theory, anything of the nature of an ultimate command. Transcending all customs, and supreme over all enactments, rose the sovereign majesty of natural law, which is one and indivisible, and runs through all creation. ' All custom,' writes Gratian, the great canonist, ' and all written law, that are adverse to natural law, are to be counted null and void.' Here, in this conception of a natural law upholding all creation, we may find once more a Stoic legacy to the Christian Church. ' Men ought not to live in separate cities, distinguished one from another by different systems of justice '—so Zeno the Stoic had taught—' but there should be one way and order of life, like that of a single flock feeding on a common pasture.' Zeno, like St. Paul, came from Cilicia.[1] Like St. Paul, he taught the doctrine of the one society, in which there was neither Jew nor Gentile, neither Greek nor barbarian. We shall not do wrong to recognize in his teaching, and in that of his school, one of the greatest influences, outside the supreme and controlling influence of the Christian principle itself, which made for the dominance of the idea of unity in mediaeval thought.

Before we proceed to draw another negative conclusion from the principle of the one community, we must enter a brief caveat in regard to the conclusion which has just been drawn. We cannot altogether take away the State

[1] Cf. E. R. Bevan, *Stoics and Sceptics*.

from the Middle Ages by a stroke of the pen and the sweep of a paradox. There were states in mediaeval Europe, and there were kings who claimed and exercised *imperium*. These things caused the theorists, and particularly the Roman lawyers, no little trouble. It was difficult to reconcile the unity of the *imperium* with the multiplicity of kings. Some had recourse to the theory of delegation, and this seems to be the theory of the *De Monarchia* of Dante. But there was one contemporary of Dante who said a wise thing, prophetic of the future. *Rex est in regno suo*, wrote Bartolus of Sassoferrato, *imperator regni sui*. In that sentence we may hear the cracking of the Middle Ages. When kings become 'entire emperors of their realms' (the phrase was used in England by Richard II, and the imperial style was affected by Henry VIII), unity soon prepares to fly out of the window. But she never entirely took flight until the Reformation shattered the fabric of the Church, and made kings into popes as well as emperors in their dominions.

We may now turn to draw another conclusion from the mediaeval principle of unity. To-day the world recognizes, and has recognized for nearly four centuries, not only a distinction between States, but also a distinction between two societies in each State—the secular and the religious. These two societies may have different laws (for instance, in the matter of marriage), and conflicts of duties and of jurisdictions may easily arise in consequence. The State may permit what the Church forbids; and in that case the citizen who is also a churchman must necessarily revolt against one or other of the societies to which he belongs. The conflict between the two societies and the different obligations which they impose was a conflict unknown to the Middle Ages. Kings might indeed be excommunicated, and in that event their subjects would be compelled to decide whether they should disobey excommunicated king or excommunicating pope. But that was only a conflict between two different allegiances to two different authorities; it was not a conflict between two different memberships of two different societies. The conflict between the two societies—Church and State—was one which could hardly arise in the Middle Ages, because there was only a single society, an undivided Christian commonwealth, which was at one and the same time both Church and State. Because there was only one society, baptism counted as admission both to churchmanship and to citizenship, which were one thing, and one only, in the Christian commonwealth; and for the same reason excommunication, which shut the offender from all religious life, excluded him equally and by the same act from every civil right. The excommunicated person could not enter either the Church or the law court; could not receive either the eucharist or a legacy; could not own either a cure of souls or an acre of soil. Civil right and religious status implied one another; and not only was *extra ecclesiam nulla salus* a true saying, but *extra ecclesiam nullum ius* would also be very near the truth. Here again is a reason for saying that the State as such can hardly be traced in the Middle Ages. The State is an organization of secular life. Even if it goes beyond its elementary purpose of security for person and property, and devotes itself to spiritual purposes, it is concerned with the development of the spirit in its mortal existence, and confined to the expansion of the mind in the bounds of a mortal society. The Middle Ages thought more of salvation than of security, and more of the eternal society of all the faithful, united together in Christ their Head, than of any passing society of this world only. They could recognize kings, who bore the sword for the sake of security, and did justice in virtue of their anointing. But kings were not, to their thinking, the heads of secular societies. They

H 2

were agents of the one divine commonwealth—defenders of the Faith, who wielded the secular sword for the furtherance of the purposes of God. Thus there was one society, if there were two orders of ministering agents; and thus, though *regnum* and *sacerdotium* might be distinguished, the State and the Church could not be divided. Stephen of Tournai, a canonist of the twelfth century, recognizes the two powers; but he only knows one society, under one king. That society is the Church: that king is Christ.

Under conditions such as these—with the plurality of States unrecognized by theory, even if it existed in practice, and with distinction between State and Church unknown and unenforced—we may truly say with a German writer, whose name I should like to mention *honoris causa*, Professor Tröltsch, that 'there was no feeling for the State; no common and uniform dependence on a central power; no omnicompetent sovereignty; no equal pressure of a public civil law; no abstract basis of association in formal and legal rules—or at any rate, so far as anything of the sort was present, it was a matter only for the Church, and in no wise for the State'.[1] So far as social life was consciously articulated in a scheme, the achievement was that of the clergy, and the scheme was that of the Church. The interdependencies and associations of lay life—kingdoms and fiefs and manors—were only personal groupings, based on personal sentiments of loyalty and unconscious elements of custom. A mixture of uniformity and isolation, as we have seen, was the characteristic of these groupings: they were at once very like one another, throughout the extent of Western Europe, and (except for their connexion in a common membership of the Church Universal) very much separated from one another. But with one at any rate of these groupings— the kingdom, which in its day was to become the modern

[1] *Die Soziallehren der christlichen Kirchen*, p. 242.

State—the future lay; and we shall perhaps end our inquiry most fitly by a brief review of the lines of its future development.

IV

The development of the kingdom into the State was largely the work of the lawyers. The law is a tenacious profession, and in England at any rate its members have exercised a large influence on politics from the twelfth to the twentieth century—from the days of Glanville, the justiciar of Henry II, to the days of Mr. Asquith, the prime minister of George V. It is perhaps in England that we may first see the germs of the modern State emerging to light under the fostering care of the royal judges. Henry II is something of a sovereign: his judges formulate a series of commands, largely in the shape of writs, which became the common law of the land; and in the Constitutions of Clarendon we may already see the distinction between Church and State beginning to be attempted. With a sovereign, a law, and a secular policy all present, we may begin to suspect the presence of a State. In France also a similar development, if somewhat later than the English, occurs at a comparatively early date. By the end of the thirteenth century the legists of Philippe le Bel have created something of *étatisme* in their master's dominions. The king's court begins to rule the land; and proud of its young strength it enters the lists against Boniface VIII, the great prophet of the Church Universal, who proclaimed that every human creature was subject to the Roman pontiff. The collapse of Boniface at Anagni in 1303 is the traditional date of the final defeat of the mediaeval papacy. Everywhere, indeed, the tide seemed on the turn at the close of the thirteenth century. The Crusades ended with the fall of Acre in 1291. The suppression of the great international order of the Templars twenty years later marked a new leap of the encroaching waves. The new era of the modern national State might seem already to have begun.

But tides move slowly and by gradual inches. It needed two centuries more before the conditions in which the modern State could flourish had been fully and finally established. Economic conditions had to change—a process always gradual and slow; and a national economy based on money had to replace the old local economy based on kind. Languages had to be formed, and local dialects had to be transformed into national and literary forms, before national States could find the means of utterance. The revival of learning had to challenge the old clerical structure of knowledge, and to set free the progress of secular science, before the minds of men could be readily receptive of new forms of social structure and new modes of human activity. But by 1500 the work of preparation had been largely accomplished. The progress of discovery had enlarged the world immeasurably. The addition of America to the map had spiritual effects which it is difficult to estimate in any proper terms. If the old world of the Mediterranean regions could be thought into a unity, it was more difficult to reduce to the One the new world which swam into men's ken. Still more burdened with fate for the future generations was the vast volume of commerce, necessarily conducted on a national basis, which the age of discoveries went to swell. Meanwhile, men had begun to think and to write in national languages. Already by the reign of Richard II the dialect of the East Midlands, which was spoken in the capital and the universities, had become a literary language in which Chaucer and Wyclif had spoken to all the nation. Still earlier had come the development of Italian, and a little more than a century after the days of Wyclif, Luther was to give to Germany a common speech and a common Bible.

It was little wonder that in such times the old unity of the Christian commonwealth of the Middle Ages shivered into fragments, or that, side by side with a national language, there developed—at any rate in England and in Germany—a national Church. The unity of a common Roman Church and a common Romance culture was gone. *Cuius regio eius religio.* To each region its religion; and to each nation, we may add, its national culture. The Renaissance may have begun as a cosmopolitan movement, and have found in Erasmus a cosmopolitan representative. It ended in national literatures; and a hundred years after Erasmus, Shakespeare was writing in England, Ariosto in Italy, and Lope de Vega in Spain.

In the sixteenth century the State was active and doing after its kind. It was engaged in war. France was fighting Spain: England was seeking to maintain the balance: Turkey was engaged in the struggle. It is a world with which we are familiar—a world of national languages, national religions, national cultures, national wars, with the national State behind all, upholding and sustaining every form of national activity. But unity was not entirely dead. Science might still transcend the bounds of nations, and a Grotius or Descartes, a Spinoza or a Leibniz, fill the European stage. Religion, which divided, might also unite; and a common Calvinism might bind together the Magyars of Hungary and the French of Geneva, the Dutchman and the Scot. Leyden in the seventeenth century could serve, as The Hague in the twentieth century may yet serve, if in a different way, for the meeting ground of the nations; it could play the part of an international university, and provide a common centre of medical science and classical culture. But the old unity of the Middle Ages was gone—gone past recall. Between those days and the new days lay a gulf which no voice or language could carry. Much was lost that could never be recovered;

and if new gold was added to the currency of the spirit, new alloys were wrought into its substance. It would be a hard thing to find an agreed standard of measurement, which should cast the balance of our gain and loss, or determine whether the new world was a better thing than the old. One will cry that the old world was the home of clericalism and obscurantism; and another will say in his bitterness that the new world is the abode of two other evil spirits—nationalism and commercialism. One thing is perhaps certain. We cannot, as far as human sight can discern, ever hope to reconstruct unity on the old basis of the Christian commonwealth of the Middle Ages. Yet need is upon us still—need urgent and importunate—to find some unity of the spirit in which we can all dwell together in peace. Some have hoped for unity in the sphere of economics, and have thought that international finance and commerce would build the foundations of an international polity. Their hopes have had to sleep, and a year of war has shown that 'a synchronized bank-rate and reacting bourses' imply no further unity. Some again may hope for unity in the field of science, and may trust that the collaboration of the nations in the building of the common house of knowledge will lead to co-operation in the building of a greater mansion for the common society of civilized mankind. But nationalism can pervert even knowledge to its own ends, turning anthropology to politics, and chemistry to war. There remains a last hope —the hope of a common ethical unity, which, as moral convictions slowly settle into law, may gradually grow concrete in a common public law of the world. Even this hope can only be modest, but it is perhaps the wisest and the surest of all our hopes. *Idem scire* is a good thing; but men of all nations may know the same thing, and yet remain strangers one to another. *Idem velle idem nolle in re publica, ea demum firma amicitia est.* The nations will at last attain firm friendship one with another in the day when a common moral will controls the scope of public things. And when they have attained this friendship, then—on a far higher level of economic development and with an improvement by each nation of its talent which is almost entirely new—they will have found again, if in a different medium, something of the unity of mediaeval civilization.

BOOKS FOR REFERENCE

W. J. Ashley, *An Introduction to English Economic History*, vol. i, pt. 2, ch. 3 ; vol. i, pt. 2, ch. 6. Longmans.
Lord Bryce, *The Holy Roman Empire*. Macmillan.
A. J. and R. W. Carlyle, *Mediaeval Political Theory in the West*. W. Blackwood.
H. W. C. Davis, *Mediaeval Europe* (Home University Library). Williams & Norgate.
Encyclopaedia Britannica (11th edition), articles on 'Crusades' and 'Empire'.
J. N. Figgis, *Churches in the Modern State*, Appendix I. Longmans.
Bede Jarrett, *Socialist Theories in the Middle Ages*. T. C. and E. C. Jack.
E. Jenks, *Law and Politics in the Middle Ages*. Murray.
F. W. Maitland, *Political Theories of the Middle Ages*, translated from Gierke's *Das Deutsche Genossenschaftsrecht*. Maitland. Cambridge University Press.
R. L. Poole, *Illustrations of Mediaeval Thought*. Williams & Norgate.
H. Rashdall, *Universities of Europe in the Middle Ages*. Clarendon Press.
A. L. Smith, *Church and State in the Middle Ages*. Clarendon Press.
H. O. Taylor, *The Mediaeval Mind*. Macmillan.
E. Tröltsch, *Die Soziallehren der christlichen Kirchen* (II. Kapitel).
P. Vinogradoff, *Roman Law in Mediaeval Europe*. Harper.

V

UNITY AND DIVERSITY IN LAW

You know the story of Sophocles' *Antigone* : how, when two brothers disputed the throne of Thebes, one, Polynices, was driven out and brought a foreign host against the city. Both brothers fall in battle. Their uncle takes up the government and publishes an edict that no one shall give burial to the traitor who has borne arms against his native land. The obligation to give or allow decent burial, even to an enemy, was one which the Greeks held peculiarly sacred. Yet obedience to the orders of lawful authority is an obligation binding on every citizen. No one dares to disregard the king's order save the dead man's sister. She is caught in the act and brought before the king. ' And thou,' he says, ' didst indeed dare to transgress this law ? ' ' Yes,' answers Antigone, ' for it was not Zeus that published me that edict ; not such are the laws set among men by the Justice who dwells with the Gods below ; nor deemed I that thy decrees were of such force that a mortal could override the unwritten and unfailing statutes of heaven. For their life is not of to-day or yesterday but from all time, and no man knows when they were first put forth.'[1]

There you have the assertion of a law supreme and binding on all men, eternal, not to be set aside by human enactment.

And now turn to this passage from the traveller and historian Herodotus, an almost exact contemporary of Sophocles. He has been telling how Cambyses, king of

[1] Sophocles, *Antigone*, 449–57 (Jebb's translation).

the Persians, has been wantonly insulting the religion and customs of the Egyptians. 'The man must have been mad,' he says:

'For if one was to set men of all nations to make a choice of the best laws out of all the laws there are, each one upon consideration would choose those of his own country : so far do men go in thinking their own laws the best. Therefore it is not likely that any but a madman would cast ridicule on such things. And that all men do think thus about their laws may be shown by many proofs, and above all by this story. For when Darius was king he called to him the Greeks who were at his court and asked them, 'How much money would you take to eat your fathers when they die ? ' And they answered that they would not do this at any price. After this Darius called the men of an Indian tribe called the Kallatiai, who eat their parents, and asked them in the presence of the Greeks, who were told by an interpreter what was said, 'How much money would you take to burn with fire your fathers when they die ? ' And they cried with a great voice that he should speak no such blasphemy. Thus it is that men think, and I hold that Pindar spoke rightly in his poem when he said that law was king over all.'[1]

There you have law, king over men and gods, but a capricious monarch commanding here this, there that.

This capricious arbitrary aspect of law was a thing which much impressed the Greeks. They contrasted the varying, artificial arrangements made by mankind with the constancy and simplicity of nature. We speak of nature and convention; they contrasted things that are by nature with things that are by law. It was a contrast that bore fruit later on.

Now law, whose arbitrariness and variety so much impressed the Greeks was the law not so much of this place or that, as of this or that community and its members. This is a conception quite different from that of the modern

[1] Herodotus, iii. 38.

world. We may paraphrase ' English law ' by saying the law of England, because it is the law which will be applied (with, it may be, some exceptions or modifications) by the English courts to all persons, be they English or aliens, who come before them. But Athenian law is not in this sense the law of Athens, nor, to begin with, is Roman law the law of Rome. What we find is a law of Athenian or Roman citizens. The stranger to the city is a stranger to its law. As a matter of principle he is without rights by that law. His life is not protected by the blood-feud which his family can pursue, or by the compensation with which it may be bought off. His marriage with a citizen will be no marriage, or at best a sort of half marriage. He can acquire no land within the city's territory, and what goods he brings with him are pretty much at the mercy of the first taker.

Such, at any rate, is the theory of the 'law of citizens'.

We need not, it is true, believe that it was logically formulated in primitive times and ruthlessly applied. Some of its applications were the result of positive legislation due to a growing consciousness of the self-sufficiency of the city state and of the privileges of citizenship, as when Athens passed a law excluding from citizenship the offspring of citizens who had married foreign wives. But in its broad outlines the principle is sufficiently borne out by the exceptions which were necessary to make human intercourse possible. The stranger within your gates is protected just because he is within your gates, and you throw your protection about him, as is indeed your duty, for suppliants and strangers come from Zeus. The foreigner, even at a distance, may have a citizen as representative who can and will defend his rights. A stranger may be allowed to take up a permanent residence in the city, and by the mediation of a patron or guardian enjoy private rights not much inferior to those of a citizen. His legal

V UNITY AND DIVERSITY IN LAW

position will not be very different from that of a woman citizen, who needs the like mediation. Cities may, again, by treaty confer on each other's citizens reciprocal rights of legal protection.

In the middle of the third century B.C., Rome, after its first successful war against Carthage, took special measures to deal with the problem of the alien litigant. The great and growing commerce which came from all parts of the Mediterranean called for something more than a mere admission to treaty privileges. A special officer was from henceforth appointed to deal with the law-suits to which foreigners were parties, and the judgement was given by a body (which we may compare with our jury) which might include fellow-citizens of the foreign suitor.

But here a difficulty arose: what law was to be applied to a transaction between a Roman and a foreigner, or between two foreigners? The Roman law, the law of citizens, had been codified two centuries earlier, and its outline had been hardened by the practice of two centuries. The forms for a transfer of property, for instance, were rigid and solemn; the foreigner would hardly know them, and if he did, his alien hand could not effectively do the prescribed acts nor his alien mouth speak the almost sacred words. The answer was that behind the forms of the law of this city or that, there was 'a law of the men of all nations'. The common elements in the ordinary transactions of life, in whatever form they were clothed, could be taken into account and given effect to. Thus, side by side with the ownership according to the law of Roman citizens, the solemn words of promise which only a Roman citizen could utter, the marriage which only a Roman citizen could enter into, there might be property, contract, marriage to which any one, citizen or alien, might be a party.

This 'law of the men of all nations' (*ius gentium*) was

of course not an international law, it was a law administered by Roman officers, and it was coloured by Roman conceptions, however much it may have drawn from a comparison of foreign laws with which the Romans were brought into contact. In turn it reacted upon the more narrow law of Roman citizens (*ius civile*), broadening its conceptions and enabling it to free itself from primitive formalism. It also made easier the task of Roman governors who were called upon to administer the various laws of the different countries which came to form the Roman empire.

The gradual extension of the citizenship (completed at the end of the second century A.D.) to the whole of the inhabitants of the empire made possible, at least in outward appearance, the application of a uniform system of law throughout what was then the civilized world, though beneath an apparent uniformity local traditions and customs survived to the end, at any rate in the east. The ' civil law ', as the Roman law in its final form has been called down to the present day, consists of elements of the narrowly Roman and the more universal law inextricably interlaced.

This Roman solution of the problem of the foreign litigant is of much more than merely practical importance. The Stoic philosophy which grew up amid the decay of the old city life, whose adherents spoke of themselves as citizens of the world, had fastened upon the old antithesis of law (or convention) and nature, and formed the conception of a law of nature, which should have a reasonable basis and a validity superior to the arbitrariness of the city law. To this ideal conception the Roman law of the men of all nations gave a body and a reality. Stoicism became the ' established ' philosophy of Rome, and Roman lawyers well-nigh identified the ' *ius gentium* ' with the ideal law of nature, describing it as that which natural reason has established among all men. Yet for at least one of the great classical lawyers, whose words have been enshrined in Justinian's legislation, the identification was incomplete. By nature, it was said, all men are free, and mankind has departed from what natural reason requires, in permitting slavery. Thus the law of nature must be sought in something more universal than the practice of mankind. More than fifteen hundred years later in an English court an argument against the recognition of the rights of a slave-owner was successfully founded on the law of nature.

Before the Roman law had been put (at Constantinople) into the final shape in which it is preserved to us, the Roman empire in the west had already been broken up by barbarian invasions. The invaders brought with them their tribal laws and customs, rude, often cruel, narrow rather than simple, for simplicity is the work of civilization. They did not understand, and could not adopt, the law of the world into which they had come. Yet neither could they, if they would, force their laws upon the conquered inhabitants. Among these the old civilization lingered on in a degenerate form, and with it the Roman law. One of the first things that happened was that the conquerors drew up for their Roman subjects short codes of the Roman law as it survived in a debased form, as they drew up statements of their own law for their followers. For a long time each man, according to the community to which he belonged, had a 'personal' law. As late as A.D. 850 we hear that in France it might happen that five men met together and each would have a different law. Of course such a state of things means before very long that there must be at any rate one set of common legal rules which must be applied throughout a territory, namely rules to decide which kind of personal law is to be used when there is a dispute between two persons whose personal law is different.

Gradually the different populations within the same area coalesce, and law from being personal becomes local. But the local area will not be the same for all purposes. The law or custom which determines the rights of the small, often unfree or half-free tenant, whether as between him and his neighbour or as between him and his lord, may extend no further than a very small area, such as in England we call a manor. The law by which great men held their land from a king, though perhaps not uniform throughout the kingdom, will cover a much larger area. The fact that a great man may hold land in far distant places, it may be in different kingdoms, and that men of this class have connexions with different parts of Western Europe will lead to the formation of common notions of feudal law, which make possible even the scientific study of a law of feuds, though no complete uniformity was ever attained.

England was the first western country to attain political unity with a territory substantially the same as at the present day; and the determination of the English kings that in the more important matters justice should be done throughout the land in the king's name, either by his courts at Westminster or by judges sent by him to the counties, secured the formation of an English Common Law which left comparatively little play for local custom, and which at an early time became strong enough to resist attempts to introduce foreign law. As early as the time of Henry III the barons proclaimed with one voice that they would not have the laws of England altered in favour of a rule—the legitimation of bastards by the subsequent marriage of their parents—which in one form or another has been adopted in Western Christendom, and even in the neighbouring kingdom of Scotland.

In France political unity was reached only later and bit by bit, and when it came the difference of law in the

V UNITY AND DIVERSITY IN LAW

various provinces was too firmly established to make uniformity possible until the time of the Revolution. In Germany the shadowy unity of the Holy Roman Empire was never enough to afford any effective central administration of justice. National law in the strict sense was impossible under such conditions : the most that can be expected is such a degree of unity as results from common traditions inherited from more primitive times, and a community of language and national feeling.

Amid local and national diversities of law there were at any rate two unifying influences, the Roman and the Canon law. In some parts of Europe, as in the South of France and Italy, the traditions of the Roman law had never died out, and in a debased form, with much admixture of the law of the invaders, it had come to form the basis of the local law. In others it was the barbarian law which formed the groundwork. But just as behind the new languages, whether in the main founded on Latin or on Teutonic, Latin remained the medium of intercourse between the countries of the West, and the instrument of thought and learning, so Roman law remained a tradition which was ever ready to exert an influence. It is not only in law courts that law is learnt and developed. Transactions have to be drawn up in writing, and will largely be made in Latin, and founded on precedents. The grants of land to and from ecclesiastical bodies especially will be in a form which borrows much from Roman or romanesque models ; and they will form models for the transactions of others. Even the formulation of native law in the early codes will be carried out by men who know of no written law except the Roman. In the twelfth century Roman law becomes a subject of University study throughout Western Europe, in Italy, at Paris, even at Oxford, and forms a part of that international learning which scholars carry from land to land. Men trained in the Roman law rise to high positions in the public service. As judges and administrators they will not forget what they have learnt as students or taught as doctors. Yet it would be easy to exaggerate its influence, great as it was. It was certainly more as a form and method of legal thought than as an actual source of legal rules that it made itself felt, for instance, in our own country, and the strength and cohesion which it helped to give to our law enabled that law later to resist its further advance.

The Canon law was the law of the Western Church, a truly international society. It was formed largely on the model of the Roman law, and it largely borrowed from it, though it is full of non-Roman elements. It governed not merely what we should call purely ecclesiastical matters, but dealt or attempted to deal with other things, such as marriage and the disposition of the goods of the deceased. Our own law of marriage and divorce, and of probate of wills, has a history which goes back to the ecclesiastical law of the Middle Ages. Like the Roman law it exercised an influence as a model and a repository of maxims, all the greater because in every country it was a law in actual force within a sphere of which the boundaries were constantly being disputed between the lay and the church powers.

The beginnings of modern Europe with which we associate such things as the revival of learning and the Reformation brought with them on the Continent the event which is known as the reception of Roman law. The traditions of the ancient world had been seen in mediaeval times through mediaeval eyes, and had been moulded to mediaeval needs. The new age insisted on going back direct to the classical tradition. It was the actual Roman law of Justinian, not the Roman law as interpreted by mediaeval commentators, that was to be

V UNITY AND DIVERSITY IN LAW 131

studied and applied. The break-up of the institutions of the Middle Ages, the growth of absolute monarchical power, the centralization of government, all favoured the tendency. Roman law contained doctrines eminently pleasing to an absolute ruler, e. g. 'the decision of the monarch has the force of law' In Germany above all, where law was divided into countless local customs, the movement had its fullest effect. Roman law comes to be the law which is to be applied in the absence of positive enactment or justifiable custom. The native law finds itself driven to plead for its life, and is lucky if it can satisfy the conditions which are required to enable it to continue as a recognized custom. In every country of the West outside England, in greater or less degree, the Roman law comes in as something which will at least fill up the gaps, and will purge or remodel the native law. Even in Scotland texts of the Roman law may be quoted as authorities. The strength of our own law, and the successful resistance of our public institutions to monarchical power saved us alone from a 'reception', in the continental sense, of Roman law. And even our Blackstone will quote Roman law with respect where it tends to confirm our own rules.

If this reception was a movement which brought about a greater unity in the form and substance of the laws of Western Europe, there was another factor at work which tended in the opposite direction. The claims of the Empire to universal authority become more and more unreal: the claims of the Pope are either rejected entirely, or the ecclesiastical sphere is strictly delimited. The State becomes sovereign. For this purpose it makes no difference whether it is a High Court of Parliament or an absolute monarch which is the supreme authority: law comes to be thought of as the command of a sovereign person or assembly. 'No law', we are told, 'can be unjust', for law is the standard of justice, and there is no other standard by which the justice of law can be measured. The fact that there is in every State a sovereign power which can make and unmake the law at its pleasure makes possible the creation of a uniform law for all the subjects of a State, and so far as the State coincides with the nation, makes for the creation of a national unity in law. Thus Frederick the Great gave a code to Prussia, thus Napoleon gave France a code which swept away the diversities of the provincial customs; yet it served more than merely national purposes, for it found its way not only into the countries conquered by him, where it survived his conquests, but even into lands where he never held sway. Our French fellow-citizens in Quebec use an adaptation of it as a statement of their law. It took longer before Germany as a whole obtained a uniformity of law. The very strength of the national aspirations roused by the war against Napoleon stood for a time in the way of codification. The great German lawyer of that time, Savigny, thought of national law as a half-unconscious product of the national feeling of right. The Code of Napoleon had been a revolutionary code, founded (imperfectly, no doubt) on the doctrines of the rights of man; codification for Germany would mean the adoption of something abstract, not speoifically national. It was only a century of extraordinary fruitful learned activity, bringing with it at the same time a new and intense study of the Roman law, and a revival of the knowledge and application of the native conceptions of law, that made possible the German civil code which came into force fifteen years ago.

England has never seriously undertaken the work of codification, and its law, uniform and national already in the Middle Ages, has become in the modern world something far wider than a merely national law. The English settlers in the new world brought their law with them.

To-day English law, modified no doubt by State and Federal legislation, is the Common Law of the great republic of the United States. The colonies which still remain within our Empire are territories of the English law, save where, as in South Africa or Quebec, civilized settlers had already established and retained their own law. Throughout these lands, it matters little under which flag, an English lawyer finds the Courts speaking a language which he understands.

Thus it came about that the world, which derives its civilization from Western Europe, may be divided into lands of the English law, and lands where in outward form at least the law is Roman. And yet we must not make too much of this division. In the first place it cuts across national boundaries. It unites us with the United States of America, it separates us from some of our own colonies while it unites them with continental Europe. In the second place law is, like language, a form of thought; and diversity of form, though it hinders, does not prevent a unity of substance.

Among the forces which have made for unity something should be said of the conception of a law of nature. The phrase has been out of fashion in this country since the days of Bentham and Austin, who laid stress upon the positive, one might say arbitrary, character of the only law which they would recognize as law in the proper sense of the word. I am not concerned here to discuss its philosophical validity. But it has never been lost sight of. It is one of the inheritances of the Roman law tradition. Alike in the Middle Ages, and since their close, it has been the subject of speculation and an influence guiding the legislator, the thinker, and the administrator of law. There is a whole literature upon it on the Continent. It bulks pretty largely in Blackstone: you can see its influence on the judges of the eighteenth century in this country; the founders of the American Republic put a good deal of it into their constitution, and American judges will still refer to it without shame. What it really means is a standard by which the law here and now may be judged, a standard founded on the needs of human nature. That the standard becomes a different one, as the needs and possibilities of humanity develop, has not prevented the seeking after such a standard.

It is perhaps only another way of putting the same thing to say that law has developed and is developing constantly by reference to the pursuit of ends more or less consciously arrived at by mankind. So far as these ends are common, and I take it that in the main, amid national and individual diversity and conflict they are common ends, law has been formed for their attainment. On the whole what men have asked law to do for them has been the same at any given stage in civilization. The eighteenth century asked for liberty, property, and happiness. We are putting a rather different meaning, or perhaps a different stress on the words, not only here but throughout the civilized world, and the main movements of legal change are in the same direction everywhere.

One word about the two kinds of law known as Public and Private International law.

The fact that the laws of different countries are different gives rise to problems whenever the Courts of one country have to deal with a set of facts where some foreign element is involved, for instance a citizen or an inhabitant of another country, or property which is in another country, or a contract or transaction which took place abroad. Now we have long got past the stage at which the Courts could simply disregard the foreign element, could say this man is a foreigner, therefore he has no rights; or this event took place abroad, and therefore we will treat it as if it had never happened. On the other hand it will not do for the Court to apply simply its own law. Grave injustice would be done, for instance, if a transaction made on the faith of law which will give a certain effect to it, were treated as made under another law which will give it a different effect or no effect at all. For this reason the Courts of every country have formed rules (sometimes called Private International Law; sometimes, and as some hold, more properly, called 'Conflict of Laws') by which they determine how far, where a foreign element is involved, the foreign law is to be carried out rather than the law which the Court applies in ordinary cases. These rules are not the same in every country, because differences of opinion are possible as to what justice requires. But the very existence of such rules shows that the Courts hold that the world of law is one, however much diversified, and that no one territorial law can blindly go on its way without taking account of its neighbours.

International law in the more proper sense of the word, that is Public International Law, or the law which governs the relations between States, is a very different thing. Something of the kind was not unknown in the ancient world; the Greeks, for instance, had rules against the poisoning of wells, the proper treatment of envoys, and the making and keeping of treaties. But in its modern form it dates just from the time when States were waking up to the consciousness of sovereignty, and when the horrors of the wars which followed the Reformation showed that even sovereign powers ought to conform to some rules of conduct. It has been the work in its origin of writers and teachers of law, and has been built up more recently by agreement between States. Unlike the law between man and man, which modern states enforce by organized compulsion, there is no standing organization whose business it is to see that it is kept. It is not true to say that for this reason it is not law at all, for in primitive times the recognized rules of private law were enforced not by State sanction but by the action of individuals, with the support of the opinions and at times the active help of their neighbours and friends. But a law which is defied with success and impunity is no law. The reality and strength of International Law has lain in the fact that its breach brought at least the risk of suffering, through the common disapprobation of civilized nations ; its preservation and maintenance for the future must lie in a certainty of disaster, not greatly less than that which awaits the transgressor of private law.

Books for Reference

Jethro Brown, *The Austinian Theory of Law.* Murray.

Maine, *Ancient Law.* Murray.

Pollock and Maitland, *History of English Law.* Cambridge University Press.

Vinogradoff, *Common Sense in Law.* Home University Library. Williams & Norgate.

Vinogradoff, *Roman Law in Mediaeval Europe.* Harper's Library of Living Thought.

VI

THE COMMON ELEMENTS IN EUROPEAN LITERATURE AND ART

For some hundred years past it has been common to lay great stress upon the importance of national characteristics in art. This has been very natural, for they represent one main aspect and justification of the revolt against the conception of the one permanent and immutable standard of perfection of the Neo-classicists of the Renaissance. Lessing and Herder, who were the critical protagonists of the new world, had indeed a knowledge and admiration of ancient art which was probably superior to that of the classicists, but they refused to admit that art was bound to follow the forms of antiquity, and maintained rather that its forms would necessarily change with the changing conditions of the world, and with the varying characteristics of different nationalities or races.

From their time down to our own, then, this conception of art, as being coloured or affected strongly and continually by nationality, has become almost a commonplace of criticism, and it will not be denied that there is real importance in the conception. For though nothing is really art which is not distinctive and personal and unique, yet just so far as the personality of the artist is conditioned by his nationality, so far also will his artistic work reflect the characteristics of his nation or country. And yet, while this is true, it really needs very little consideration to see that when we consider a great work of art, we are very little concerned with the question of the nationality of the artist, but with something which is deeper and larger than his nationality. The great artist no doubt represents life under the forms or terms of his concrete experience, but it is life and the world itself which he represents. He is not greatly concerned with the merely superficial or passing aspects of human nature and the world, but with that which is essential and continuing under these terms.

It may indeed be urged that there is some real and fundamental difference between the art of the East and that of the West, but as we have come to know eastern art better, we have become more doubtful even of this, and are rather impressed with the unity of the artistic expression even of East and West. I am far from wishing to say that nationality or race has no significance in art, but I think that we have been in danger of greatly exaggerating its importance. I am at least certain that we have very constantly made too much of the supposed differences in the literature and art of the different European countries, and that we must make clear to ourselves that European art and literature are really one.

It is not unimportant to observe this at the present time, to consider whether literature and art are dividing or uniting forces. As far as we can understand, what indeed seems a little unintelligible, the Germans desire to impress upon Europe their culture or civilization, an attempt as absurd as it would be impossible, for German culture is, after all, only a part of the great European civilization, and the part cannot take the place of the whole. But on the other hand it is not less important for us to understand that what we desire to do is not to destroy those elements which Germany contributes to European civilization, but only that they should take their natural and appropriate place in that greater unity which is enriched and enlarged by the contribution of every separate

VI EUROPEAN LITERATURE AND ART

national society. European art is one; that is, the common characteristics are far more important than the national differences. And further, we often take to be national, characteristics which happen to show themselves at one time in one place, while they may have existed at another time in another place. The history of European art is in a great measure the history of successive influences or movements which were for the most part common to all Europe, but which did not always exactly synchronize in the different European countries.

So far as there is such a thing as nationalism in literature it is wholly modern, while in mediaeval literature and art there is hardly anything of it. This may seem strange to those who imagine that it is only the railway and the steamship which have brought the world together, but the truth is that the movement of ideas and fashions was probably at least as rapid in the Middle Ages as it is to-day. However this may be, the fact is, I think, clear, that when we come to examine mediaeval literature we find that it is practically homogeneous, that whether we look at it in England or France, in Germany or in Scandinavia, it has practically the same qualities. I do not speak of Italy yet, for Italian literature is the latest-born of the great European literatures, it has not at least come down to us in any forms earlier than those of the thirteenth century.

Mediaeval literature is known to us primarily under two forms, the heroic epic and the romance, and it is to these that we must first turn our attention. We know the heroic epic in different languages throughout a period which extends roughly from the eighth to the twelfth centuries. The earliest example is the English Beowulf; among the latest are the German Nibelungenlied and some of the French Chansons de Geste, which belong to the end of the twelfth century. This epic literature is not least interesting to us because it has, as far as we can judge, no trace of that great classical influence of which you have already heard, and which plays so great a part in the later developments of European literature. Now what is the epic? Its materials are the stories of northern mythology, the traditions of the great migrations which overthrew the Roman empire in the west, and the legends which grew up round the name of Charles the Great. They are stories of the gods and demigods, of the Burgundian and the Hun, of the English people possibly while still settled on the Baltic coasts, of the conflicts of the Frank and the Saracen, of the earliest settlers in Iceland; and they vary in their temper and their tone.

But they all represent the sense of the glory and splendour of the great fighting man, of the stout heart, which rises with rising danger and is never so great or so splendid as when it faces overwhelming odds and defies the inexorable fates. The epic poet is so possessed by this sense of the greatness of human nature that it does not matter much even whether the man is wrong or perverse: he loves the obstinacy of Roland, who will not, till too late, sound his horn to call Charlemagne and his armies, but prefers to face the enemy, and if need be to die, by himself, rather than to ask for help; he is filled with the sense of the magnificence of the stark figure of Hagen, who had indeed treacherously murdered the great Siegfried, but whose heart is so high and his hand so heavy, that when he is overpowered, and Chriemhilda at last avenges upon him the murder of her husband, the old knight standing by kills Chriemhilda herself—it was not meet that so great a fighter should be slain by a woman. These are the men of the epics.

And beside them stand the figures of women great and gracious, women for whose love men die and perish, but

VI EUROPEAN LITERATURE AND ART 141

who themselves also can hate and love passionately and fiercely. It has sometimes been said by those who only know the epics in one or other of the various languages, that women and the love of women have no place in the epic, but belong to the romance, but this is a mistake. In the mediaeval epic there is little talk about emotion, but in the Nibelungenlied and in some of the Icelandic sagas the woman is, like Helen in the Homeric epic, the motive and source of all the action.

The epic is the story of great and heroic figures, abstracted in that sense from the common or ordinary circumstances of life, but the background of the action is always realistic and even detailed in its realism, so that, just as again in the Homeric poems, we can frequently reconstruct the life and manners of the time to which the poems belong from that which they tell us. And it is impossible to say that there is any really national difference between the epics as we find them in different languages ; they are indeed the expression of the temperament and personality of the great artists who produced them, and they are each unique and individual in proportion to the greatness of their authors, but in their general characteristics they are the same.

There are few changes in the history of literature more remarkable than that which came over European art in the later years of the eleventh century and the beginning of the twelfth. The epic is concerned with the world of action, the romance is occupied almost exclusively with the world of feeling and emotion. For this is the real character of the romance. It has sometimes been said that the essence of the romance lies in the strange and mysterious circumstances of the world, in stories of mystery and wonder, of fairyland and magic. And it is quite true that it often uses these forms of human experience. But this is not its real quality. From the story

of Tristan and the 'lais' of Mary of France, down to
the *Vita Nuova* of Dante, that with which it is occupied
is the human heart, its hopes and fears, its joys and
sorrows, its exultation and despair. We have only to
read the earliest and greatest forms in which the story of
Tristan and Iseult have come down to us to see this for
ourselves. It is indeed true that we can see or that we
can conjecture that behind the present romance there
may have lain an epic story of the hero's actions, but
what we see now is nothing but the story of the 'infinite
passion', the 'infinite pain' of the human heart. It is
the story of their fatal love, of the passion which drives
them out of the homes of men into the wilderness, the
fatal passion which separation only makes deeper, which
nothing can change, nothing can end, the story of a
man and woman to whom the world is well lost for love.
And if you wish to see the whole meaning of life as the
romance actually understood it, you have but to turn
again to that 'lai' of Mary of France, which tells us in
a few lines how Tristan and Iseult, long parted, succeed
in meeting in the forest for a few moments—meet and
then part—and over it all there is nothing but a certain
exquisite sentiment of love and pain, of love and tears.

This romance poetry is indeed strange, so strange that
no one has yet succeeded in finding or explaining its real
origin. Only the day before, the great artists were singing
the gallant deeds of men, but now they can see nothing,
think of nothing but the human heart. And what is
perhaps strangest of all, this great reality of feeling, of
passion, is presented under the form of a world almost
wholly unreal and conventional. The men and women
of the epic were great heroic figures of larger stature, of
greater passions than the common run, but they were
quite real people, moving and acting in the real world.
The figures of romance are for the most part, but for the

VI EUROPEAN LITERATURE AND ART 143

intense reality of their love, the unreal, conventional figures of a world of knights and ladies, of unreal and conventional actions. We understand the epic world, we see and recognize their people, their dwellings, their ways of acting and thinking, but the romantic knights and ladies are mere conventions.

The truth is that the chivalrous or romantic world is unreal, partly perhaps because the artists are occupied with nothing but the emotions, and profound though these are, it is perhaps because of their abstraction that the romance ended in the strange allegorical movement of the thirteenth century. In the hands of the later and lesser poets, the romantic method finally loses almost all sense of personality, and becomes a picture and analysis of abstract emotion. It is to these abstractions that Guillaume de Lorris gave a new life and a singular grace in the personifications of the *Romance of the Rose,* and the charm and grace of his art carried Europe off its feet, so that for nearly three hundred years it tended to dominate European poetry. Even the greatest artists of these centuries, Dante and Chaucer, at least started with this method, and at the very end of the fifteenth century William Dunbar in Scotland still used it with grace and vivacity.

But I have lingered too long in the Middle Ages. I have done so because, if we could only make more clear to ourselves the homogeneity of the Europe out of which we all came, it would, I think, greatly help to clear up the superstitious exaggeration of the conception of nationality in art. There is not time to deal with it, or we might stay to observe that the characteristic of mediaeval literature is that of all mediaeval art and life. To myself, indeed, it is clear that the notion that the people of the Middle Ages desired or worked for a unified political organization is indeed a great mistake. But, on the other hand, it is equally certain that in general civilization, as in religion, there was a real unity, and that it was only very slowly indeed that the self-conscious nationalities of the modern world were formed out of the welter of the confused races and tribes of Europe : indeed, in some parts of Europe this development was not reached till the nineteenth century and in south-eastern Europe it is only coming to-day.

European art still transcends nationality ; in its essence it is differentiated by the personality of the artist, not by the distinction of nationality. This may seem at first sight a paradox, for you may be inclined to say that surely the modern national literatures are in many ways different, you will say that there is surely some great difference between Dutch and Italian painting, some great contrast between English and French poetry. Many people used to speak, perhaps some do still, of the warm and passionate and romantic south, and of the cold and ungracious and passionless north. But this is merely a delusion. Dante is not more imaginative or passionate than Shakespeare.

What is it then which has produced this impression ? The answer to the question and the best evidence of the unity of European art will perhaps be found in examining some of the great movements in its history, since the time when the civilization of the Middle Ages reached its highest point in the thirteenth century.

With the fourteenth century we come to the beginning of a movement which culminated in the greatest literature of the modern world, in the drama of England and Spain. But its beginnings are at first sight strangely different from its fulfilment, and it is almost impossible therefore to find any phrase or term under which we can justly represent it. The first great master of the new world was

VI EUROPEAN LITERATURE AND ART 145

Dante, but not the Dante of the exquisite sentiment but artificial form of the *Vita Nuova*, but the great imaginative realist of the *Divine Comedy*, the artist who could portray the passion and pain of Francesca and her lover, and with equal power the masterful figure of Farinata, whose dauntless soul not hell itself could quell; who could pass from the vivid drama of the fierce contemporary life of Italy to the infinite peace of those to whom ' la sua voluntade è nostra pace '. For indeed it is this which places Dante among the supreme poets of the world, that there is no aspect of the reality of human life and experience which is strange to him, and which the greatness of his imagination cannot make living to us. It has often been said that Dante is the greatest and most representative artist of the Middle Ages, but so far as this is true, and it is only partially true, it may make plain to us that there are no boundaries of time in art any more than of race or country. Dante is the first great artist of a new world, but it was not till three centuries had passed, it was not until Shakespeare, that the whole meaning of the new literature was made clear. The new literature has been thought to begin with two great artists, an Italian and an Englishman: with Boccaccio in the south and Chaucer in the north.

What is, then, the characteristic quality or note of the *Decameron* and the *Canterbury Tales*? It is not, as some absurd persons think, to be discovered in the licentiousness or grossness of some of these tales, this only represents one aspect of their realism, and indeed in this they do little more than continue the characteristics of what we know as the ' Fabliaux ' of the Middle Ages. The quality of the new art lies just in this, that there is nothing in human life which is uninteresting or insignificant to these great artists, that they are bound by no traditions, hampered by no conventions. They had begun as artists of romance, and the romantic sentiment of life never ceased to interest and move them, but they had learned to go beyond the romantic conventions, and to find the material of their art in everything which was part of the reality of life. To them, as to the other tale-writers of these centuries, it was quite immaterial whether they were retelling a story which had come down from immemorial antiquity, or relating something which had happened but yesterday in their own town or village, and they knew nothing of distinctions of class or rank or circumstance; it is the universal human interest which arrests them. The example which we shall find most representative is that which is to us English people the most familiar, that is the ' Prologue ' to the *Canterbury Tales*. Was there ever anything greater of its kind than this ? Who can ever forget these figures: the Knight, the Franklyn, the Prioress, the Wife of Bath? As we read there passes before us all the company of human life, wise and foolish, grave and gay, good and bad. Chaucer and Boccaccio are the greatest artists of what has often been called the ' realistic ' type, they are at least very easy to distinguish from the epic and romantic artists.

They are great artists, but it is also clear enough that their powers and their insight into human life were limited. What they began was carried out to its fulfilment by the great dramatists of the sixteenth and seventeenth centuries. For this is indeed the relation of the tale-writers to the dramatists, that they furnish the materials upon which the dramatists built up their presentation of human life, or rather, the elements which are transformed by the imagination of the great dramatists from bare ' realism ' into the highest expression of reality. No doubt the dramatists take into their work other materials and influences, but the substantial quality whether of the tragedy or the comedy is intimately related to that of the tales. How often were the great dramas built up on materials which

VI EUROPEAN LITERATURE AND ART 147

they drew from Bandello or the other Italians who continued the tradition of Boccaccio, or from similar northern sources. But the great dramatists gave their stories a life, a passion, a breadth and fullness which is far removed from that of their sources. In their hands, or rather in their creative imagination, we see not merely the external circumstance, the bare fact, but we see all the fullness and completeness, all the exquisite grace and beauty, all the passion and terror of human experience. We may call Boccaccio and Chaucer ' realists ', but it is only in Marlowe and Webster, and above all in Shakespeare, that we reach reality itself.

We all know the world of Shakespeare, how he ranges from Falstaff to Hamlet, from Bottom to Lear, from Mrs. Quickly and Doll Tearsheet to Rosalind and Imogen and Cordelia; we know how to Shakespeare, and in a lesser degree to some of the other great Elizabethans like Marlowe and Webster, there is nothing common and insignificant in life, nothing which the creative imagination of the artist cannot transform, transmute, from mere dross into pure gold. We say, and we say rightly, that here is the greatest thing that England has brought forth, and we think of it as representing the splendid youth and the first maturity of a great nation.

But now, do we remember and understand that alongside of the English drama there is another drama, not indeed so great as that of Shakespeare, but greater, I think, than that of any other Elizabethan, the drama of Spain, of Lope de Vega and Calderon, a drama of the same character, inspired by the same spirit, living under the power of the same creative imagination, a drama in which the same vivid reality is informed by the same breath of magical romance. In the tragedy of Lope de Vega, in the comedies of Calderon, with all the distinctive individuality of the great artists, and of each great work of art, we have a poetic drama which is in its essential characteristics the same as that of England.

And yet how different were the circumstances of the two nations, Spain was decadent, bankrupt, defeated; England was rising to the supreme heights of its greatness under Elizabeth and Cromwell. At the end of the sixteenth century, Spain had passed its splendid meridian and was falling into the grey obscurity of a clouded evening. It had quickly lost the great place which for a few years it had held in the world, every day brought a new failure, every year a new disaster; the great Armada had perished miserably on the dunes of Flanders and Holland, on the cliffs of Scotland and Ireland; a handful of valiant Dutchmen had defied its power and broken its wealth; the real enemy of Spain, that is France, had gathered itself together after forty years of ruin and misery, and had driven out the Spanish power. Indeed, so great, so overwhelming, was—as we can now see it—the ruin, that Philip II, who to the English imagination has stood for the embodiment of cruel and masterful malignity, has become to the historical student one of the tragic figures in history, a sincere, stupid, bigoted man, vainly striving to hold together the great empire which had been created by Ferdinand and Isabella, by Cortez and Pizarro and Charles V.

England, on the other hand, was rising from obscurity to its place as the mistress of the seas; Englishmen were raiding and plundering the New World, which Spain and Portugal had looked on as their own; England was sending out its sailors and merchants to all the seas, and to all lands, from the frozen north to the Indies.

And again, Spain was possessed by a fierce and passionate love for the old religious order, it was the one country in which devotion to the forms and conceptions of mediaeval religion had proved unshakeable, while England

VI EUROPEAN LITERATURE AND ART   149

was the representative power of the new religious temper, and was soon to hold almost the foremost place in the new intellectual life of Europe.

And yet the drama of Spain is in all its most essential and intimate characteristics the same as that of England; represents on the one side the same overwhelming sense of the tragic conflicts of life, the same sense of the greatness, the splendour of human nature, which is most triumphant when most it seems to fail; and on the other side at least something of that exquisite, that almost unimaginable grace of the romantic comedy, of the world of Portia and Viola and Beatrice and Miranda. I do not think that the unity of the great art of Europe, the comparative insignificance of merely national characteristics and historical circumstances can find a more convincing illustration.

I could wish that I were able to deal adequately with the parallel movements of painting and sculpture during these centuries, but I have neither the capacity nor is there now the time to deal with them. This much only may be said, that the movement of these arts is very closely parallel during these centuries, from the fourteenth to the seventeenth, to that of literature. I cannot discuss the characteristics of mediaeval sculpture and painting, but I would remind you that the notion that these were merely conventional and abstract is just as mistaken as the notion that mediaeval literature deals only with conventions or allegories. It is of course obviously true that the ecclesiastical or religious purpose served by the greater part of the decorative art of the Middle Ages which has survived to us, limits and restrains its subjects and its forms. But no one who is at any pains to consider mediaeval sculpture and mosaic painting can fail to see that alongside of much which became conventional, and was fixed in what has been called the ' Byzantine ' style, there is an immense amount of work both in sculpture and in mosaic which expresses the determination of the mediaeval artist to represent the world as he experienced and saw it, and that the main obstacle to the free expression of this spirit was not the acquiescence or satisfaction of the mediaeval artist in conventional forms, but the lack of technical dexterity. This will become evident to any one who will turn his attention, in studying the mosaics, from what are no doubt the somewhat conventional and hieratic figures of saints and angels to the realistic attempts to portray the stories of the Bible. And it will be clear to any one who will study, for instance, the sculpture of Wells or Amiens or Chartres that by the thirteenth century the artists were rapidly learning how to represent the world as they knew it, and something of its grace and beauty. If we say that the history of the plastic arts in Europe from the fourteenth to the seventeenth centuries is the history of the discovery and presentation first of reality, and then of reality as transformed by the highest imaginative conception of beauty, this must not be understood to mean that reality and beauty had been absent from those arts in the Middle Ages.

If then we trace the development of Italian art, we shall first observe in such work as that of Masaccio in the Brancacci chapel at Florence just the same characteristic interest in the appearance and the varieties of human life as we find in the work of Boccaccio and Chaucer, and in the succession of the great Tuscan and Umbrian and Venetian painters and sculptors the same transformation of the bare reality of life by the magic of the imaginative sense of beauty and of passion as in the great drama. It is not, I think, merely fanciful to say that the real counterpart of the English and Spanish drama is to be found in the Italian painters and sculptors of the fifteenth and sixteenth centuries and in the Flemish artists of the early seventeenth. It is certainly true that each of these great artists had his own individual and distinctive genius, but the exquisite grace and beauty of the Umbrians and Tuscans have never been matched save in the romantic comedy of Shakespeare, and the presentation of the tragic passion of the human soul in *King Lear* has only once been equalled, and that is in the dreadful beauty and horror of the Night and Day, the Evening and the Morning of Michelangelo.

I do not think I need say much about the classical movement in art and literature, for we all know that it was international. It was begun by Petrarch, not indeed the Petrarch of the sonnets, for these are only a later form of the Troubadour lyric, and do not show any special trace of the classical influence, but the Petrarch whose letters were the first summons of Europe to a new and indefatigable work of the rediscovery of the ancient world. It was an Italian with whom the classical movement began, but it was only in the hands of two northern artists that it achieved a satisfying development in literature: the one a Frenchman, Racine, the other an Englishman, Milton. Neither are, I imagine, really classical at all, but of the two, Milton, as he was by far the more learned in ancient art, was also probably nearer to the ancient world both in form and in spirit.

Nor need I say anything about the deplorable ravages of the movement of good taste and common sense, which produced Boileau and, in some measure, Pope. It did some good, but far more evil, but happily it is long past and dead and done with, and we can afford to remember the little good and to forget the evil. Good or evil, it was at least very clearly a European and not a national movement.

I must ask you now to consider the extraordinary changes which passed over Europe in the eighteenth century, to trace the beginnings of that change which culminated in what we generally call the Romantic movement.

We all know, though not as well as we should, the work of Defoe, and beside Defoe there stands a painter whom also we all know, the great Hogarth. We all at least have read *Robinson Crusoe*, and we have probably all seen Hogarth's engravings of the good and bad apprentices, and the series of paintings in the National Gallery known as the 'Marriage à la mode'.

What is it now that we find in Defoe and Hogarth? An infinite multitude of detail—we all remember the 'three Dutch cheeses' and the 'fowling-pieces' which Robinson carefully ferried on his raft from the wreck to the island—an unsparing presentation of all the ugly and sordid realities of life; you might almost say, by preference the ugly realities, the squalid vices, the stupid and brutal ferocity of human nature. It is not a pretty or a pleasing world which we see in Hogarth or in Defoe's *Colonel Jack*. But they are great artists. If you see human nature often on its most repulsive side, in its harshest and most repellent form, at least you see in their novels or pictures, the world as they saw it in the streets and taverns, in the police courts and prisons of their day, as for that matter you can still see it everywhere in town or country. The world which they see may often, perhaps usually, be ugly, but at least there is no conventional prettiness, there is no smug veneer of an artificial good taste which refuses to call a spade a spade, and which deliberately turns away from those things in life which are irritating to its sense of decorum and propriety.

Here there is something new, and we can imagine a defender of the nationalist conception of art saying that

VI   EUROPEAN LITERATURE AND ART   153

here at last we have an obvious example of the revolt of northern realism against the southern or classical grace. But there could not be a greater delusion. For though it is true that the new realism was not fully developed all over Europe until the eighteenth century, it had its beginnings in the sixteenth century, and not in the ' cold ' north, but in the ' romantic ' south. The first signs of the new movement are to be found not in England or in Flanders, but in Spain in the sixteenth century. It was the *Lazarillo de Tormes*, the first of the Picaresque novels which struck the new note, which turned from the fantastic and conventional world of the romances in which Don Quixote had nourished his soul, and from the heroic world of beauty and grace of the dramatists, to the bare and hard reality of the life of the beggar and the vagabond. Not even Defoe himself ever surpassed the clearness and precision of the *Lazarillo*, and it was the first work of a type, whose slow development can be traced in almost every country in Europe: in England, in the realistic attempts of Greene and Nash and Deloney, in Germany in *Simplicissimus*, in France in the *Roman comique* of Scarron and in the *Gil Blas* of Le Sage, who was an almost exact contemporary of Defoe.

And all this can be traced just as clearly in the history of painting. The great Italian painting had ended with the gorgeous magnificence of the Venetian school, with Giorgione and Titian and Tintoretto, and its mastery passed for a few years to Flanders, to Rubens and Vandyck ; but in the painting of Spain and of the Low Countries in the later seventeenth century we find ourselves in another world. The little beggar boys of Murillo may perhaps show a somewhat mannered realism, but the Spanish painting, as a whole, while it would be absurd to try to describe it under any one phrase, shows very clearly the determination to present the reality of the world under terms which are very different from those of the great Italians of the fifteenth and sixteenth centuries. And when we turn to the art of the Low Countries in the latter part of the seventeenth and in the eighteenth centuries, leaving for the moment out of account the new art of landscape painting, we find ourselves in the same world as that of Defoe and Hogarth.

What was this, then, that had come to European art and literature? Clearly what we see is the transition from the heroic world of the tragedy, from the splendid beauty and force of the Italian painters, from the infinite grace of the romantic comedy, to some other artistic apprehension of the world. The movement was not indeed wholly dependent upon a reaction, but in its development it corresponds with the reaction against the continuance of a great tradition which had become merely a convention, when it had lost its vitality and sincerity. The best examples of this may perhaps be found in Dryden's attempt to carry on the heroic tradition in English tragedy, and in Voltaire's strenuous and meritorious efforts to continue the work of Racine and Corneille. They meant well, and their tragic dramas are not without merit, but it is clear enough that they could not bend the bow of Ulysses. They were great artists, as we can see clearly enough in *Absalom and Ahitophel*, or in *Candide*, but their genius lay in other directions. 'Il faut cultiver notre jardin' is a great judgement of life, one very wholesome and necessary for all time, but it was not the mood of Othello or of Hamlet.

European art had to come down from the empyrean, and though the descent was great, yet it gained new life by once again touching mother earth.

No doubt, however, the harsh reality of Hogarth and Defoe was not the whole of life, and, by a strange transition, before the middle of the eighteenth century we find the

VI EUROPEAN LITERATURE AND ART 155

novelists and, though they are less important, the dramatists, turning from the faithful and minute study of the outward appearance and form of things to the study of sensibility and emotion, and the world, which had seemed so hard and unmoved, was dissolved in tears.

We find this a strange and even a ridiculous spectacle, the men who had prided themselves on their common sense and reasonableness, whose literature had sparkled with wit and epigram, blubbering and crying like great children; but whatever we think of it, that is what happened. The first artist of the new type was a Frenchman, Marivaux, and his *Vie de Marianne* is a study of a young woman who is the embodiment of sensibility and self-consciousness, an amiable and virtuous girl, who is hardly able to enjoy the good that life brings her, for fear lest she should miss the opportunity of renunciation. The first great novel of sentiment is also French, the Abbé Prévost's *Manon Lescaut*, and here indeed we are in the deep waters of affliction; there are but few moments between the beginning and the end of his sad story when the hero is not in tears. And yet it is a great novel, for there are few studies of human nature, as absorbed and almost lost in emotion, which are more moving.

These novels, however, which appeared between 1730 and 1740, are overshadowed by the works of the great Englishmen, by Richardson and Sterne and Goldsmith, for these are not artists of England alone, but of all Europe, known and loved and imitated in every country in Europe. The sorrows of *Clarissa*, the pathetic or maudlin humour of Sterne, the idyllic grace and gentle laughter of Goldsmith, these, as they moved every heart, influenced even the greatest of European artists. The influence of *Clarissa* on Rousseau, of Goldsmith on Goethe and Jean Paul Richter need no exposition.

The sentimental movement reached almost its highest

level in the great and morbid genius of Rousseau, who was himself the living embodiment of the movement. Far more than even his creations, more than Julie or Saint-Preux, was he himself possessed by an emotionalism which finally became a disease. But, strangely enough, it was the Olympic genius of Goethe which gave its supreme form to the treatment of life under the terms of feeling. In *Werther* this whole phase of art passed beyond itself into the tragedy of the vain and hopeless efforts of an honest but over-sensitive nature to control his emotion and to master his life. Not indeed that it was with *Werther* the movement ended: it was continued in Byron: it was perhaps the most important element in what the Germans call specifically their *Romantische Schule*, and in the work of the French Romantic artists from Chateaubriand to Alfred de Musset. If you wish to see it in painting you have only to look at the work of Greuze, and at the engravings in our grandmothers' 'Forget-me-nots'. In spite of all its absurdities this sentimental movement played a great part in preparing men for the great revolution itself, for it opened men's hearts, it set free their emotions; if the realism of Defoe and Hogarth had enabled men to escape from convention and the mannerisms of good taste into a world of reality, the emotional movement gave this reality fullness and content, represented a larger and more intimate apprehension of life.

This brings us to another aspect of the art of the seventeenth and eighteenth centuries, to the poetry and painting of 'nature', to the beginnings of that great artistic movement which culminates in Wordsworth and Turner, and whose influence dominated all Europe in the eighteenth century and continues to do so in our own time. It seems a strange thing, but it is true, that it was not till the seventeenth and eighteenth centuries that there appeared a school of painting which took landscape, and a poetry

VI   EUROPEAN LITERATURE AND ART   157

which took 'nature' specifically for its subject. There is indeed frequent reference to 'nature' in the poetry of the Middle Ages and of the sixteenth century, and this is often significant in the early English poetry and charming in the romances and in Petrarch and Chaucer, while in Dante and the Elizabethans, and especially in Shakespeare, it reaches an almost incomparable beauty; yet in all these it is, as in the backgrounds of the great Tuscan and Umbrian painters, exquisite and significant and true, but not the prime subject which engages their attention.

There are indeed two great poets in whom we begin to feel that the background begins to be almost as important as the figures of the foreground; Spenser is genuinely interested in his stories of chivalry and honour, and in his moral allegory, but we sometimes wonder whether the most important thing in his poetry is not the chequered light and shade of his forests, the picturesque splendour of his castles, and the gloom of his caverns and dungeons. Spenser's poetry is like a tapestry on which indeed some story of human life is presented, but which is in the end a great work of decorative art, to which the immediate subject contributes form and pattern and colour, but in which it is in a measure lost.

In Milton the matter is different: no one can doubt that he is a great artist of human life and fate; even if *Paradise Lost* were to leave us in some uncertainty, the *Samson* would convince us all. But, while I think this is true, it is also clear that not only in the grace of his earlier poetry, but in the maturity of his genius, in the *Lycidas* and even in the *Paradise*, Milton is at least as great an artist of nature and its beauty as he is of life. And near Milton there stands a poet, lesser indeed, but individual and unique, that is Henry Vaughan, who had unhappily strayed into the 'metaphysical' maze, and who helplessly enough tries to endue himself with the giant armour of Donne, but who, when he is himself, is one of the most exquisite and gracious poets of nature.

We may perhaps, without being fanciful, find a parallel to these poets in the great Venetian painters of the sixteenth century, in whose work we see the landscape of Venetia and the Cadore compelling more and more our attention, as not a mere background, but as an integral part of the picture; but it was not till the seventeenth century and the Flemish and Dutch painters that we see the transition complete, and the artist sets before us not some scene in human life, but simply the beauty and splendour of 'nature' herself.

It was not till Thomson began to publish *The Seasons* in 1726 that the development was complete in poetry. Thomson is a difficult poet to appreciate rightly, for though his subject was 'nature' his method was often as conventional and artificial as that of any Augustan; but he was a lover of the fields and woods, and his imagination, if it is not very powerful, is often very sincere. What was begun by Thomson was carried on with greater sincerity and reality by Cowper, and was transformed by the imagination of Gray and Collins. We sometimes think of this development as specifically English, and it is true that in Wordsworth and Shelley the poetry of nature grew into something which is unique and unmatched, but we must not think of the poetry of Wordsworth as though it were the only form under which nature can be presented. That would be to ignore the qualities, in England of Keats and Tennyson, and in Europe of great artists in whom the treatment of nature assumed other forms. The great poetry of nature began in England, but it was carried on in all the European countries, and for more than a century it was dominated mainly by the genius of Rousseau in France and of Goethe in Germany. I cannot here pretend to deal with the treatment of nature in Rousseau, or with the outcome of his influence first in Bernardin de Saint-Pierre and Chateaubriand, and then in the elegiac beauty of Lamartine and de Musset's *Nuits*; nor can I deal with the poetry of nature in Goethe, and its lesser but often beautiful expression in the German 'Romanticists', and in Heine. It is only possible here to remind ourselves that neither the poetry nor the painting of nature belongs to any one country, but is an intimate part of all modern art.

And thus at last we come to the great revolution itself, that great revolution in art and thought and life, of which the political and social revolution is one form, and of which we are all the children. In this, all the elements of which we have been thinking are gathered up and come to perfection; reality, sentiment, nature. And this was of no one country or nationality. The first and also the greatest artist of the revolution is Goethe himself, for it all culminates and reaches its highest expression in *Faust*. The passion for freedom, for the complete experience of life, for life itself, and not mere knowledge or mere words—this is the motive which drives Faust till he is willing to make his bargain with any power which will give him this. The infinite, the insatiable desire of the human soul, which can never be wholly satisfied, which can never reach its term, this is the passion which possesses Faust, this is the rock upon which the hopes of the poor devil are shipwrecked, the poor devil who in the limitation of the merely critical and negative temper cannot understand that Faust can never be satisfied, will never say to the moment, ' Verweile doch, du bist zu schön.' For the drama of *Faust* is not a drama of damnation, but of redemption, and though the breadth and scope óf the whole conception pass beyond all presentation in complete and rounded form, the great tragedy of Gretchen takes us from the splendid but abstract world of ideas into the simplest experience of human life, where Faust becomes human through love itself, but too slowly, too late to avert the tragedy.

If Goethe represents the great humane conceptions of the revolution most profoundly, Wordsworth comes very near him in the depth of his knowledge of humanity, and in his supreme sense of the unity of all life and nature with the living spirit who is in all things; and the great romantic artists of France are governed by the same sense of nature and love and the spiritual, and in Victor Hugo this reaches a level only just below that of Goethe himself.

You must not misunderstand me, nationality has real meaning, it has something akin, but distantly, to personality; but in the main it affects the more superficial aspects of art. In painting and sculpture the European artists use a language which we can all understand, imagine life and nature under terms which we all feel and know to be true. And, though in literature the language creates a real difference, and causes a difficulty in recognizing the unity which lies behind the difference, yet the moment we begin to overcome that difficulty we find ourselves in a world intelligible, familiar, moving to us all; and intelligible just in proportion to the greatness of the artist.

It is idle for us to dispute about the relative greatness of our national arts, for their greatness lies not in national idiosyncrasies, but in the personality of the artist, and in the single, the unique quality of the particular works of art, and these belong not to this country or nation or to that, but to us all. It is not to Frenchmen only that the intellectual passion of Pascal, or the hatred of shams and the love of the honest man of Molière or of Voltaire, appeal, but to us all. It is not only Germans who under-

VI EUROPEAN LITERATURE AND ART

stand the splendour of human experience, and the infinite pathos of the mistakes of the human heart, but we all. And the spectacle of the tempest in the heart of Lear, that tempest of the soul, of which the storms of nature are but a faint reflection, or the exquisite serenity and humanity of the recognition of Cordelia, these are not the prerogative possessions of England, but they speak to the heart and soul of the whole world.

We may be divided from each other by many things, material or political, but in the supreme art and poetry we rise above all these distinctions and are only men and women, with the earth under our feet and the heavens above us.

Books for Reference

The subject treated in the essay may be considered in relation to the following works:

Beowulf; *The Song of Roland*; *The Nibelungenlied*.
Tristan and Iseult (Thomas, or Béroul); Mary of France, *Lais*.
Dante, *Divina Commedia*.
Boccaccio, *Decameron*; Chaucer, *Canterbury Tales*.
Shakespeare; Lope de Vega; Calderon.
Defoe, *Robinson Crusoe*; Le Sage, *Gil Blas*.
Marivaux, *Marianne*; Prévost, *Manon Lescaut*.
Richardson, *Clarissa*; Goethe, *Werther*.
Goethe, *Faust*; Wordsworth, *Michael*, &c.
Victor Hugo, *Légende des Siècles*.

There are English translations of the greater number of these.

VII

SCIENCE AND PHILOSOPHY AS UNIFYING FORCES

SOME political thinkers have taken the State for the highest form of human association. Humanity is for them a mere abstract idea. It is no organized whole; owns, they think, no common allegiance, pursues no common aim. To find such an organized whole, such an allegiance, such an aim, we must look to the State and to nothing beyond it. We find such a whole in Germany, in France, in England, but not in anything common to the three and to other States as well. This opinion, due in its modern shape to Hegel and his followers, is false to history, false in political theory, and mischievous in ethics, but it is nowhere more false than in relation to the world of thought. The essential unity of Western civilization as an intellectual, moral, and spiritual commonwealth is indeed illustrated—unfortunately illustrated as it happens—by this very theory of the State which denies it. For the theory is of German make. It arose out of the historical conditions of Prussia in the early years of the nineteenth century, was fostered in Germany by the peculiar method by which the unity of the nation was effected, and, setting out from its home, has permeated much of the thought of the West, effectively combating the Liberal humanitarianism which was the especial contribution of England to the movement of the nineteenth century. The reaction of the German idea of the State on the English conception of liberty is the dominating influence of the last forty years in English political thought and progress. There can hardly be a more striking testimony to the reality of that unity which the theorists who embody it seek to depreciate or deny.

When we speak of unity in this connexion we may mean one of three things. There is a unity of character or type. There is the unity involved in continuous unbroken descent from a common origin, and there is unity of effective interconnexion and mutual dependence. These senses of the term unity are confused by some writers, but must clearly be distinguished before any useful inquiry can be made. Unity of character, for example, is a different thing from continuity of historical development, for a civilization might radically change its character in the course of generations. It might lose all the specific features of its own family and come into closer resemblance with others of quite distinct parentage. Again unity of character is not the same thing as the effective interconnexion and co-operation of different centres. On the contrary, such co-operation is of most value where there is marked difference of character, where, for instance, a lack of a quality in one nation is counteracted by a surplus in another. Thus these three forms of unity are distinct, but if distinct they are not unrelated. Naturally, where there is a common origin, many traits of the primitive unity of character are likely to persist, and where there is effective intercommunication, many differences may be rubbed off. So, where we start with unity of origin, we are likely to find some measure of unity in other respects, and this is what we do find, in fact, in the case of Western civilization. It does possess a certain unity of character, and this is largely due to unity of origin, and is maintained in spite of marked divergences, which have not impeded an effective intercommunication but have tended rather to add interest and value to the results which that intercommunication has produced.

Section I.—Unity of Character

There is a certain unity of character running through all civilization, and indeed through all humanity. Certain fundamental institutions and principles of organization are common to East and West, to the ancient and modern world, to civilization and savagery, and there is not the least evidence that the similarities are the result of historic connexion. On the contrary, they arise from a human nature which is fundamentally the same, adjusting itself to conditions of life which are fundamentally the same. But of course it is only the broadest and most general characters that are thus common to all the world. Within them there is every sort and degree of specific difference. There are types within types, worlds within worlds, and what we call Western civilization is one of these. That is to say, it is at the present day a family or group of nations sharing in common certain things which distinguish it from the rest of the world, such things, for instance, as a certain degree of social order, a certain outlook upon life, certain fundamentals of religion and ethics, and an industrial organization based on applied science. Now to mention any of these points is at once to provoke a criticism. In each respect, it will be said, the nations of Western Europe and the lands that have been colonized from them differ vastly among themselves. The social order of Germany is by no means that of England. The industrial development of southern Italy is very different from that of Belgium. The Prussian outlook upon life—this in particular will be emphasized just now—is quite another thing from the French. This is true enough, but once again it means only that there are further specific differences within the genus. We could pursue the differences as far down as we like. For the United Kingdom, say, is by no means

VII UNIFYING FORCES

one homogeneous whole. Even within England alone deep contrasts reveal themselves between the agricultural South and the industrial North. Yet we do not hesitate to think of the English character, English institutions, the English type as distinct from the rest of the world, and we are right in so doing because there is a real unity pervading all the differences. Just in the same way at a higher remove there is a certain unity of character pervading the deeper and wider differences that appear in the various centres of Western civilization.

Section II.—Unity of Origin

This unity of character is very largely due to continuous descent from a common cultural ancestor. The civilization of the West is fundamentally one not because the peoples of the West are one racially. They are not so. They comprise every branch of the Aryan family and a considerable admixture of quite other stocks. Their civilization owes its common characteristics mainly to a common origin and continued interaction. That is why it is in the mass a community of ideas, for ideas pass from man to man and from nation to nation more readily than institutions, more readily far than character, more readily perhaps than anything except material goods. In the realm of ideas Western civilization forms a single commonwealth of informal but of exceeding democratic constitution. This freedom, indeed, it owes in large measure to its international character, for there are constantly arising local and temporary dictators, arbiters of fashion in the ideas of politics, philosophy, and even of science. Within a narrow circle such a dictator often has it all his own way, but it is seldom that he can maintain a prolonged ascendancy throughout the international commonwealth unless there is some pretty solid foundation for his doctrine.

This commonwealth has its foundations in the past. It derives in the first instance from the unity of mediaeval Christendom, where it enjoyed the advantage of a common language of learning, the gradual loss of which is imperfectly compensated by the possession of two or three modern languages alone by the educated man of the present day. Through mediaeval Christendom and through the Arabic schools, which can hardly be regarded as a part of Western civilization but in the Middle Ages were rather its teachers, it derives from the Greco-Roman world, and through the Greco-Roman world from the Greeks themselves. The Greeks in their turn were aware that they owed the rudiments of their science to the ancient civilizations of the Nile and the Euphrates. Thus in the intellectual world there is a continuity stretching back six thousand years or more to the beginnings of recorded civilization. More than once the continuity is nearly broken, but some strand is always preserved, and it is in this continuity in the world of ideas that we get the main evidence of such progress as human history reveals.

The foundations of material civilization were laid in Egypt and in Babylonia, where the progress made in agriculture and the industrial arts implies a considerable body of empirical knowledge of physics and chemistry at an early date. We have Egyptian textbooks of arithmetic dating from the eighteenth and perhaps from the twelfth dynasty. We have texts dealing with the rudiments of geometry. Empirical chemistry appears to be of Egyptian origin, the word itself is referred to the Egyptian term for black earth—and to have passed to the Arabs, who made it into a quantitative science, without greatly interesting the scientific mind of Greece. Careful astronomical records extending over thousands of years were kept both in Egypt and Babylonia, and upon them a considerable body of astronomical knowledge was built

VII UNIFYING FORCES

up. But there is no evidence of a scientific interest detached at once from theology and industry. In theology itself Egyptian learning early became dissatisfied with the popular deities, and sought for a unity of the godhead either in some one supreme deity such as the sun or, more often, in a mystical identification of all the gods as so many incarnations or impersonations of a single principle. But though these and kindred speculations were not without influence on Greek thought, the entire achievement of Egypt in this direction, so far as known to us, was of little importance as compared with that of other oriental civilizations.

Thus without underestimating a debt which the Greeks themselves acknowledged, it remains true to regard science and philosophy alike as in essence an original creation of the Greek genius. What grew up in Greece during the sixth and fifth centuries B.C. was the spirit of disinterested inquiry proceeding on rational methods. By the term disinterested I mean detached from ulterior objects. Geometry for the Greek was something more than the art of land measurement, astronomy something more than a means of regulating the calendar or foretelling an eclipse. It was a study of the nature of the heavens, an attempt to penetrate the construction of the material universe. So with geometry. It might begin as an investigation of the relations of particular triangles, squares, and oblongs, but it developed into an attempt to grasp the nature of space relations and to understand them as depending on simple common principles. This is to say that in the hands of the Greeks these subjects first became sciences. But a still greater subject also became in their hands matter for disinterested rational inquiry. They developed what Aristotle called the science of Reality, or, as we call it, Philosophy—the attempt to approach by the rational criticism of experience the problem of the nature and origin of the universe and of man's place therein. They propounded the fundamental questions which still occupy the highest intellects of mankind. They laid the foundations of method and bequeathed to Europe the terminology which all exact thinking requires. Even when we speak of method we are using an Aristotelian term, and when we distinguish one subject from another we are employing the Latin translation of the word which Aristotle introduced. In a word, modern thought, scientific and philosophic alike, has a unitary origin. It is derived from the Greek.

The mode of this derivation is not simple, and would require considerable space to examine in detail. In outline it must suffice to say that the Greek culture was spread over the Eastern Mediterranean through the conquests of Alexander, and that as its capital Alexandria gradually replaced Athens. It flowed westward with the Roman conquests, when, as the Roman poet said, captured Greece took captive her barbarous conqueror and introduced the arts into rustic Latium. It shared in the general decline which accompanied the rebarbarization and final collapse of the Roman Empire. But now occurred a division in the stream of historic tendency. The fortunes of East and West were separated. The Western Empire was overrun by Germanic tribes, and after the sixth century the tradition of the old culture was maintained for the most part in the monasteries. Greek was forgotten in the West. Greek authors were known only in Latin translations, and science and philosophy came to a standstill. In the East the Mohammedan conquests brought the Arabs into touch with Greek learning. They preserved the tradition and extended the work, and it was the contact with Arabic culture through the crusades which initiated the first renaissance in the West in the twelfth century. There followed the epoch of the great mediaeval systems, the rediscovery of Aristotle and the attempt to fuse the Christian faith with the Aristotelian system. The later Middle Age was the period at which Western civilization was most distinctly a cultural unit, the scene of a great attempt to unify all the aspects of life, the religious, the philosophic, the political, on the basis of a religious faith made articulate and systematic with the aid of Greek philosophy, speaking the Latin tongue as the common possession of all educated men.

The paradox of thought is that while unity is its ideal, freedom is its necessary condition, and endless divergence the inevitable consequence. There could not be much thinking about matters of faith without heresy, nor about matters of politics without disaffection, rebellions and new political grouping. Heresy and schism broke up the mediaeval unity and reinforced the political tendencies making towards the modern state system. The rise of modern literature displaced the classics from their unique position as literary models. After the seventeenth century the habit of writing in the vernacular tended more and more to oust Latinity, and culture in each country began to assume more of a distinctively national character. Specific national characteristics began to appear in science and philosophy as well as in literature and education, and a large part of the history of modern thought depends on the partial independence on the one hand and the frequent interactions on the other of these centres.

Section III.—Unity of Interconnexion

This brings us to the third sense in which unity can be predicated of a cultural group. The unity that depends on the interconnexion of distinct parts implies some differences of character. Western civilization has lost something of the unity of character which it owed to its common origin, though it still retains enough of it to figure as a single whole in contrast to the rest of the world. We may be sure that the differences between German, French, and English seem much less marked to the intelligent Chinese than they are to Germans, Frenchmen, and English themselves. We ourselves habitually think of China and Japan together as denizens of the Far East, and it is only personal acquaintance which makes us begin to mark the differences between them. Few Europeans, I imagine, get as far in their discrimination as to appreciate the distinctions between the Northern and Southern Chinese, which are as clear to the Chinese themselves as the difference between English and Scottish is to us. Western civilization does retain a generic unity of character, though national differences have had an increasing influence in the sphere of thought. Meanwhile the unity of interconnexion has on the whole grown closer with the spread of education, the multiplication of learned magazines and the facilities of travel. One of the most interesting chapters in the development of modern thought can be written, as Dr. Merz has shown by example as well as by precept, on the theme of the mutual influence of the great national centres of thought, and in particular of France, England, and Germany. These nations might seem as though designed, whether by nature or by the unconscious hand of political history, to be half-willing, half-reluctant complements to each other. English common sense, French lucidity, German idealism; English liberty, French equality, German organization; English breadth, French exactitude, German detail,—how much poorer the world would be if any one of these had been allowed to develop on its own lines without the criticism of the other two. What a special providence gave the easy-going Englishman a northern neighbour to lecture him on German metaphysics in his own tongue and compel him to the definiteness which he instinctively detests,

VII UNIFYING FORCES

Without Scotland as a link, the connexion between English and German thought would hardly have been effective and continuous, and it was a Scotsman who aroused the greatest of German metaphysicians—himself of Scottish descent—from his dogmatic slumbers.

This international division of labour is more significant in the regions of metaphysics and political thought than of physical science. To science, every modern nation has contributed both great names and useful journeyman work. Through the medium of the learned reviews and of periodical congresses science has become more and more international. It is still possible now and again for a great discovery like that of Mendel or an important hypothesis like that of the kinetic theory of gases to be ignored for a whole generation. But this does not seem to depend especially on difficulties of language or of international communication. There is a queer element of arbitrary fashion in the scientific world which every now and then decrees that certain people shall be ignored, no matter how sound their work, or that certain hypotheses shall be treated as matters of faith, no matter how flimsy their structure. Man does not all at once become a creature of pure reasoning by assuming the robe of science and entering the laboratory. But national prejudices are not pre-eminent among the forces which dictate these fashions. Indeed in the English intellectual world there operates, if anything, a certain anti-national prejudice. It has sometimes been easier for an Englishman to get a hearing in Germany than in England, and it is certain that in many subjects a respect is paid to German writers which they would not have been able to win if they had written either in French or in English. This is due to a certain encyclopaedic minuteness which is the peculiar property of German industry. If you want an exhaustive negative, I remember an archaeologist saying once, you must go to the Germans.

That is to say, on almost any subject you will find some German, and a German only, who has taken the trouble to go through the whole matter from beginning to end, not attending merely to what is interesting or important, but writing down *all* that is to be found out in all the authorities bearing on that subject. And this work will be insufferably tedious and, taken by itself, may be very unilluminating. But it is much less tedious for the reader than it was for the writer, and, if suitably indexed, such a work will in permanence serve as a guide-book to those who are going to exercise real thought and insight upon that subject. It is the element of disinterested drudgery which the Germans have contributed to science. Not that they have lacked men of genius, but that they have added to genius that which, Carlyle notwithstanding, it so often lacks— the infinite capacity for taking pains. Take up any scientific treatise in any language and on almost any subject, cast your eye down the references to authorities in the footnotes on a few pages at random, and you will find probably three out of four of those cited bearing German names. They will outbalance English, American, French, Dutch, and Italian added together. If you pass from quantity to quality, if you take the leading ideas contributed to the subject, you will find the balance redressed. Here French and English and others hold their own, and perhaps a little more than their own. But in bulk of work, and especially in the faithful, unrepaying service of the hard dry fact, the Germans have set a standard to the world. It may be that their very merit is due in part to a lack of certain qualities as well as to a superabundance of others. There is a want of proportion in some of these vast Teutonic treatises that takes the heart out of the English student. Some witty person has said that German science consists in demonstrating over again with enormously elaborate apparatus what an Englishman has already made plain enough to any sensible person with the aid of a gingerbeer bottle and an old sardine tin. But I suspect there is another side to the question. The German has probably worked out his figures to the twentieth decimal where the Englishman was content with the second, and it may always turn out that the twentieth decimal has its value. Be that as it may, the co-operation of both types of mind is necessary, and patient endeavour in the elaboration of detail is the peculiar function which the German academic tradition has developed in the service of the general cause of the advancement of learning.

In more speculative thought the equipoise of international co-operation reveals itself in the changes which national thought has undergone under foreign influence. In the eighteenth and early nineteenth centuries English and Scottish metaphysics developed in the main on lines of their own. It was the heyday of the so-called English school of experience. This school was influential in France, and in Germany acted as the ferment which dissolved the older academic tradition and stimulated the growth of the new idealism. German idealism first became an influence in England through the medium of Coleridge and later of Carlyle. But it had little effect on the national philosophy except in shaking the younger Mill out of the narrow rut in which he had been educated and contributing to his thought that stream of influence which throughout life he tried in vain to merge harmoniously with the paternal teaching. But in the last third of the nineteenth century new channels of influence were opened. The authority of Green at Oxford and of Caird in the Scottish universities brought the tide of Hegelian influence, on the ebb in Germany, in full flood over the intellectual world of Great Britain and America. English empiricism was rapidly swept out of existence.

Mill and Spencer, the dominating figures of the sixties and seventies were reduced to the position of dummies used for target practice by beginners. Being intelligible they could be read by the first-year student, and the exposition of their fallacies provided an easy task for the lecturer's wit. There was none so poor to do them reverence, or if any did he was relegated to a fourth class in the Final Schools. It would be a very interesting study in our object to analyse the Anglo-Scottish idealism in close relation to the German original, and measure the changes which a philosophy undergoes in the process of assimilation by a people of very different intellectual tradition. Lack of sympathy with German and particularly with Hegelian idealism disqualifies me from the task, but this much in spite of this lack I can see. The German philosophers had a hold on those large and general ideas which the English mind seems instinctively to distrust, and which English philosophy had sought to resolve away into component parts. The Englishman as a philosopher is by nature very much like the Englishman as a mechanic or as a business man. He wants to touch and see, to test and handle, before he is convinced of reality. 'I desire that it be produced' is the frequent remark of Hume—Scotsman in some respects, but very English in this—whenever he is dealing with some conception not readily verifiable in experience. English philosophy left to itself was not inclined to do justice to the subtler, more evasive notions that are not readily defined. It did not allow enough for what we may call the imponderable elements. German idealism has had just the opposite fault. It has been too ready to take its thoughts for realities, too prone to use large and perhaps vague conceptions as if they were solid coin and not tokens that needed a good deal of scrutiny to determine their value. We may see an example in a branch of

VII UNIFYING FORCES 175

political thought which has been a good deal under discussion of late To some German thinkers the conception of the State presents itself in a manner which by no means comes natural to the Englishman. To the German the State is an entity as obvious, real, and apparent as the individual citizen. It is not just the head of Germany, or the sixty-five millions of Germans, or the Kaiser, or the army, or the Government. It is just itself, the State, and it has attributes and powers, is the object of duties and possessor of rights just like any Hamburg merchant or Prussian Junker. To the natural Englishman all this seems half mystical, half superficial. Talk to him of the State and if he is to grasp the conception at all he must get it into terms of persons or things. He pictures it perhaps as the Government, perhaps simply as the income-tax collector, perhaps as the miscellaneous millions living in the United Kingdom. If he discusses its wellbeing, its success or its failure, he does so under the reserve that all this is a shorthand for the wellbeing of great numbers of men and women. If its honour and good faith are in question what he will ask is whether Sir E. Grey fulfilled a definite pledge at a given moment after the manner of an English gentleman. Now for my own part, whether through national prejudice or not, I believe this habit of checking and resolving large conceptions to be the safest and most scientific way of dealing with them. Yet I can also see that it may lead to a good deal of crudity and may lead men to ignore important elements for which they cannot readily find some concrete expression. In this very matter of the State, for example, we are dealing with an organization of individuals, and if our way of talking about it makes us overlook the flesh and blood of which it is composed, the other way may obscure in our minds the vital differences introduced by the very fact of organization. The Germans have often seen the wood more clearly when the Englishman was more careful to distinguish and name the trees. So I cannot doubt that it will prove in the end to have been good for us to have been compelled by a few leading thinkers to go to school with the Germans for a couple of generations, even at the cost of the temporary depreciation of much that was most vital in our own social philosophy. Perhaps the best thing that can be wished for Germany, and through her for Europe, in the next generation, is that she should learn as much from our tradition as we have learned from her.

The whole history of political thought in the last two centuries is a study of complex interactions between processes going forward in each of the leading nations. The liberalism of Locke and the principles of the Whig revolution profoundly influenced France, and the very fact that distance lent them enchantment and allowed them to be idealized gave them a value as a stimulus to the French critic of absolute government which they could hardly exercise at home, where their real limitations were better known. The French revolution bore on the entire thought of Europe, alike by sympathy and antipathy, producing the reactionary philosophies of Burke in England and of Hegel in Germany, and the endeavour to formulate a new and safer line of Radicalism by Bentham. Philosophical Radicalism expressed in the main by the distinct but related Manchester school had two generations of development in England, and was felt as a real influence abroad during the period of comparative peace that followed Waterloo and that raised men's hopes of an era that should put wars aside and devote itself to the essential progress of mankind. French influences again, particularly that of Comte acting through J. S. Mill, brought new life into this school as the first flush of its youth was fading. Finally, as we have seen, German influences overwhelmed it, and England, fascinated as much by the prestige of Germany as by her thought, gravitated more and more to the doctrine of the self-contained, military, Protectionist, all-powerful State. In this story of political thought events have been no less potent than arguments. The failure and success of institutions, the victories and defeats of countries identified with certain principles have repeatedly brought new strength and resolution to the adherents or opponents of those principles as the case might be in all lands. The successive steps by which Italy secured unity and freedom were a perpetual encouragement to believers in national right and liberal government throughout the middle of the century. The triumph of Germany in 1870 was a victory for autocratic power, for discipline, for unscrupulous statesmanship, for blood and iron, which effected a conversion, only half conscious and very slow in producing its result, but all the more complete for that reason, in the attitude of men to fundamental questions of social ethics. Looking back on the hundred years that separate the two European cataclysms the historian will discover a rise of liberal and humanitarian opinions to ascendancy in the earlier period and a reaction against them towards the close. The causes of such a change are multifarious and tangled, but he will, I believe, recognize the year 1870 and the victory of Bismarck as the dividing line. May it be so that he will find in the present war another turning-point from which a new movement is to begin.

Be this as it may, we may rest assured that the political thought of Europe, like its philosophy and its science, will go forward or backward as a unity. It may move by peaceful and friendly co-operation or by the stimulus of embittered rivalry. But its many centres are related by so many strands of connexion that the movement in any one of these is reflected in the rest. The liberties of England are fostered by the emancipation of the Alsatian, the Slovak, or the Pole. They are enfeebled by the victories of political autocracy or the military machine. Thinkers, it may be said, ought to be above these mundane influences. Philosophy should deal with what is in itself and eternally rational and just and wise. But philosophy as it exists on earth is the work of philosophers, who, authority tells us, suffer as much from toothache as other mortals, and are, like others, open to the impressions of near and striking events and to the seductions of intellectual fashion. Yet, if the larger thought is worth anything, it should enable those who follow it to look a little further beyond the present and a little deeper below the surface differences that distract the kindred peoples. If the thinkers are true to their thought it may be that from them will come the beginnings of the healing process which Europe will need. Much is being and will be said of the political reconstruction which is needed to restore and secure the civilized order. But the commonwealth of thought will revive of itself from the day when peace is concluded. German physiology will not be less learned, German scientists will not be less expert, German chemists will not be less pre-eminent because their military lords have plunged Europe into a disastrous war. We shall need their services, shall watch their experiments, read their records, and utilize their brains as before. Perhaps it may be some years before the international congresses can be resumed, but the internationalism of learning will revive of itself, against our wills if not by and with our wills, and in the world of science, and in this world alone, the event of war will make no difference. Conqueror and conquered will work at the same task and meet as equals. The scientific demonstration knows no more of the nationality of its originator than of his caste or colour,

VII UNIFYING FORCES

age or sex. In this one real democracy the idea, the hypothesis, the proof, whatever it may be, stands or falls on its own merits with no questions asked as to its ancestors or country of origin. In the growth of this commonwealth war is but a momentary check. Its destiny is to become wider in extent, closer in its interconnexions, and not less rich in the diversities of its national centres. Whether it is also destined to grow into a political unity the future must decide. At least we can say that for any such unity it provides the only sure and solid foundation.

BOOKS FOR REFERENCE

Merz, *History of European Thought in the 19th Century.* W. Blackwood.

Marvin, *The Living Past.* Clarendon Press.

VIII

THE UNITY OF WESTERN EDUCATION

I HAVE been asked to address you on the Unity of Education in Western Europe. The task is not an easy one, for what do we mean by unity ? It would be easy for me to spend my time in talking on the technical aspect of the subject; I could deal with curriculum and organization, with school buildings and class-rooms, black-boards, and all the material of schoolmastering, and could show you how great is the similarity in these matters in all civilized countries. I doubt, however, whether this would interest you; I doubt whether this is the unity of which you are in search. You would tell me that you asked for unity and I had given you uniformity. Uniformity you can have anywhere; in modern life all is standardized and stereotyped; you have it in the great hotel and the Atlantic liner—there you have men of all nations, they do the same thing at the same time, they eat the same food and wear the same clothes; you find it in the factory and on the battle-field. Go to a textile factory, whether in Oldham or in Chemnitz, or in Bombay, the processes are the same and the product is the same, except as there may be more or less adulteration.

And so in education, if you care to do so, you can find the mechanical uniformity of modern civilization. A new form of school-desk makes the round of the world as quickly as a new chemical process or a new battleship. The pictures on the walls of the rooms may be the reproduction of some modern German work, and the atlases you use may be second-rate copies of the products of Gotha or Leipzig; you

VIII UNITY OF WESTERN EDUCATION

can have, too, uniformity in time-table and curriculum ; but, after all, this uniformity may be merely superficial. Go along the streets of an old town and you may see the regular façade of a modern street, but behind this you will find all the variety of the mediaeval buildings which it encloses—the façade is mere paint and stucco.

Uniformity is not necessarily unity, and unity is not inconsistent with variety. That which I presume we are searching for is a more fundamental, spiritual, and intellectual unity—internal not external; not a painted and stucco resemblance, but a unity of origin and of life.

Let us see what we can learn from history.

The history of European education is centred round two institutions, the School and the University. Both have their origin in the remote past, and both have maintained themselves with singular fidelity to their original type.

The School goes back to the very origin of our civilization ; if we are to understand its nature, we must transfer ourselves in thought to those early days when the first missionaries planted in the Somerset valleys and on the stern Northumberland coast the Cross of Christ. They came to a people still on the verge of barbarism, with a language still unformed by literature, with a religion that gave no clue to the mysteries of life by which they were oppressed. They came to these men full of the enthusiasm of the Gospel—coming not only as teachers of religion, but as the apostles of a higher civilization, for they had behind them the awful name of Rome.

Wherever they came, among their first duties was to found schools in which to train men who would succeed them ; we must always remember that the education which they gave had one supreme object—it was to bring up the boys of the rude and barbarous communities in which they found themselves, to become teachers and servants of the Church. The substance of the teaching was always the same, whether in Spain, in Gaul, in Ireland or in Britain; it was the Bible, the services of the Church, and the writings of the Fathers. It was by the school that the boys were initiated into the common system of Western Christendom, and were made citizens of the greater world the centre of which was in Rome.

But if the substance and the object was identical throughout Europe, so always was the form in which the teaching was given; at a time when all learning and all religion came from Rome, the foundation of knowledge was the Latin tongue. In these early days was established the tradition that still subsists; the gateway to learning and to culture lay by the narrow road of the Latin grammar. The schoolboy who still tells out his longs and shorts can compare them with the ruder efforts of his Saxon forefathers thirteen centuries ago. Never have authors attained a fame and a circulation equal to that of the great grammarians who, during the decline of the Empire, codified the rules of Latin speech; generation after generation passed, and down almost to our own days every schoolboy began his career on the lines laid down in the works of Donatus and Priscian.

We must, however, guard ourselves against a mistake into which it would be easy to fall. It is true that in the early mediaeval days education was based on the study of the Latin language; and it was only through literature that the language could be learnt. The study of classical literature as we understand it was, however, far removed from the ideals of this time. The most authoritative teachers never neglected to warn their pupils against the moral dangers which arose from the study of heathen writers; Ovid and Cicero were only admitted under protest, and they were merely the stepping-stone to the study of Augustine and Prudentius.

On this common basis—the Bible, the Church, and the

VIII UNITY OF WESTERN EDUCATION

Latin language—was then established the education of Western Europe, and the form it then assumed it retained for over a thousand years, almost without change. By this a common cast was given to the intellect, and the nations were disciplined by common spiritual teaching. It was extraordinarily effective. It kept down, and in many countries almost destroyed, the vigorous and aspiring local and national life which, in every country, was striving after self-expression. In our own country this effect was most conspicuous. The English, illiterate though they might be, were not without the promise of a great future. In the remains of the Saxon poems we can see the beginnings of what under happier circumstances might have grown into a great national literature. Its origins were deep seated in the life of the people. It proved itself quickly able to absorb the new teaching of the Gospel, and, as the Christian Epics show, here was the basis on which might have been built a national interpretation of Christianity. All that was required was the adoption of English as the language of the Church and the School. The beginning was made when Alfred, during the few years which he secured from the Danish inroads, began his great work of founding an English literature in which the teaching of the Church and the works of antiquity were included. The attempt was ruined for the time by the renewal of the Danish inroads, permanently by the Norman Conquest. For William brought with him not only his French knights, but also Italian priests. Once more, under the influence of Lanfranc and his successors, the Church and the School were brought under the full control of the revived power of Rome, and all prospect of a spontaneous and indigenous national intellectual life was destroyed. Unity was re-established, and the School was the instrument by which England was fully incorporated in the culture and religion of the Western Church.

As it was with the School so also with the university. The second, as the first, was the creation of the Church, and even more conspicuously it was the vehicle for fostering and maintaining the control of common institutions and a common learning, and thereby of crushing out the rich variety of local life which everywhere was springing up. In its very constitution the University of Paris, the mother and model of all later universities (at least in northern Europe), showed its international character; the students who flocked to it from all countries were organized in 'nations' a system which, at least in name, still remains in many of the universities to this day; the whole instruction was and remained in Latin, and the whole course of instruction was a long apprenticeship to the study of theology. It was from the universities that emanated the great system of philosophy in which a Frenchman as Abelard, an Italian as Thomas of Aquinas, an Englishman as William of Ockham each took his part.

We may regard with admiration the great intellectual achievements of the Scholastic philosophy which, for over two centuries, dominated the official education, but we must not forget that its ascendancy implied the exclusion from all public recognition of the local and national thought and literature which now, as before, was struggling into life. The Troubadours and the Minnesänger, the Chanson de Roland and the Nibelungenlied, the Chronicles of Froissard, Chaucer, and Piers Plowman, each of them so full of fresh vigorous local life, were not only outside the official system of education, but in their essence opposed to it. This was clearly seen as soon as the free and uncontrolled mind was directed to the highest subjects of thought. National idiosyncrasies, as they found expression in the domain of philosophy and theology, produced results different from the established teaching of the school. To the

VIII UNITY OF WESTERN EDUCATION

Church truth was always one and the same. Truth was one, error was manifold; in unity was salvation, and divergence was heresy. And so every attempt at national and local thought was not only suppressed in education, but fell under the ban of discipline. In Languedoc the Albigenses ventured the assertion of their independence; Huss in Bohemia, in England Wyclif. What happened? The Albigenses were massacred, Huss was burnt, Wyclif was condemned, and his followers suffered under the new law of heresy.

This system, which had originated as a part of a great spiritual movement, long outlived its usefulness. It became an intolerable tyranny. Its effects were to be seen in the teaching of the humblest grammar school, and every boy who began the study of the Latin grammar was being initiated into the abstractions or the Scholastic logic. It became a dead and iron crust by which the mind of man was confined, and it was the school and the university which were the peculiar institutions by which this system was maintained. Unity of education there was, but at what a price had it been won.

One thing had, however, been secured: the common Christian basis of our modern civilization had been stamped upon the peoples; so long as Europe remains Europe this cannot be forgotten or obliterated. No nation can repudiate its own past, and, whether they will or no, all Western nations are irrevocably bound together by the ties of the home in which their childhood and youth was passed.

At last the change came: it came in that double revolution which we call the Renaissance and the Reformation. In considering them we must confine ourselves as closely as we can to their effect on education.

The revival of learning was essentially an educational movement, it had from the beginning to do primarily with the school. It had as its object a complete change both in the subject-matter and in the spirit of education. Always it drew its inspiration from the literature of Greece, and this meant the fullest freedom of the human intellect, freedom of speculation, freedom of inquiry on the conditions of human life, and in particular it was a revolt from the ascetic ideas of the mediaeval Church; it was the assertion of the dignity of the body and mind of man. Now whereas in Italy, its original home, this took a warp definitely antagonistic to Christian faith and Christian ethics, in Northern Europe the new classical learning was harmonized with Christianity, and classical learning was applied to the interpretation of the Bible. It was the synthesis of what mediaeval Europe had regarded as irreconcilable opponents. That was the inspiration of the school reform, and this is the guiding principle of all higher education for the next three centuries. It was a movement that originally was not local or national but European, and in its first form was not in opposition to the maintenance of the ecclesiastical unity of Western Europe. The figure in whom it reaches its clearest expression is that of Erasmus. Standing at the transition between two epochs, he was the last of the great European scholars, and belongs to the undivided Catholic Church as much as did Abelard or Anselm. The wandering scholar of the Renaissance, without father, without mother, completely freed from ties of family or country, at home equally in Deventer or Cambridge, in Basel or in Paris or in Rome, without even a native language, for to him Latin was the only vernacular (he has, I believe, left no word written in any other language), he saw the vision of a Europe still united in obedience to the one Church, but a Europe in which the culture of the humanist would go side by side with the common faith inherited from early days.

The hopes of Erasmus were not to be fulfilled. It is indeed true that he laid the foundation on which the recog-

VIII UNITY OF WESTERN EDUCATION 187

nized and official scheme of education has continued almost to our own day ; the Latin schools of Germany and the Grammar Schools of England were each alike conducted on the basis of the Church and the classics, but even before the foundations had been completed the real unity was gone. The Renaissance was met by two forces, each stronger than itself, and the common stream was broken into a number of smaller currents. These have since increased in strength till the sense of the common origin has almost disappeared.

The common mediaeval system (and in this the spirit of the Renaissance was still mediaeval) depended on the common Church, and especially in education, in the use of Latin as the universal language of learning. During the sixteenth century both were overthrown. Luther was stronger than Erasmus, and the new languages, Italian, French, Spanish, English, quickly began to encroach on the claims of Latin to be the one language of the school.

The religious revolution need not detain us. It is sufficient to recall that in many parts of Europe the divergence of creed tended to become if not identical with, at least closely to follow the boundaries of states and nations. In every land the school was still strictly under the control of the Church, acting now as the delegate of the temporal ruler, and in each country a whole body of teaching and discipline was evolved, the result of which was a fundamental difference in the attitude of mind. The English bishops, the German consistories, the Scotch presbytery, set their seal on the schools, as much as did the Jesuits and Port Royal in France. The Shorter Catechism, the English Prayer Book, the German hymns, each gave a distinct character to the religions of the country, and this character was the basis of the teaching in the schools.

Religion, which had been the great unifier, became the chief engine of separation.

Equally important was the growth of national literature. This indeed goes back far beyond the sixteenth century, but none the less it is from this time that the writers not only of imagination, but also of learning, began to express themselves each in his own vernacular. Sir Thomas More, it is true, wrote his *Utopia* in Latin, but it was in English that it had its great circulation. Bacon used both languages, but it is on English editions of his works that his fame chiefly rests. In particular we find that works on religion and theology are now produced not only in Latin, but one hundred years before Hooker would have discoursed on ' ecclesiastical polity ' in the learned language, and Pascal would never have thought of using French for discussing the philosophy of the Jesuits.

The influence of these changes upon the school is remarkable. Strictly speaking, for many generations they seemed to have little immediate effect upon it. In every country in Europe Latin remained both the subject and the vehicle of higher education, but it is just for this reason that we find that, during the seventeenth century and the greater part of the eighteenth, the schools are more and more falling out of touch with the intellectual life of the times. They continued in the old way; for them Shakespeare and Milton, Montaigne and Molière, Cervantes and Tasso, seemed to have written in vain. They maintained the form of an older period, but they had lost the spirit by which it had been inspired. Their learning remained purely classical ; but even though the new national literature was long in winning for itself a definite place in the recognized school system, the growth of this literature and the evolution of national consciousness of which it was a part could not in fact take place without altering the whole spirit of the teaching. If we are to understand how this was we must keep in mind one of the chief characteristics of what is called a classical education.

VIII UNITY OF WESTERN EDUCATION 189

The study of the classics means the study of the whole life of the two great nations of antiquity as preserved in the extant literature. Now this does not contain a definite and formulated doctrine, it does not even, as might be said of the Middle Ages, mean one attitude towards the world; it opens to the student a field of extraordinary wealth and variety, and from this each will take that which he is able to appropriate. To one it may be the mysticism of the Cambridge Platonists, to another the frank and pagan joy in life of Anacreon and Horace. Rousseau and Grote will each in his own way appropriate the lesson of Liberty, while others will turn to the story of the militant and dominant aristocracy of Rome. Goethe and Keats, Milton and Gibbon, Berkeley and Schopenhauer, will each draw their inspiration from the classics, but the result will not be to make them resemble one another, it will be to give vigour, decision, form, resolution, and dignity to the qualities of each.

And as it is with individuals, so it is with nations. The schools of all nations maintained their classical curriculum; boys still began, and often ended, their schooling with the Latin grammar, but this did not mean, as it had meant in the earlier days, that the influence was the same. There was indeed little in common between what we may venture to call the pedantry of Germany and the superficial elegancy of the Jesuit schools. And so the classical basis did not prevent the school assuming a national complexion. Let me give one illustration of the manner in which the classical teaching could take a markedly national spirit. Perhaps the most effective classical teaching that we find in the eighteenth century is that at Eton, and it was on it that was founded the great school of oratory and statesmanship. It was on Cicero and Homer and Demosthenes that Pitt and Fox and Canning and Gladstone (for the tradition continued to his day) formed their minds and their style, but they emerged from their training above all Englishmen, but Englishmen who had learnt how to give to their own national feelings a dignity of expression and nobility of form equal to that of the exemplars whom they had studied.

Now just as the finest expression of the English national spirit is found in those whose school training had been based on the classics, just as the Girondists based their revolutionary doctrines on Hellenic models, so almost at the same time the great political awakening of Germany and Prussia was inspired by what has been called the second Renaissance; and yet how profound is the divergence between Wellesley and Pitt, Humboldt and Stein, St. Just, Demousin, and Vergniaud; all were children of the common classical tradition, but how different is the use to which they put it. During the centuries that passed between the Renaissance and the Revolution, the education of the different countries had then in fact been drifting far apart. What has been done during the nineteenth century has been openly to carry into effect changes which had long been overdue and were already to a large extent operative.

It was inevitable that the new literature and thought would eventually find its way into the schools and universities. Before this change had been accomplished, a fresh and even stronger influence asserted itself. Democracy had come, and a democracy which based the state on the principle of nationality. It seized on the school as the means to hold the minds of men in fief, just as had the mediaeval Church, and in doing so enforced and perpetuated the national differences.

In the eighteenth century rulers troubled themselves little about matters apparently of such minor importance as the languages in which their subjects conversed and read. Even the French did not try to touch the German-speaking inhabitants of Alsace, and Copenhagen could

VIII UNITY OF WESTERN EDUCATION

become a centre of German letters, while French maintained itself at the Court of Berlin. All this was changed by the Revolution, and Napoleon was the first deliberately to convert the whole fabric of French schools and the university into an instrument for the organized propaganda of the cult of the Empire. Since then there is scarcely a government (always except that of England which alone has been strong enough to rest on the native and undisciplined political sense of the people) which has not followed in his path. In particular when the state is founded on the nation the school is used to develop in the children the full consciousness of nationality. That institution that was for so long the home of European unity has become the most useful agent for the perpetuation and exaggeration of national differences. It is in the school that the immigrant to the United States is taught to reverence the institutions of his new fatherland, and from generation to generation the school labours to keep alive the memory of the half-forgotten struggle of the new republic and the British monarchy. In France each successive government has used the school to force on the nation its interpretation of the national history and ideals. And the victories of Prussian armies were cemented and confirmed by the official exposition of the Prussian state and the cult of the Hohenzollern. To the school is transferred the conflict between the doctrines of authority and the revolution, of the secular state and of the Kingdom by by the Grace of God. Every nation rightly struggling to be free has seen in the school the instrument for securing the allegiance of the young, and the school has become the centre of political struggle. In Trieste and in Poland, in Alsace and in Macedonia, we find kings and politicians contending for the minds and souls of children, and it is in the school, the college, and the university that has been prepared the conflict that is now devastating Europe.

What has been done in the nineteenth century has really been only to carry into effect the change which was long overdue and was implicit in earlier years. The national culture and national authors have at length forced their way into the schools, and the result has been that institutions which originally in reality, and for so long in appearance, were the vehicles for the expression of the common European civilization, have been almost entirely won over to the cause of the national expression.

This is indeed inevitable. Education, as we have seen, can only be effective when it is the vehicle for strong beliefs, and is informed by the conscious expression of an attitude towards the world. Now, in modern days, the consciousness of a common European spirit has, in fact, almost disappeared. In its place we find the intense consciousness of the nation. Even religion has become national, and God has once again become a tribal deity. The new consciousness of the common interests of what is called Labour have no recognition in the approved teaching. If the work of the school was not to be merely the dead instruction in useless knowledge, if the work was to be directed towards informing the minds of the pupils with ideals and beliefs, it was only in the idealization of the national thought that this could be attained.

Is the older union of thought to be permanently lost? If not, you must find it again in some higher synthesis. There are many who would do so in the pursuit of mathematics and the natural sciences; in them, at least, no divisions of country can be found. The student in his chemical laboratory, the doctor in his hospital, the mathematician in his study, finds his colleagues in every country in the civilized world, and it matters not to him whether the next step in penetrating the secrets of nature have been made in Vienna, or in Paris, or Amsterdam, or Bologna.

There are many who believe that on this basis will be

established the Union of Civilization. If we look, however, more critically, we may find reason to doubt whether this optimistic view is justified. I do not share this hope and this belief, I do not look forward to a spiritual and intellectual unity of the nations established on the basis of scientific education. It is, indeed, impossible to overestimate not only the practical but also the intellectual influence of what we may call the scientific spirit. It is indeed true that those who are accustomed to the careful and systematic investigation of causes, who have been trained from their earliest years to recognize in the pomp and pageantry of the external world—and even to some extent in the working of the human mind and the structure of human society—the orderly sequence of natural law, will have a type and character of mind essentially different from those who have not passed through this discipline. The civilization (I scarcely dare to use the word culture) of those nations who have this in common will have a unity of their own, and will differ fundamentally from their own past and from that of other races.

On the other hand there are two considerations that I should like to put before you, as leading to a less important position, the one arising from the practical nature of science, the other connected with its essential intellectual origin.

It is a characteristic of all work in physical science that however it may originate in the pure desire for truth, it is very quickly available for practical use, personal comfort, the acquisition of wealth, and national efficiency. The physicist who calculates the stresses and strains of an aeroplane finds that in teaching man how to control nature he is also providing the means for his struggle, whether in peace or war, in commerce or on the battle-field. We soon find that the progress of technical skill is curiously inoperative in its effect on human thought and feeling.

Men remain the same whether they ride in a coach, or a train, or a motor-car; it matters little whether they use bows and arrows, or rifles, or hand-grenades, or liquid fire.

Now in education it is the technical side of scientific progress which almost inevitably becomes most prominent, and the greater the advance in knowledge the more will this be true. The wider the domain of knowledge the greater is the number of those who will be chiefly occupied with the use of the processes and materials that have been discovered and the smaller is the proportion of those who will have reached the border of the known, and will begin the work of exploration into the unknown. That is, the greater will be the number of those who are the servants and not the masters of science. A unity of a certain kind we shall have, the unity of those who have learned to pilot an aeroplane, to apply X-rays, to extract the phosphate from iron, or to test cattle for tubercle. All this may produce a uniformity in the machinery of life, it passes by untouched the motives of action, the beliefs, affections, and interests. How many illustrations of this do we see around us! What more glorious illustration of the power of the human intellect can be found than the later developments of electricity, but scarcely had the discoveries been made when we find them seized upon by the man of affairs, and wireless telegraphy becomes the subject of speculation on the Stock Exchange, and a chief instrument of war. That which the chemist finds in his laboratory is, within a few years, sometimes even a few months, found again in the factory, and perhaps on the field of battle.

Do not let it be supposed that I would underrate the possibility of a deeper unity, but if we would find it we must carry our analysis further back. The progress of science is in truth not a cause but a result, not an ultimate fact but the symptom of a state of mind. It springs from that which was brought into Europe consciously at the Renaissance and which we may call the spirit of Greece. It is that to which we owe not only the investigation and subjection of nature, but equally with it all progress in every department of thought, the analysis of society, whether political or economic, the investigations of the working of human reason, the probing of human passions, and their record in art and literature.

What is this spirit? Is it not the confidence in the spirit of man, the spirit which in intellectual matters bends to no authority, and recognizes no limit to its enterprise, which probes all things, tests all things, and follows fearlessly where the argument leads it? This is what I mean by the spirit of Greece, it is that which Sophocles has immortalized. Of all this, what we call science is but a part, perhaps at present the most striking and important part, but still a part only; to look to it as the key of our civilization and the sole basis of our education would be to set up a partial and, therefore, a false ideal. An ideal, moreover, which, if pursued to its logical conclusion, would become the basis for the most appalling tyranny, by which the free spirit of investigation, to which we owe all our scientific progress, would be buried in the structure that itself had reared. For what is the end to which it must lead? Is it not a society which is held together.by technical skill, a society of organized efficiency, where each individual holds his place, not as a living spirit, but as a slave of the great machine, tied throughout his life to the perfect performance of his limited and specialized task? I can imagine such a society; it is the ideal which some modern German writers have definitely put before us. It may be that this will be the Europe of the future, a Europe with a common government and a universal system of education by which each child will be trained to take his allotted part in an organized slavery. I hope I shall not live to see it.

None the less, a unity there is, but it is a deeper unity than this. It is the unity inherited from the past. Here we may find, not indeed a superficial uniformity, but a real unity of life and spirit. No civilization can repudiate its own origin, and whatever the future may have in store the childhood of Europe was nourished on the Bible and Christianity, and in the more mature years there was added the impulse to the boldest use of the human intellect that came from Greece. These two elements give us that which is the peculiar characteristic of Western Europe, and as we are told that the growth of each individual repeats the evolution of the race, so the education of each individual repeats in childhood and boyhood the education of the nation. It is from these two elements that the whole of modern culture springs, and it is from them that again and again they regain their strength.

And if we recollect this we need not be much disturbed by our apparent differences and misunderstandings. After all, they are the necessary result of freedom, and what do the Bible and Greece mean but moral and intellectual freedom? We want no formal and artificial unity: to us change, progress, conflict and division are the breath of our life. Just as the cluster of little towns in the Aegean islands and valleys prized before all things their political and intellectual independence, so is it with these small countries nestling on the shores of the Atlantic. Politically they have always refused to acquiesce in the establishment of any common authority over them, whether it comes from outside or even from among themselves, and so also they always repudiate the ascendancy of any single or partial intellectual doctrine. Each party and each nation adds its own contribution ; all have a common origin, and all spring from the same root. Since the bonds have been relaxed and the dominion of the Universal Church overthrown, we see nothing from the rivalry of political systems

VIII   UNITY OF WESTERN EDUCATION   197

and passing schemes of thought ; they chase each other like the storms which arise from the Atlantic and pass in quick succession over our shores. It is this change and succession which is to us the breath of our life: we know nothing of the steady static weather of the great continents, where rain and drought have each their measured and settled space : and we know nothing, and will know nothing, of the formal and authoritative rule combining all Europe into one realm, whether political or intellectual. For we know that unity and permanence does not belong to this life, and our nearest approach to truth is to be found not in a settled system but in the thousandfold interactions of half-truths and partial systems.

> Life like a dome of many-coloured glass
> Stains the white radiance of eternity
> Until death shatters it to fragments.

A unity there is, but it is the unity of the countless and varied flowers that carpet the meadows in spring, the unity of the common spirit of life which animates them all.

Books for Reference

Leach, *The Schools of Medieval England.* Methuen.
Mullinger, J. Bass, *The Schools of Charles the Great.*
Paulsen, *Geschichte des gelehrten Unterrichts.*
Rashdall, *Universities in the Middle Ages.* Clarendon Press.
Foster Watson, *Grammar Schools.* Cambridge University Press.
Woodward, *Erasmus.* Cambridge University Press.

IX

COMMERCE AND FINANCE AS INTERNATIONAL FORCES

COMMERCE and finance are departments of life in which mankind approaches nearer to unity than in any other. They are practical expressions of the instinct of self-preservation which is the first law of nature. They spring straight from the acquisitiveness which is a universal characteristic of human nature and indeed of animal and vegetable nature. Every living thing wants to acquire food. Adam Smith indeed restricts the trading instinct to mankind. 'The propensity', he says, 'to truck, barter, or exchange one thing for another ... is common to all men and to be found in no other race of animals, which seem to know neither this nor any other species of contracts. Two greyhounds in running down the same hare have sometimes the appearance of acting in some sort of concert. Each turns her towards his companion or endeavours to intercept her when his companion turns her towards himself. This, however, is not the effect of any contract, but of the accidental concurrence of their passions in the same object at that particular time. Nobody ever saw a dog make a fair and deliberate exchange of one bone for another with another dog.'[1]

Mr Cannan, in his edition of the *Wealth of Nations*, very judiciously points out in a note on this passage that 'it is by no means clear what object there could be in exchanging one bone for another'. Probably if one rummaged the literature of dog stories one would find

[1] *Wealth of Nations*, Bk. I, ch. ii.

plenty of examples of commerce between dogs, and when they perform tricks to get food, we detect the germ of the exchange of a service for a commodity.

When a bee takes honey from a flower and leaves in exchange the pollen from a flower of an opposite sex, it may be said to be at once a merchant, a carrier, and a matrimonial agent, and the brilliant colours with which flowers attract these merchants have been compared to the advertising posters of the human trader. But however the case may be in the animal and vegetable world, there can be no question that the trading instinct appears at a very early stage of human development. In boys the instinct to trade or swop articles appears long before they feel any inclination to fall in love or to give much serious thought to religion. The classical example is given by Mark Twain, who relates how Tom Sawyer exchanged one of his own teeth, which had been pulled out that morning, for a tick in the possession of Huckleberry Finn, and then ' the two boys separated, each feeling wealthier than before '. In fact, of course, they both were wealthier than before, because each had got something that he wanted more than the article with which he had parted; and this pleasant result sums up the whole genesis and basis of commerce.

But though commerce is thus merely an expression of an instinct which is primitive and universal, it does not follow that it is its only or even its earliest expression. Perhaps its earliest and most natural expression was through robbery, with or without violence. A primitive savage who saw something that he wanted would probably, if strong enough, hit its owner on the head and take it, and this short and simple method of acquisition still occasionally reappears in the realms of the most highly civilized diplomacy. Nevertheless, at a very early stage its limitations became obvious, and quite at the dawn of recorded history we find commercial transactions referred to as an established branch of human intercourse. The Old Testament story has not gone far before it tells us of buying and selling. In the twenty-third chapter of Genesis we find a very interesting bargain recorded between Abraham and Ephron. Sarah had died in Kirjath-arba :

' the same is Hebron in the land of Canaan : and Abraham came to mourn for Sarah, and to weep for her. And Abraham stood up from before his dead, and spake unto the sons of Heth, saying, I am a stranger and a sojourner with you : give me a possession of a buryingplace with you, that I may bury my dead out of my sight. And the children of Heth answered Abraham, saying unto him, Hear us, my lord : thou art a mighty prince among us : in the choice of our sepulchres bury thy dead ; none of us shall withhold from thee his sepulchre, but that thou mayest bury thy dead. And Abraham stood up and bowed himself to the people of the land, even to the children of Heth. And he communed with them, saying, If it be your mind that I should bury my dead out of my sight ; hear me, and intreat for me to Ephron the son of Zohar, that he may give me the cave of Machpelah, which he hath, which is in the end of his field ; for as much money as it is worth he shall give it me for a possession of a buryingplace amongst you. And Ephron dwelt among the children of Heth : and Ephron the Hittite answered Abraham in the audience of the children of Heth, even of all that went in at the gate of his city, saying, Nay, my lord, hear me : the field give I thee, and the cave that is therein, I give it thee ; in the presence of the sons of my people give I it thee : bury thy dead. And Abraham bowed down himself before the people of the land. And he spake unto Ephron in the audience of the people of the land, saying, But if thou wilt give it, I pray thee, hear me : I will give thee money for the field ; take it of me, and I will bury my dead there. And Ephron answered Abraham, saying unto him, My lord, hearken unto me : the land is worth four hundred shekels of silver ; what is that betwixt me and thee ? bury therefore thy dead. And Abraham hearkened unto Ephron ; and Abraham weighed to Ephron the silver, which he had named in the audience of the sons of Heth, four hundred shekels of silver, current money with the merchant.'

In this very early and curious example of a bargain we find the seller continually expressing reluctance to sell and asking the buyer to accept as a gift the commodity that he wants. It appears from the sequel that this is merely an example of Oriental politeness. At any rate, the end of the bargain was that Abraham paid the money, four hundred shekels of silver, which is described as 'current money with the merchant', thus apparently showing that this system of payment in metals was already a regular feature of commercial transactions. Coined currency had not yet been developed, for we may note that Abraham weighed the silver.

When we come to the days of Solomon we find something like a developed international trade. The fifth chapter of the first book of Kings describes how Solomon, on taking the throne of his father, sent to Hiram, king of Tyre, and stated his purpose to build a house unto the name of the Lord his God, asking Hiram to send his servants to hew cedar trees out of Lebanon, and saying that he would give hire for Hiram's servants according to all that he should appoint. Hiram replied that he would do all that Solomon desired concerning timber of cedar and concerning timber of fir. 'My servants shall bring them down from Lebanon unto the sea: and I will convey them by sea in floats unto the place that thou shalt appoint me, and will cause them to be discharged there, and thou shalt receive them : and thou shalt accomplish my desire, in giving food for my household. So Hiram gave Solomon cedar trees and fir trees according to all his desire. And Solomon gave Hiram twenty thousand measures of wheat for food to his household, and twenty measures of pure oil: thus gave Solomon to Hiram year by year.'

According to this arrangement it would appear that

Solomon paid for the timber that he imported by exporting to Hiram wheat and oil, but it is shown in a later chapter that the transaction was not a purely commercial one. At the end of twenty years, when Solomon had finished the building of the temple, he gave Hiram as further consideration twenty cities in the land of Galilee, 'and Hiram came out from Tyre to see the cities which Solomon had given him; and they pleased him not. And he said, What cities are these which thou hast given me, my brother? And he called them the land of Cabul [explained in the margin as meaning "displeasing" or "dirty"] unto this day. And Hiram sent to the king sixscore talents of gold.'[1]

Apart from this transaction between the two kings, Solomon appears to have developed a very considerable foreign trade, presumably exporting wheat and oil and other agricultural products. His imports appear to have been various. Chapter ten of the first book of Kings states that 'the king had at sea a navy of Tharshish with the navy of Hiram: once in three years came the navy of Tharshish, bringing gold, and silver, ivory, and apes, and peacocks.'... 'And the king made silver to be in Jerusalem as stones, and cedars made he to be as the sycomore trees that are in the vale, for abundance. And Solomon had horses brought out of Egypt, and linen yarn: the king's merchants received the linen yarn at a price.'

The whole question of Solomon's balance of trade is a very interesting one, and deserves the attention of some Hebrew scholar who may be able to throw light upon it. In these days it is rather difficult to see how a purely agricultural country could have found the means of paying for all these articles of pure luxury which Solomon imported so freely. It must be noted, however, that 'all the earth sought to Solomon, to hear his wisdom, which

[1] 1 Kings ix.

God had put in his heart. And they brought every man his present, vessels of silver, and vessels of gold, and garments, and armour, and spices, horses, and mules, a rate year by year '. From this it appears that Solomon was able to exchange his wisdom for a very considerable part of the imports which came into his country, and so perhaps we may take it that Solomon's wisdom is the earliest recorded example of what is now known as an invisible export. A modern equivalent would be the articles which English writers contribute to American newspapers and are paid for, ultimately, by the shipment to England of American wheat and cotton. It is also interesting to note in these days, when personal economy and simplicity of life are so freely preached, that Solomon's very luxurious imports were followed by evil consequences, imports of an enormous number of strange women, and a consequent turning away of his heart after false gods.

When we come to secular history, the very first chapter of the first book of the first history ever written deals with a question of commerce. Herodotus, who has been called the Father of History, opens his work with a few introductory words stating that ' these are the researches which he publishes in the hope of thereby preventing the great and wonderful actions of the Greeks and Barbarians from losing their due meed of glory, and withal to put on record what were their grounds of feud '. And then he plunges straight into his story, as follows : ' According to the Persians best informed in history, the Phœnicians began the quarrel. This people, who had formerly dwelt on the shores of the Erythræan Sea, having migrated to the Mediterranean and settled in the parts which they now inhabit, began at once they say, to adventure on long voyages, freighting their vessels with the wares of Egypt and Assyria. They landed at many places on the coast, and among the rest at Argos, which was then pre-eminent above all the states included now under the common name of Hellas. Here they exposed their merchandise, and traded with the natives for five or six days; at the end of which time, when almost everything was sold, there came down to the beach a number of women, and among them the daughter of the king, who was, they say, agreeing in this with the Greeks, Io, the child of Inachus. The women were standing by the stern of the ship intent upon their purchases, when the Phœnicians, with a general shout, rushed upon them. The greater part made their escape, but some were seized and carried off. Io herself was among the captives. The Phœnicians put the women on board their vessel, and set sail for Egypt. Thus did Io pass into Egypt, according to the Persian story, which differs widely from the Phœnician: and thus commenced, according to their authors, the series of outrages.'[1]

Commerce is thus a striking example of the unity of mankind, being a practically universal form of human activity which arises as soon as man verges from the earliest stages of barbarism. In the case of individuals it is easy to see how this desire to exchange commodities between one individual and another meant so great an increase in human efficiency that it had only to be thought of to be universally adopted. The primitive savage, doing everything for himself, building his own hut, killing or finding his own food, and making his own clothes, such as they were, was an extremely versatile and self-sufficing person. At the same time the comforts that he enjoyed were probably not very satisfactory. His hut was almost certain to be draughty and to let in rain through the roof; his hunting and finding of food must have very often left him with his larder empty, and the state of his wardrobe was probably simple rather

[1] Rawlinson's translation.

than satisfying. It would inevitably happen that certain members of the tribe would show greater efficiency than others in doing a certain one of these various businesses which are essential even to the simplest form of human life. Thus the tendency to specialization begins to show itself. The skilful hut-builder builds huts not only for himself but for other members of the tribe; he acquires further skill by constant practice and the huts are more quickly built and better when finished. The other tribesmen, in effect, pay him by supplying him with a certain amount of food and clothes. The tendency for specialization would make very rapid progress, and it is easy to see how at a very early date and in the most primitive communities there would be bowyers, arrow-makers, and leather-dressers, and how various kinds of artificers would arise, supplying the wants of the community in some special line, and receiving from the community all the commodities which they required apart from those which they produced themselves. The individuals of the community thus become mutually dependent, and live by one another's production. Hence comes unity, and with it a fresh cause of disunion, owing to the likelihood of quarrelling over the exchanges effected.

As progress developed and the communities at a greater distance became acquainted with one another's wants and the various kinds of goods that certain districts supplied, this tendency to specialization and consequent exchange of goods would grow in an ever-widening circle. Instead of the tribe being a commercial unity, the zone in which the interchange of goods went on would widen as far as the geographical and other boundaries allowed it. In the same country one district would be found to be specially well adapted for agriculture, and another for pasture; another, being well supplied with metals, would naturally provide a race of smiths and producers of rough tools for industry, and the exchange of commodities between districts with these various capacities would mean that the specialization of production would go steadily further, and that a whole town or village would be found in which the great majority of the inhabitants were at work upon one particular form of industry, relying for the other kinds of commodities that they required upon the activity of a similar community living in the next valley or on the other side of the river. This widening-out process would naturally extend itself over the borders of different countries. Obstacles to this process would be found in the differences of language and probably in the difficulties of transport. On the other hand, it would be greatly stimulated by the different ideas of value that prevailed in different communities. Value depends upon the extent to which anybody wants a thing, also on what he thinks it is worth, that is to say, the number of commodities in his possession with which he is prepared to part in order to secure it. Obviously commodities coming in from foreign countries, and being unknown or rare in the country in which they are offered, if they are otherwise at all attractive, possess a certain amount of what is called scarcity value, which makes them easily saleable by adventurous merchants who arrive with the cargo.

The stories of fortunes made by merchants who travelled among simple native tribes with cargoes of glass beads and were able to exchange these gaudy baubles for gold or rubber or other commodities which are valuable in civilized countries, have often been told, and opportunities for trading of this kind must have been very much more frequent when communication was comparatively difficult. Value to a great extent being determined by local convention and local habit, the profits of the trader were likely to be considerably increased the further he got from his home market. If he took away with him plenty of things which were in abundant supply at home and consequently cheap, he would almost certainly be able to bring back a large number of things which were plentiful in a faraway community, and consequently cheap for him to acquire, and scarce in his own district and consequently sure of a good market. This difference of standard of value in different countries was a great stimulus to foreign trade, also a great help to bringing mankind together, though it sometimes ended in disillusionment. It has been asserted that even within the memory of man an English merchant traded with a primitive community in which gold and silver were exchangeable weight for weight. For some years he did a very pleasant and profitable trade by taking a cargo of silver and bringing back with him the same weight in gold, the value of which in England happened to be sixteen times as great, or more. Unfortunately, when he made his last voyage he was met at the mouth of the river by a friendly native, who informed him that the community was waiting for him with tomahawks, and he hastily put to sea again. For the rest of his life he cherished a grievance against this curious people with which he had dealt, according to his own view, on perfectly equitable terms, having sold them a commodity at a price to which they were accustomed, and which they regarded as quite correct, with the result that they proposed to murder him because they found that the price was not in accordance with that current in other parts of the world.

By this business of exchange of commodities between one community and another, the process of specialization or division of labour which has already been referred to as its basis has been developed to extraordinary lengths. Its effect has been to increase enormously the wealth available, while at the same time the concentration of the individual has narrowed down his work so that he now no longer specializes on making one commodity, but on making a part of a fraction of a commodity.

Adam Smith's chapters on division of labour are so well known that there is no need to point out the very great economic benefits that arise from it. Clearly, any man who spends all his working time upon one particular process of productive activity acquires thereby a skill and rapidity in carrying out his part of the operation which would be impossible to any worker who has to carry the manufacture of an article from the beginning to its end. Just as we saw, when the primitive savage left off doing everything for himself and took to building huts for the rest of the community, that the huts became much more water-tight and comfortable, so the process goes still further, and building becomes very much more rapid and very much more cheap and efficient when a large number of specialists are set to work on the various very different processes required for the construction of a house. The consequence is that the production of goods is very greatly cheapened and made much more rapid, but at the same time the worker tends to become an artisan instead of a craftsman, and his work is likely to be much more monotonous and much more trying. Instead of seeing his product grow under his hand from its beginning to its end, with constant changes in the nature of its call on his energy and care, he is employed during the whole of his working time on some mechanical process, with the result that he himself becomes something very like a machine. What he has gained in the power to make and acquire commodities cheaply and quickly is offset to a certain extent by the less interesting and varied nature of his work.

It also follows that as the worker becomes a specialist he becomes dependent upon other members of the community for the supply to him of a large number of things which he requires for his own existence. If he spends his life in making one commodity or in making part of one commodity, it is clear that his requirements of all the things that are necessary for life apart from what he makes himself can only be satisfied by the willingness of the community to take the commodity that he makes in payment for those which it produces and of which he is in need. When he works for himself, he only makes things that he knows himself to need; when he works to sell to others, he has to speculate on the hope that the others will want what he makes.

Commerce thus not only shows the unity of mankind by being a universal feature of his existence, but increases that unity by making each individual dependent upon the exertions of his fellows, and on their willingness to take from him stuff which he is turning out ; but if commerce thus promotes unity, it also tends to create a certain amount of friction and disagreement between one man and another when differences of opinion arise concerning the value of the product which each man is making, that is to say, concerning the amount of goods which the rest of the community is prepared to give him in exchange.

This consideration is also very strongly evident with regard to international trade. Here the division of labour is assisted by the difference in the products of different countries. There can be no doubt that the exchange of commodities between one nation and another tends to bring them together and to promote unity and harmony of interests. At the same time it is also likely to be fruitful in quarrels and bickering. We saw that Hiram was very much dissatisfied with the cities in Galilee which Solomon presented to him in the course of their semi-commercial transactions. He appears to have retaliated by making Solomon a very handsome present in gold ; but Hiram seems to have been a very exceptional person, and it is probable that most traders who are dissatisfied with the consideration received would not have been so generous in expressing themselves.

International commerce has also been a fruitful cause of disunion rather than unity when various nations have quarrelled with one another concerning the right to trade with a third people. If one nation is trading with another greatly to its profit, it feels that it has a grievance when it finds that a neighbouring nation is sending cargoes to the same destination and undercutting it and taking the cream of the trade. After religion, it is probable that trade has produced more bloodshed than any other form of human activity. At the same time there can be no doubt that on the whole its influence has been strongly on the side of unity and that it has done more to break down international barriers than any other influence that has operated in the course of history. The trader, as such, believes entirely and whole-heartedly in the unity of mankind. All that he wants to do is to buy his products as cheaply as he can and to sell them at the best possible price. Whether he buys at home or abroad, or whether he sells at home or abroad, is a matter of complete indifference to him except that, as has been shown, owing to variations in value in different parts of the world, he is probably likely to be able to make larger profits from foreign trade than in commerce at home. National preferences sometimes induce him to encourage home industry by buying home products when foreign goods would have paid him better, but in so far as this happens, he ceases to be a trader as such and becomes a mixture of trader and patriot. As buyers and sellers, however, mankind is, on the whole, singularly free from international prejudices. It was thought at one time that importation of foreign goods into England would be considerably checked by insisting upon marks of origin, that is to say, that imported goods should

IX INTERNATIONAL FORCES

be stamped as such. This expectation, however, seems to have been entirely disappointed, since most buyers were not concerned with the question of the country whence the commodity that they bought came, and only considered whether it suited their purses and was what they wanted. Sometimes there is actually a prejudice in favour of foreign goods, and, curiously enough, this is found to be so even in countries in which a protective policy has been very highly developed. It is, or was a few years ago, common to see in American newspapers, flaming advertisements heralding sales of imported goods, which were definitely stated to be such obviously because the sellers thought that they were likely to be able to sell them better because they were stated to be so. It is also a proud boast of English manufacturers that in many countries on the Continent it is common, or was until quite lately, for native manufacturers to sell their goods more easily in their home markets by describing them as English. Political and national prejudice seems to be overruled by the common human desire for something new and strange, and consequently, in spite of all friction that has arisen from international trade, and of the number of wars which have had their origin in commercial questions, there is good reason for the assertion that on the whole commerce has been a mighty promoter of intercourse among the nations and of the unity of mankind. If it had not been for commerce, the cheapening and quickening of communication could never have been carried out. The trader goes first, and after him the traveller and the tourist.

This claim can be made with perhaps even more certainty when we proceed to the realm of finance. If commerce is international and unifying, finance is perhaps even more so. Finance, of course, arises out of commerce and is an essential part of its machinery. By finance we mean the machinery of money—money-dealing and money-lending.

Money becomes necessary as soon as the exchange of commodities, which is the meaning of trade, becomes fairly developed. At first, primitive peoples exchanged their commodities one for another, but a difficulty arose when out of a pair of possible traders one had something which the other wanted but the other had not. For example, if the arrow-maker had arrows to sell and wanted to buy fish, there obviously could be no bargain if his friend who wanted to buy arrows had only got deerskins to give in exchange. It was essential to the development of trade that some commodity should be hit on which could always be taken in exchange and so form a circulating medium. We have seen from the twenty-third chapter of Genesis that a certain weight of silver had in Abraham's time begun to assume this function. Economic text-books tell us that many other commodities had the form and function of money before the metals came into use. Until quite lately there were many places in which the use of an agreed medium of exchange had not been adopted to facilitate the purposes of commerce. Jevons begins his very interesting book on money by relating how

Some years since, Mdlle Zélie, a singer of the Théâtre Lyrique at Paris, made a professional tour round the world, and gave a concert in the Society Islands. In exchange for an air from *Norma* and a few other songs, she was to receive a third of the receipts. When counted, her share was found to consist of three pigs, twenty-three turkeys, forty-four chickens, five thousand cocoa-nuts, besides considerable quantities of bananas, lemons, and oranges. At the Halles in Paris, as the prima donna remarks in her lively letter, . . . this amount of live stock and vegetables might have brought four thousand francs [£160], which would have been good remuneration for five songs. In the Society Islands, however, pieces of money were very scarce ; and as Mademoiselle could not consume any considerable portion of the receipts herself, it became necessary in the meantime to feed the pigs and poultry

IX INTERNATIONAL FORCES 213

with the fruit,'[1] and so her receipts consumed one another.

This is an example of the inconvenience which the invention of money overcame. In primitive communities it took the form of cowry-shells or tobacco or gunpowder or any commodity which was in universal request in the place. All the seller wanted to do was to be able to obtain for his product a certain amount of stuff which he could rely on being able to exchange for other things that he wanted. In the end the precious metals, with their strong appeal to human vanity, and their utility for adorning temples and so propitiating divine favour, ousted all other commodities which had been used for money; and they are now to a great extent ousted by pieces of paper, which still, however, represent claims to so much gold.

The discovery of a circulating medium enormously facilitated the progress of commerce, and it was not long before a class of people grew up who specialized in this particular form of business and became financiers and moneylenders. Bankers and financiers were known in Rome and Athens, and we know that some machinery existed by which the monetary claims of one country on another could be settled by something that fulfilled the functions of the modern bill of exchange. The actual provision of metallic currency has from the earliest times been almost entirely under the control of the government which took into its own hands, as an essential part of the police protection which it gives to the people, the coining of currency, stamping the coin in such a way that anybody who took one might know that he was getting a certain weight of a precious metal. But the money-dealing business very soon developed the machinery of credit by which anybody who had an enterprise or a venture out of which he expected

---

[1] Jevons, *Money as Mechanism of Exchange*, p. 1.

to make an attractive profit could, if he had sufficient property to pledge, provide himself with the means to finance it between the day that he started on his operations and the day when he brought home his profits : and this business also became international, though not, perhaps, as rapidly as commerce had overstepped the boundaries between one people and another.

In the *Merchant of Venice* we find Antonio trading with all the countries of the then known world,

> From Tripolis, from Mexico, and England,
> From Lisbon, Barbary, and India,

but we do not find that Shylock was lending money on at all the same international scale. When communication was slow, difficult, and untrustworthy, money-lending at a distance was made very risky, because it was impossible for the lender to keep the watchful eye on the borrower's operations and credit that is required if he is to feel comfortable in his venture. For a Lombard Street banker to lend money to a merchant in Cheapside payable at a year hence was, until comparatively lately, a much safer enterprise than to lend it to a merchant in Paris, because the local borrower was always under the lender's observation. If he were overtrading or living on too lavish a scale it would at once be noticed and reported.

Nevertheless, international finance made steady progress through somewhat obscure beginnings. We know that Philip II of Spain was heavily indebted to moneylenders all over the Continent, and that by his famous repudiation he carried consternation throughout Europe.[1] Edward III was also heavily indebted to Florentine bankers, and he also omitted to pay his debt ; and it is said that the descendants of the Florentine bankers still have a claim

---

[1] Motley, *United Netherlands*, ch. xxxiii.

against the English Crown in consequence[1]; but it was not until after the creation of stock exchanges and the machinery of a public market in securities that international finance became a question of general importance.

Here also the effect has been for unity combined with a good deal of disunion. Twenty years ago it used to be said that feeling in the Western States of America was very strongly anti-English because most of the Western farmers were indebted to English moneylenders, and on the whole it may be said that the relations between the borrower and lender are not likely to be so friendly and so likely to promote unity as those between buyer and seller. There is really no logical reason why this should be so: the basis of the bargain between the two is exactly the same. In commercial transactions one man sells to another because the other man wants something that he has got more than he does. It is exactly the same with the borrower and lender of money. A man borrows because he wants money and is prepared to pay a rate of interest for it. The lender lends because he has money to lend and wants to earn interest on it. Nevertheless there is something in this relationship which seems to produce discord. It is not many years since the Australian newspapers used to talk of England as John Bull Cohen, implying that the English money market made more than it ought to do by developing, with the help of its financial resources, the production and commerce of the young countries of the world. Perhaps it is human to feel a grudge against a creditor, because the money has to be paid back, whereas a commercial bargain is done with. Nevertheless, after allowing for all the friction that money-lending seems to produce, there can be no question that the establishment of the international market in securities has enormously widened the world's output of commodities, and it has

[1] Thorold Rogers, *Economic Interpretation of History*, ch. xx.

greatly promoted that unity of interests which has brought mankind together more than anything else.

Englishmen are always supposed to be particularly insular. Nevertheless, any one who looks at the Official List daily published by the London Stock Exchange and sees the enormous number of Government and municipal loans from all parts of the world, the number of foreign railways, and the number of foreign enterprises of all kinds which are dealt in on the London Stock Exchange, cannot avoid the conclusion that this practice of investing money abroad, which has been followed here to a greater extent than in any other country, must have very greatly widened the Englishman's horizon and forced him to confess that at least from one point of view dwellers in foreign countries have some right to exist. At any rate, in practice English investors not only have shown that they do not recognize international barriers, but there have even been times when foreign securities have actually been preferred to English. A few years ago it was reported by stockbrokers that many of their clients would not invest money at home and insisted whenever possible that it should be placed abroad. To such an extent has this process been carried on that it is now calculated by statisticians that no less than four thousand millions of English money have been placed outside England, about one-half of this having been lent to foreign countries, and about one-half to our own colonies. Here again, as in commerce, there arises a possibility of quarrelling, not only between the lender and borrower but also between rival groups of lenders in different countries. When an economically backward country is being developed with the assistance of capital from nations which are at a further stage of economic progress, the moneylender is supposed to acquire a certain amount of political prestige and privilege which makes other nations, which have an eye to increasing their influence in the borrowing country, jealous concerning such operations. A curious example was presented not long ago by China. China wanted to borrow, and probably the only countries which had any genuine surplus of capital available for export were England and France. Nevertheless, owing to the political side issues involved, Russia, Germany, and the United States also all insisted on taking part in the business of lending money to China. China was compelled to borrow more money than it wanted, so that all these so-called civilized Powers could share in the operation, and the absurdity of the position was increased by the fact that some at least of the Powers which lent the money would have had to borrow it somewhere before they could do so.

This freedom with which England has furnished financial resources to the rest of the world is sometimes called in question as having had, or being likely to have, bad effects upon the activity of production at home. It is quite clear that the progress of international commerce and the division of labour among nations by which commodities of all kinds have been very greatly cheapened could not have been carried out if England and other comparatively far developed countries had not supplied the necessary capital for the development of the relatively backward parts of the earth. If English money had not gone into building railways in America, Canada, Argentina, Australia, and all over the world, and supplying capital to the farmers and others who opened up these countries, food could not have been nearly as cheap as it is or as it was before the war, and clothes and other necessaries of life would have been at a very different price. In fact, it may be said that if England had not acted as she has, as the world's financier, the development of the world's trade to anything like its present scale would have been altogether impossible. If we could feel sure that the distribution of the world's production had been as satisfactory as the wonderful increase in its output, there would be no question that all classes in England had been very greatly benefited by its financial activities abroad. As it is, it is sometimes argued that English capital going abroad stimulates production in other countries and increases the demand for labour there, but that the demand for labour in England and its reward might have been on a higher scale if English capital had been kept at home. This is a question which is, happily perhaps, outside my province at present, but it is one which demands serious attention. This much can be said, that the years in which English capital has gone abroad with the greatest rapidity have also been those in which our export trade has been most active, and it is obvious that this must be so, because when England exports capital it does so in the form of lending money either to a foreign Government or to a foreign municipality, or to some company, English or foreign, which is conducting some enterprise in a foreign country.

In whatever way the money is lent the result is that the country to which it is lent is given so much buying power in England and consequently its demand for English goods is to that extent stimulated. It does not follow, of course, that the whole amount of money that it borrows is actually spent in England. It is possible that the Canadian railway which is raising money in England may spend it by buying steel rails in Belgium, but in practical fact the net result is that somebody or other abroad is given a claim on England which finally, by some roundabout process, takes effect in a demand for English goods and services. At the same time, when one does admit that international finance is essential to international commerce and that the specialization, which is an essential product of commerce, is thereby quickened, we have to remember that the objections, such as they are, which can be put forward against the division

IX INTERNATIONAL FORCES

of labour among individuals cannot be overlooked altogether when the division of labour is applied to nations.

Dr. Bowley, in his book on England's foreign trade, puts the matter dramatically as follows :—

The limit to the indefinite division of labour is to be found in the social, intellectual, and moral objections to specialization. It is not pleasant to contemplate England as one vast factory, an enlarged Manchester, manufacturing in semi-darkness, continual uproar, and at intense pressure for the rest of the world. Nor would the Continent of America, divided into square, numbered fields, and cultivated from a central station by electricity, be an ennobling spectacle.'[1]

This is a picturesque expression of the objections to the unity of mankind if carried too far through the process of specialization. While admitting their force, it is not necessary to admit that the specialization process need go quite to that length. Even if England became one vast factory, it need not necessarily follow that it must work in semi-darkness, continual uproar, or at intense pressure, but it is all to the good that a specialist of Dr. Bowley's eminence should call our attention to certain things which have to be guarded against. On the other hand, we may contend that if England became one vast factory, it would only do so because it paid it so well to do so, that that vast factory might be made more in accordance with William Morris's ideal than the picture of Inferno drawn by Dr. Bowley. We might imagine England one vast Garden City, dotted over with factories, each of which might be as beautiful as a cathedral, embowered and surrounded by fruit trees and gardens, in which a highly educated and technically trained population would work for five or six hours a day, and spend the rest of their time in intellectual

[1] *England's Foreign Trade in the Nineteenth Century*, by A. L. Bowley.

leisure and healthy exercise and home life under ideally happy conditions.

It is interesting to note that the result of the present war is likely, if anything, to check the export of capital for a time, not only owing to the very obvious reason that for the present all our available capital is going into the war and for some time to come will have to go into expenses connected with the war, but also because this war has set a new precedent with regard to the duty of belligerents in the matter of making payments to one another. In olden times, when war was a gentlemanly business, trade and finance were very little interrupted by it. At the time of the Crimean War the Russian Government punctually paid the interest due on Russian loans to English holders and thereby established a prestige amongst English investors which was cherished for several decades. Now that nations have taken to going to war with tooth and nail, throwing their whole available population into the field and using every possible device, military, commercial, and financial, to beat their enemies, any such pleasant decencies as paying money due from one country to another in the shape of interest or otherwise have been abandoned. When the war is over it is possible that investors will remember this fact to a certain extent and will be more chary than they were before of investing their money abroad at any rate in any country with which there is the remotest possibility of our being involved in war.

War has also shown the great inconvenience that arises when the mutual dependence of nations one on another for certain products leaves them crippled because international exchange is interrupted. International trade and finance, in their full and free development, have been shown to depend on the assumption that peace is secure. Unless the present war should be so ended as to secure peace for all time, it seems likely that all nations will aim at being able to rely, at least for the essentials of life and of defence, on home production or on a supply from countries with which war may be regarded as impossible. If this be so, then unity through trade and finance will be less universal, but more close-knit in its narrower scope.

Books for Reference

A. L. Bowley, *England's Foreign Trade.* Swan Sonnenschein.
C. K. Hobson, *The Export of Capital.* Constable.
W. S. Jevons, *Money and the Mechanism of Exchange.* Kegan Paul, Trench, Trübner & Co.
Smith's *Wealth of Nations*, chs. i–iv.

X

INTERNATIONAL INDUSTRIAL LEGISLATION

WE have learned to look upon the doctrine of interdependence of classes within the nation as a truth self-evident to all eyes unblinded by wilful prejudice or ignorance of that disabling kind charitably defined by the Roman Catholic Church as invincible. To say that unemployment in the mills of Lancashire or the shipyards of the Clyde not only affects the happiness and well-being of cotton operatives and boiler-makers and the great businesses which are carried on by their means, but depresses the national vitality and puts a drag on the national energy throughout the kingdom—to assert that no people can be wholly strong and vigorous while any corner of its territory or any layer in its social strata remains in the possession of a group physically weak, mentally undeveloped, and morally below the standard of ethics which, as a people, it has tacitly agreed to accept as necessary, seems to many of us in these days to state truisms. Yet it is not so long ago that facts which we now presume to be familiar, at least to every undergraduate, were the dangerous discovery of the few who, in an age when people said ' Socialist ' as Mr. Pecksniff said ' Pagan ', had the temerity to point out, that in things human and political as in mechanics, a chain was and could be no stronger than its weakest link. Even now, in the reaction, often only half conscious, of the employing class against any force which tends to raise the employed to a social plane less removed from that on which they themselves move, in the genuine dislike of education, concealed under ceremonial phrases in days of peace but breaking into fire and fury when the natural man is roused by a touch of excitement, we can see how skin-deep in many cases is the general belief in the widely proclaimed creed that economically as well as spiritually, we are all members one of another. And if the truth of our interdependence as citizens has won acceptance slowly and grudgingly, because the facts that prove it lie other-where than on the surface, it is easy to understand that the interdependence which is international, resulting as it does from the meeting, and crossing, and twining in the web of national life of innumerable fine threads drawn from the utmost corners of the civilized world, has scarcely yet come within the consideration of the ordinary man as an influence from which he cannot escape, and with which, therefore, he is bound to reckon. That, doubtless, is why international movements in general arouse so little interest in the mind of the average reader of newspapers. He does not regard them as practical. The persons engaged in promoting them he defines as cranks, dividing them into two classes, of whom one may be dismissed as harmlessly absurd, while the other ought probably to be suppressed as dangerous.

The events of the first week of August 1914, where the interdependence of countries is concerned, might and did throw some light on the journalistic mirror into which civilized man looks morning by morning, but it was light of the crudest kind. The result of the illumination, in numerous instances, was only to make a great number of people reflect with astonishment on the number of things which this country is in the habit of purchasing from abroad, comment with indignation on her folly in not having made them all at home, and, when passion rose sufficiently high, express a resolution that, however deeply they might need the enemy's products, they would never buy any of them again. To do them justice, this was not the attitude of the men confronted with the actual difficulty of inventing substitutes for raw materials of which the source had suddenly dried up. Those who sat in factory offices ruefully contemplating models of goods to the making of which Germany, Belgium, and Austria had hitherto sent some indispensable contribution, did not, even while they set about inventing something that should replace this contribution, belittle what they had lost. They knew, and said, that while they were confident of producing a working substitute, they did not pretend to offer in every case the precise quality which seemed to be the special gift of the German, or Belgian, or Austrian trader. Perhaps it was not after all only sheer laziness on the part of the British manufacturer, and sheer lack of patriotism on the part of British governments which induced our commercial leaders to concentrate on one field of production and abandon another. To each nation, as to each man, his gift. Some realization of this law may have come instinctively to practical workers engaged in practical tasks.

If the organizers of production among us have not been forward in the past to promote international action in the matter of labour legislation, this is not from any failure to realize the effect of inequality of industrial conditions upon nations competing in the markets of the world. This effect was naturally greatest in cases where the countries concerned were geographically contiguous and engaged in direct rivalry with one another in respect of manufactures falling under the same trade category. Here is the perfect case of competition, in which any circumstance tending to lessen production on the one side is immediately counted as an advantage to the other. But the pressure is felt even where the territory of the rival is situated at the other side of the world, even where the article produced belongs to a different class of manufacture. In normal times long distance transport is easy and long distance freight rates cheap, so that the question of distance, although still to be reckoned with, is no longer a determining factor in the sum of consideration. Again, the network of prices which controls the ultimate cost of production of any finished article is so complex that it is difficult in many cases to rule out this or that set of industrial conditions in one country as being without importance for a given factory in another. The price of a pair of corsets sold retail in Paris may have been subtly influenced by a strike of smelters of iron ore in Silesia ; and your china tea-set may be dearer to-morrow by reason of a sudden outbreak of foot and mouth disease among the herds of the Argentine. Quite naturally, therefore, it has come about that manufacturers, in opposing proposals to make existing labour legislation either more stringent in detail or wider-reaching in scope, have put forward, as their principal objection, the plea that such reforms in favour of the worker would place British industry at a disadvantage with that of countries where the action of the manufacturer remained comparatively unfettered. The distrust, as well as the dislike of long hours as a means of increasing production, together with the belief that healthy and pleasant surroundings conduce to the development of the worker's powers as well as to the satisfactory maintenance of his physical condition, has made remarkable progress among the more intelligent of the employing class since the twentieth century began. But there is still, in nearly every trade, a considerable mass of masters who rarely think and never experiment, who turn a deaf ear to the representations of their managers and foremen when these, coming into direct personal contact with the employed, take note of results due to over-strain which are invisible to the head of the business in his office, and who continue to suppose, with their fathers, that limitation of the working period necessarily restricts output and spells commercial loss. Such men, hearing that their own manufacture is produced, let us say in Russia, by men working twelve hours a day to their men's nine, and paid at a considerably lower rate than that which obtains in their own works, would certainly not dream of drawing any other conclusion than the, to them, obvious one that the result of this difference must be a lowered cost of production. Inquiries which should prove, as did those of Sir Alfred Mond's firm when confronted with such a case, that the cost of production per ton was actually higher under the long hour and low wage system would never be instituted by them, and their results, when made by others, leave them sceptical if not suspicious.

Recognizing this mental attitude in a large section of the business men of every country, and bearing in mind that, in order to secure the efficient administration of labour laws, the legislator must be able to carry with him at least the general consent of the majority of those employers to whose trades they apply, it becomes clear that if we would remove all objection to complete and adequate protective law for the workers we must first dispel the fear of the manufacturer that such law would handicap him unfairly in the international market. And what way so apt to this end as the bringing of his competitors under a law similar in character and as far as possible uniform in its provisions?

It is a proof of the prescience of Robert Owen that, even before he had succeeded in planting the first small seed which was to grow into the flourishing tree of British industrial legislation, he had grasped the necessity and formulated the demand for international action in the matter of Factory Laws. Owen's labours at home have, naturally enough, bulked so large in the estimation of historians and publicists in their writings on this subject, that the continental side of his activities has received comparatively little attention at their hands. Nevertheless his correspondence with European governments on the abuses and needs of industrialism as it existed in the early years of the nineteenth century are among the most remarkable he ever wrote; and his appeal to the Congress of the Holy Alliance in 1818 shows how thoroughly prepared he was to treat national reform as the first step to a system which should be international. Had the statesmen of his time, too busy in their making and unmaking of kingdoms to heed his arguments and appeals, turned their attention from those high matters (in which, after all, their achievement was for the most part neither brilliant nor beneficial) to the homelier details of their people's lives, social progress would have been indefinitely hastened, and we might have been spared the sorry spectacle of one industrial nation after another committing the blunders and painfully learning the lesson of its predecessors at the cost of much avoidable human suffering. For, in this matter of industrial legislation, as in many others, men are astonishingly slow to learn by example. Perhaps the most remarkable case in point that has occurred is that of Japan, at this hour still in course of being worked out before our eyes. Here we have a nation brimful of intelligence, quick of apprehension, with a genius for selecting from the polity and procedure of other States exactly those features best fitted to promote prosperity and efficiency and an unmatched power for assimilating and reproducing them in the form suitable to its own tradition of development, following the Western Powers along the crooked path of their early dealings with industrialism and allowing the very conditions which stunted and degraded the Lancashire cotton operative of the 'thirties to be created in the mills of Osaka.

Since the days of Owen ideals of industrial conditions have mightily grown and developed. This was inevitable, since the standards of social comfort and hygiene have undergone complete transformation during the last century. But the important points to note are, first, that it is not only ' reformers ' who put forward these ideals, but that they have become to a large extent common to all classes of the people, and, secondly, that the raising of the standard which proceeded at a slow, irregular rate for, roughly speaking, a hundred years, quickening in one decade and remaining almost stationary during the next, is now proceeding with comparative rapidity. Already such a rate of mortality and sickness as was common in the trades technically called dangerous twenty years ago has come to be regarded as monstrous and would no longer be tolerated with patience. This acceleration in the raising of industrial standards is doubtless largely due to the conscious participation of the workers themselves in the business of providing for their own protection ; but it may also be referred in some degree to a quickened conscience and a more intelligent appreciation of the importance of the manual worker in the national economy on the part of the public as a whole. The same movement has been taking place, in different degrees according to their differing circumstances, among the other industrial peoples of the Old World and the New. The quicker this advance on the part of some nations the more keenly was the failure of others to make progress in the same *ratio* felt by those belonging to the first group. An uneasy consciousness that the backward nations were beginning to constitute an obstacle to progressive domestic legislation on the part of the advanced nations began to manifest itself. It appeared that the lame ducks were setting the pace for the whole fleet, and it was seen that self-defence no less than concern for the welfare of the human race at large demanded the devising of some machinery by which the movements of these laggards should be quickened.

Thus, seventy years after Owen had appealed in vain to the Powers in session at Aix-la-Chapelle, a definite step was taken towards an international agreement directed to the benefit of the working classes of Europe. It must not be supposed that during this interval no inheritor of Owen's tradition had been found or that his doctrine had been altogether forgotten for want of a preacher. Now and again prophets arose who, if they did not share Owen's genius, were at least his equals in sincerity and energy. Dr. Ernst Francke, in the article reprinted from the *Economic Journal* of June 1909, which I have recommended for reference at the end of this chapter, names one of these devoted pioneers, Daniel Legrand, an Alsatian manufacturer who for thirty years did his best to induce France, Great Britain, Prussia, and Switzerland to agree on a minimum of industrial legislation. Some very useful work in the same direction was done, during the years following the Franco-German War, by a Belgian publicist; and in 1876 Colonel Frey, President of the Swiss Federal Council, took the first official step in the direction of international labour treaties, by a speech in the Council recommending that Switzerland should take the lead in an endeavour to establish them. To the Swiss Government belongs the honour of addressing the first circular note to the governments of Europe proposing the calling of a conference as a first step towards this end. This conference never met. The idea of international labour legislation was in the air, and voluntary societies composed of social reformers were beginning not only to discuss but to support it. The international meetings of organized workmen, such as the miners and cotton operatives, in different countries had familiarized the continental mind with the possibility of common action between peoples in respect of labour questions. Nowhere did the proposal for the conference arouse more general interest than in Germany, where the present German Emperor, then at the beginning of his career, was showing an active interest in German conditions of industry. It seemed that he too desired to call a conference, and on his request that he should be given precedence in the matter, the Swiss Government gracefully gave way. So it fell out that the first conference on workmen's protection met in Berlin, at the invitation of the German Government, in March 1890. There were fifteen delegates, all the governments of Europe, except those of Russia and the Balkan States, being represented. The chair was occupied by the then Minister of Commerce, Freiherr von Berlepsch, a man of broad and enlightened views and singularly sympathetic character, who subsequently became one of the founders of the International Association for Labour Legislation, and has probably, more than any other individual, secured the success of its biennial meetings.

At this conference, which the German Emperor stated in precise terms to have been called in view of the problems raised by international competition, a wide range of subjects was discussed by the delegates of the different States, including employment in mines, Sunday work, child labour, the employment of women and young persons, and administrative measures. While on many points agreement was found to be possible, and the general principles which should underlie industrial legislation were accorded ready acceptance, there was enough of objection, reservation, and allegation of constitutional difficulty to prevent the conclusion of anything in the nature of an international treaty. At the time the conference appeared to have failed of its object. Subsequent events have, however, shown that this was not the case. The failure to frame an official agreement probably showed that the ground had not yet been sufficiently laboured, and that further action in the direction of inquiry and discussion was necessary before the taking of so novel a step could be justified to the official mind; but it is certain that the recognition by the representatives of all the Western States that international action in labour questions was desirable in itself, and a goal at which governments should aim, not only laid the foundation for future State action, but gave to the voluntary work of obtaining the materials for building on that foundation an impetus and a sanction which it could have obtained in no other way.

That work was speedily set on foot and continued during the next ten years. It was greatly aided by the action of the International Labour Congress held at Zurich in 1897, when the trade unionists who composed the gathering passed resolutions in favour of the establishment of an International Labour Office, and by the Congress of Brussels which assembled at the invitation of Freiherr von Berlepsch, soon afterwards. At the latter gathering, which included a number of distinguished members of parliament, men of science, lawyers, and economists from France, Germany, Austria, Switzerland, Holland, and Belgium, the view that for the present progress must be made by the way of private initiative prevailed, and the creation of three national committees, having for their object the foundation of an international association for labour legislation, quickly followed. These committees, which had their head-quarters in Brussels, Berlin, and Vienna respectively, were by the good offices of Professors Cauwès and Jay enabled to call an international congress in Paris in the year of the Great Exhibition, and at this congress the Association was actually founded, and its statutes, provisionally drafted by Professor Mahaim and presented by the Belgian committee, were adopted. A president, a general secretary, and an international committee were provisionally appointed. The functions of the Association were also defined. It was designed to serve as a bond between all those who, in industrial countries, are convinced supporters of the principle of protective legislation ; to facilitate the study of labour legislation by the publication of the labour laws of the different States, and of reports on their administration ; to assist in the compilation of international statistics of labour and of all studies tending to bring into harmony the existing national industrial codes ; and finally, it was charged with the duty of organizing the meetings of international congresses in which labour legislation should be considered. A very important part of its business was to consist in the publication in German, French, and English of a periodical collection of all labour laws newly in force in different countries.

This has been, from the first, the work of the International Labour Office, the fixed head-quarters of the Association, which serves as an exchange and clearing-house for all information pertinent to the Association's work. It is in perpetual session at Basle, and to it all reports and inquiries are addressed by the national sections, while from it issue circulars for the sections' consideration and requests for national investigation of problems which appear ripe for international treaty. The spade work of the Association is done by the national sections in their own countries, all action of the Association being necessarily based in the first instance on tHe reports received from them at headquarters. There are now fifteen[1] such national sections— an increase of eight on the original group of seven formed in 1901. The actual membership of the Association has trebled in ten years. The seven sections to which belongs the place of honour at the head of the roll, are those of Germany, Austria, Hungary, Holland, Belgium, France,

[1] These figures represent the position at the last meeting of the Association held at Zurich, 1912.

and Switzerland. Great Britain did not form a section till 1904, and it was not till 1910 that the British Government sent official representatives to the biennial meetings. The official representatives constitute a very important element at those gatherings. They attend the plenary meetings and take part in discussions, often contributing hints on their governments' attitude towards a given reform which are invaluable to those who are framing or modifying proposals with a view to government acceptance ; and are also frequently present at the sitting of commissions charged with the consideration of detail, where they can hear the opinions and arguments of experts on every important point in debate. When resolutions are before the conference they do not vote—although in respect of voting right they stand on the same footing as other delegates. But on occasion they are not afraid to express opinions on the merits and tendencies of those resolutions which may have a determining effect on the votes of their fellow members, and I have known a few weighty words from such a man as M. Arthur Fontaine,[1] commending a proposal on which feeling was largely divided, to turn the scale at once in its favour.

The delegates of a section are elected by the section itself. They may be either men or women, and their number is in proportion to the size of the section, the maximum figure being eight, as far as voting delegates are concerned, but substitute members and experts may be present in addition. The following is a list of the fifteen sections represented at Zurich in 1912 : Austria, France, Germany, Great Britain, Hungary, Italy, the United States, Belgium, Holland, Switzerland, Denmark, Spain, Sweden, Norway, and Finland. In addition the following countries and dominions sent government representatives only : Russia,

[1] The distinguished Permanent Head of the French Labour Office.

Rumania, Greece, Turkey, Portugal, Brazil, Mexico, and the Australian Commonwealth.

A brief account of the Association's method of doing business may be interesting. Meetings are held once in two years, in the month of September, different towns in Switzerland being selected in turn for the place of assembly. The four conferences which I personally attended as British delegate took place in Geneva, Lucerne, Lugano, and Zurich. There are two plenary assemblies, the first having as chief business, apart from the hearing of introductory addresses, the appointment of the five commissions into which the conference splits up for actual work; the second meeting to receive the reports of these commissions and their recommendations, and decide upon the adoption or rejection of the latter. The trilingual rule is followed, delegates addressing the assembly either in French, German, or English, as they prefer, each speech being followed by a brief *résumé* in the other two languages from the interpreter. In the commissions, by an unwritten but generally accepted custom, French and German are the only languages used. (Latterly the representatives of the United States of America, with the individualistic courage that becomes them, have shown a disposition to rebel against this custom and defy it; but the close of the Zurich meeting left it uncertain whether in this particular the New World will be able to prevail over the Old.) In the dignified speech-making of the General Assembly the recurrent changes of language, if a little disconcerting at first, can be faced with tolerable equanimity; but when it is a question of the quicker verbal sword-play which goes on in the commissions, the member imperfect in the tongues finds his position occasionally difficult. The sympathies of every humane person must go out to the expert who, having just made a telling *exposé* of his case in French well practised for the occasion, encounters a crushing rejoinder in German of which he can barely follow the general drift.

The composition of these commissions—in which all the real work of the conferences is done—is truly heterogeneous. A commission may represent a dozen nationalities ; it will certainly contain specimens of every social class, members of the most varied shades of thought in politics, religion, and sociology. I can still remember the constituents of my first commission at Geneva in 1906. Our subject was the night-work of young persons. At the head of the table was a professor of Civil Law in the University of Louvain. On either side of him sat a Catholic clerical member of the German Reichstag ; a German Protestant pastor from Bavaria ; a distinguished Parisian engineer ; an Austrian nobleman interested in social reform ; a Hungarian man of science ; a Dutch factory inspector ; a Swiss Trade Union secretary ; and myself. We were a motley crew, but the strange ' pattern ' which we must have presented to the observation of any higher intelligences interested in our deliberations had no effect on the goodwill and good humour with which they were conducted.

The range of subjects considered at international meetings is very wide. It includes all questions relating to the labour of women, young persons and children ; matters of health and hygiene, with special reference to the use of poisonous material in industry, and the regulation of dangerous trades ; workmen's insurance ; the establishment of wages boards and minimum rates as preventives against sweating ; the extension of the ten-hours' day and the Saturday half-holiday to be the legal rule in all industrial countries ; and the introduction of the three-shift system and the eight-hour working day in continuous industries. As it is obvious that questions so large, touching so deeply the domestic life and habits of every people, cannot possibly be settled either out of hand or all at once, the Association's study of each separate problem is always prolonged and, according to the circumstances and the difficulty of the case, more prolonged in one instance than in another. Like the old pioneers of National Factory legislation, the Association has proceeded along the line of least resistance : not because it lacks courage, but for reasons of sheer prudence. If it was to become, in the words of M. Millerand, the present French Minister of War, one of its oldest and staunchest members, ' the laboratory in which international treaties are made ', it was clear that it must not propose for international acceptance reforms which even among the most progressive peoples were looked upon as doubtful or dangerous. Accordingly it chose for the subject of its first great efforts two reforms in relation to which it could count with certainty upon a considerable amount of sympathy, and proposed international legislation prohibiting the night-work of women in factories, and the manufacture, importation, and sale of matches made with white phosphorus. Information on both these subjects was collected by means of the national sections ; the Association in conference drew up proposals and recommendations to the governments concerned ; the governments consented to a diplomatic conference at Berne, and the conventions concluded in 1906 were the happy result of their meeting.

But it must not be supposed that these results were reached without difficulty. Even as regards so comparatively simple a reform as the abolition of the night-work of women—to be carried out, after considerable ' delays ' in favour of those countries in which night-work by women had hitherto been an accepted industrial custom —the adjustment of the change to the varying circumstances of each State proved a delicate business, and agreement could never have been reached but for the willingness of the more backward States to make substantial sacrifices and encounter possible risks. For this reason, the allowance of some years of grace before adherence to the treaty should become practically binding was a measure almost of necessity. It would have been unreasonable and might have been cruel to insist on Belgium and Hungary assimilating their practice in such a matter to that of Great Britain without ample time to prepare for the change. Thirteen States adhered to this treaty.

The difficulties in the white phosphorus case were at first sight even more striking, and, to begin with, only seven States — Germany, France, Denmark, Holland, Switzerland, Italy, and Luxemburg — were signatories of this convention. Of these, the first five had previously prohibited the use of white phosphorus within their own frontiers. Room was, however, left for the entry of other States into the convention at a subsequent date, with the result that the scope of the treaty has been gradually extended, and that we now find ourselves fairly within sight of the banishment from manufacture of one of the most deadly of all industrial poisons, and the consequent disappearance of an industrial disease peculiarly dreadful in its nature and symptoms. The tardy adhesion of the United Kingdom to this treaty remains a matter of regret; but the procedure of the Indian Government and of all the British self-governing dominions in following the mother country when at last she determined to take action has done much to redeem that tardiness. Obviously, it was the prohibition of the importation and sale of phosphorus matches in India and the Dominions which has forced the Scandinavian and Belgian manufacturers who were opposing complete prohibition to seek for substitutes for white phosphorus. At the present moment only Japan and Sweden among manufacturing countries stand outside the convention, the United States, whose constitution forbade her to impose prohibition by direct legislation, having brought about the desired result by the imposition of a prohibitive tax.

Is this all ? it may be asked. If the question be of treaties signed, sealed, and ratified, the answer must be 'Yes'. On the subject of the night-work of boys and the hours of women and young persons, proposals were actually considered and conventions drafted by an official conference at Berne in 1913. The draft conventions were far from admirable : their framers went so far in the spirit of compromise to meet the objections of the backward States that the provisions laid down, had they been accepted without modification, would have tended to depress rather than to raise the standard of international opinion on the questions to be affected by them. We need not, therefore, feel much regret that the war has swept them, with so many other pre-war schemes, into the wastepaper-basket. The vast question of minimum rates of wages and their regulation by the State is obviously still too much in the experimental stage of its solution (even in this country where experiments have been boldest) for it to be possible to make it the subject of international agreement. As a subject of international discussion it has had its place, and an increasingly important place, for at least eight years past in the studies of the sections and the discussions of the Association meeting. Upon no question has public international opinion ripened more rapidly. In 1906, at Geneva, where the conditions of home workers were first under discussion, a few daring delegates met in corners and whispered under their breath the words ' Wages board '. By 1910, at Lugano, an English woman delegate was elected joint president of the Association's Home Work Committee, 'as a recognition of Great Britain's achievement in passing the first Trade Boards Act ' ; at Zurich, in 1912, a two-day conference on the legal minimum wage preceded the meeting of the Association, and a whole sheaf of minimum wage bills introduced by private members into the Chambers of different countries was before the delegates, together with an official measure of the French Government. To watch this change of attitude was to see international thought in the making. To appreciate its full significance, it is necessary to bear in mind the different aspects presented by the 'sweating' difficulty in this country and in the great industrial States of the Continent. The French or German social reformer sees it mainly, if no longer exclusively, as a problem of home work. Now home work in Great Britain is a by-product of a strictly limited class of industries, affecting a comparatively small class of the population; in France and Germany it forms a highly important section of the general industrial structure, it is interwoven, to an extent rarely grasped by British students, with the life, and habits, and productive power of the nation. Much more courage—and greater freedom from prejudice—was required in the one case than the other. The remarkable advance towards definite action on the part of the State in relation to the establishment of minimum rates for home workers which took place between 1906 and 1913 could not have been achieved in so short a time but for the labours of certain voluntary associations led by men of insight, candour, and indefatigable devotion. In this connexion the pioneer work of the late Comte de Mun and Professor Raoul Jay has been of inestimable value. Realizing themselves, as did few unofficial reformers, the wide nature of the movement in which they had engaged and the impossibility of confining it in its sweep and effects to a section of the manual workers, they succeeded in gradually bringing home to the ablest among their fellow-workers the necessity for closing the gulf which French mental habit had fixed between factory and home workers and preparing to treat both classes on a similar footing of equity. In Germany, —where, as we might expect, there was less forwardness to launch unofficial schemes and a disposition to work rather from the first through authoritative channels—experiments were being made under the Home Work Act which, if of little value in themselves, seemed the earnest of much better things.

If this result only had been attained, the meetings of the Association and the labours of the sections would not have been in vain. But far more was in process of achievement when the work of the Association was interrupted by the catastrophe of the European War. The adoption in all industrial countries of the ' English week ', with its half-holiday so much coveted by the continental worker—the establishment of a uniform working day—the gradual introduction of the eight-hours shift into such ' continuous industries ' as steel-smelting and glass-blowing—an international agreement to eliminate the use of lead from many branches of the pottery industry and to limit and safeguard its use in all others,—these were only some among the questions which study and investigation and discussion had brought to a stage at which the Association could look upon them as fit matter for potential international conventions in August 1914. Now that its activities are, for the most part, in suspense, it is well to remember that its greatest achievement was the proof, again and again renewed, that it is possible for persons of twenty different nationalities, holding the most diverse opinions on nearly every subject under the sun, not only to act together but to find common motives of action so strong as to break down every sundering barrier of political doctrine and religious creed. Whatever of suspicion or antipathy might flourish outside the boundaries of the international association, these evil weeds have never taken root inside them.

X INDUSTRIAL LEGISLATION 241

Is it Utopian to dream, when the days of peace shall have returned, of a reconciliation within its borders for those between whom at present the great gulf of division seems hopelessly fixed?

BOOKS FOR REFERENCE

History of Factory Legislation, Harrison and Hutchins. Macmillan. Revised edition.
Frederic Keeling, *Child Labour in the United Kingdom*. P. S. King.
Clementina Black, *Sweating*. Duckworth.
R. H. Tawney, *Studies in the Minimum Wage :* (i) *Chainmaking ;* (ii) *Tailoring*. G. Bell & Sons.
J. A. Hobson, *Work and Wealth*. Macmillan.
Edward Howarth and Mona Wilson, *West Ham : A Study*. Dent.
Sir Thomas Oliver, M.D., *Dangerous Trades*. John Murray.
Annual Reports of International Association for Labour Legislation (British Section), 1906–14. To be obtained of the Secretary, Queen Anne's Chambers, 28 Broadway, Westminster.
Ernest Barker, *Nationalism and Internationalism*. C.S.U. Pamphlets, Mowbray, Oxford.
Dr. Bauer, *International Legislation*. Mowbray, Oxford.
Ernest Francke, ' International Labour Treaties,' *Economic Journal* (June, 1909). Reprinted separately, Macmillan.
Albert Métin, *Les Traités Ouvriers*. Armand Colin : Paris.
E. Mahaim, *Le Droit International Ouvrier*. Librairie Recueil-Sirey : Paris.
Fagnot, Millerand et Strohl, *La Durée légale du Travail*. Félix Alcan : Paris.
Paul Boyaval, *La Lutte contre le Sweating System*. Félix Alcan: Paris.
 Students might also consult the following Reports :
Le Travail à Domicile en France. Ministere du Travail : Paris.
Le Travail à Domicile en Belgique. Ministère du Travail: Bruxelles.

XI

COMMON IDEALS OF SOCIAL REFORM

EARLIER ages were more able than ours to believe in the good old days. We, knowing more of the past than our forefathers did, can find in it no golden age. But our eyes do not rest even upon the present. In the nineteenth century men thought they were at the end of a process, and their evolutionary creed was often only a polite method of saying what fine fellows they were. Now we look forward. The future seems to us longer than the past and more important than the present; and we ourselves seem to be at the beginning rather than at the end of time. A knowledge of the past has made it impossible to believe that growth has stopped, and we understand how different the future may be, in part at least, by perceiving how different even this grimy and blood-stained present is from the still more inhuman past.

Among the recorded changes the Economists write of an increasing interchange of goods, and we can see as well an increasing interchange of ideas across the frontiers of States. Music, painting, literature, and science have all been influenced; and ideas concerning political, economic, and social facts have been affected by that interchange which has developed our philosophy, our science, and our art. No one nation has originated all; and each nation has depended on hints and hypotheses which have arisen in others.

But the interchange of ideas on social life has led to an increase of ideals, which are plans of action emotionally appreciated and therefore motive forces. Some of these

XI COMMON IDEALS OF SOCIAL REFORM

are the Utopias of individual thinkers; but we shall consider here only those more powerful ideals which are shared, however vaguely, by many. In this case also, as in the purely intellectual sphere, the fire spreads from group to group, from nation to nation; and as the interchange of ideas increases knowledge, so the exchange of enthusiasm makes action more powerful. A really effective ideal, however, cannot arise except from the perception of definite evil. Vague discontents may cause such revolution as leads to reaction; but the clear sight of evil is the only source of reform. We may take it for granted, then, that although an ideal is nerveless if it is not passionate, it is futile unless it is based on knowledge. Therefore a hint must be given of the evils from the knowledge of which ideals of social reform now rise. That all is not well in the relations of man to man or of group to group must be fairly obvious to any one with imagination enough for sympathy. General dissatisfaction and universal cures for society are childish; but the perception of this and that evil gives rise to different plans for reform which all originate in the enthusiasm which is an ideal. We may put aside the long history of the growth of this shared enthusiasm for better relations between men, whatever their ability, their rank, their race, or their government.

The common ideals of the present are the result of a gradual development, but we shall consider them here as attempts to deal with existing evils and plans for a better future.

Some social evils of the present are perhaps as old as any settled civilization. Such are disease and personal violence. Some are due to forces which have come into existence recently, owing to increased communication and accumulated wealth. Such are extreme poverty and the dehumanizing of social relations. With both kinds of evil we are moved to deal, and we are not deterred from the attempt to reform even long-established evil; for we feel that we do not know what is possible. Nothing is inevitable. This is not the place to give in detail the description of those evils which are being dealt with. It is enough if we recognize that it is no abstract or airy theory of equality or human nature which moves us to action. All real theories are intensely personal: and no theory has ever yet moved men unless they saw through it to the crude facts. However it may be phrased in a theory of society, we recognize it as evil that disease, leading to premature death, should be as common as it is. As a social evil it may be said to disturb seriously the relations between men. We see also that it is a social evil that men should use fraud or violence in compelling labour or in the pursuit of riches. Of the newer social evils there is the physical and spiritual deterioration which seems to result from the massing of men in great cities. There is also the dehumanizing of the relations between master and man. And this is like in kind to the dehumanizing of all functions in the vast institutions of modern times. The director of a company comes to regard himself as part of a machine; and so does the shareholder. So eventually does the agent of the State. Until at last we reach the immense evil that human action is done for which no moral responsibility is felt. How then shall we act? What has been done and what is still hoped for? The answer to such questions will be a statement of ideals.

One may speak of ideals of social reform from two different points of view; either with respect to (1) the changing sentiment which produces movements for reform or with respect to (2) the institutional change which embodies that sentiment. The two are complementary parts of one historical movement : and it is difficult to divide them as cause and effect. For sentiment, becoming enthusiasm, certainly causes institutional change, and yet the reformed institution invariably creates a new sentiment. The province of law and of social custom is to lead as well as to register—a dynamic as well as a static influence, to increase order and to incite to liberty. In actual life, therefore, it is often impossible to separate the sentiment from its embodiment in measures of social reform.

For purposes of study, however, one may divide. We may put aside the moving sentiments—the passions, however faint, which urge men to wish for a better future—and we may consider first the particular instances of reform.

One definite and in some sense new departure in the results of the shared enthusiasms of nations has been the industrial legislation of recent years. That has been already dealt with. But, although in an economic age such as ours industrial reform may seem the most striking, it is not the only effect of our shared enthusiasm and later ages may not think it the most important. There has been reform of social evils owing to the interchange between nations of ideas on education, religious toleration, medicine, and sanitation, the treatment of criminals, the suppression of slavery and many other subjects. All these and many more reforms are, as it were, registered in institutional (legal or administrative) change.

Perhaps it is better to begin with a definite instance of the working of an ideal, lest it may seem that we are speaking only of an empty aspiration. We may take as an example the reforms connected with medicine and sanitation, and those only in so far as they have been officially established by the joint action of states. This is a very restricted embodiment of a social ideal, since of course we may find the same use of common labour between men of different races in the private contest with disease or in the municipal preventive medicine which in every great city owes much to investigators and practitioners of other nations. But it is better to take the most tangible effect in purely governmental action.

The French Government proposed an international conference, which met in 1851, to deal with infectious disease; and a second conference met in 1856. In 1865 the outburst of cholera in the East led to a third congress at Constantinople. Great Britain opposed treaties for regulating quarantine, &c., because of the delay which might be caused to the pursuit of shipping interests. But at last a treaty was made in 1892 at Venice for protection against cholera. Further and more effective treaties were agreed to by civilized states in 1897 and 1903. A bureau of information concerning infectious disease was established at Paris; and commissions to supervise were established in Turkey and Egypt. With regard to sleeping sickness Great Britain took the initiative; and a conference met in 1907, in London, at which six countries were represented. So much with respect to disease; we may now turn to examples of the joint action of states as regards crime.

The African slave traffic has been dealt with since 1885 (Berlin Conference) by the European States acting together on certain general principles. And what is known as the White Slave traffic was the subject of arrangement between fifteen states in the conference at Paris in 1902.

Again, the reform of prisons and penitentiaries has been much assisted by international congresses since 1846. The last was held in 1910 in America, at which twenty-eight states were represented. A secretariat has been established at Berne for the exchange of expert opinion and for making suggestions to governments.

These are examples of a very numerous class of reforms undertaken by the *joint action* of governments. They are all comparatively recent and most of the twenty-eight unions between governments for concerted action have been established during the years of European peace between 1871 and 1914. In these instances the States of Europe have put their precious sovereignties into their pockets; although the lawyers and diplomatists explain the situation in the old terms.

With respect to all these movements for social reform three points must be noticed: first, the initiative in most reform has come from private enterprise and not from diplomacy or governments. Secondly, this private interest has spread from the few of one nation to the few of another before any effective result was attained. Thirdly, the states have not acted together because of any general theory of international action, but simply because certain social evils could not be dealt with at all by any state acting separately. Whatever hampers common action, then, also hinders effective reform in dealing with disease or crime. I need not elaborate the conclusion.

There are also instances of governmental action being *directly influenced* by the practice of other states, even when there has been no common action. The two most striking reforms of recent years have been in education and religious toleration. Of education enough has already been said. The interest from our point of view here is chiefly in the effect of education on social structure. It is increasingly evident that of all forces for transforming a nation, education is the most powerful; but no one nation can transform its education effectively without respect to the mistakes and successes of its neighbours. This has been perceived and acted upon. The influence, for example, of

Germany on England is sufficiently well known. German
precedents were quoted in the House of Commons in the
early days of state education for England: and the
Education Acts of 1870 and 1876 were largely due to
the impression made in England by the success of state
education in Prussia. Coleridge, Carlyle, and Matthew
Arnold definitely acknowledged a debt to Germany. But
Germany owed something to England in the perception
of the value of surroundings and corporate life in schools.
France also was affected by English education; and, in
fact, French educators had to come to England to find
the thing for which the French gave us the name—*Esprit
de Corps.*

The United States have been very definitely influenced
in their University education both by Germany and
England; and their Government has in primary education
certainly established for all states the transforming
possibilities of a school system. It must be remembered
that the crudity of civilization and its apparent corruption
in the United States are European not American. It is
because Europe has neglected its duty, enslaved and
brutalized its peoples, that social and political evil enters
with the immigrants; and all this mass of European
incompetence, the result of neglect or evil-doing in Ireland,
Poland, the Slavonic Countries and Italy the Government
of the United States exorcises with education: and the effect
is spreading beyond the frontiers of the States. A further
effect of influence passing from nation to nation has been
the change with regard to the relations of State and
Church. In England it is some years since the State
persecuted in the supposed interest of religion; but we
remember that the abolition of tests against Roman
Catholics was as late as 1830 and as against Jews as late
as 1850. Even the most backward of European countries
have been affected by the general feeling. In 1874 Austria

rich and the poor. I do not mean those with £3,000 a year, and those with £160 a year. It is not a question for the Exchequer. I mean that great numbers in all ' civilized ' nations are ill-fed and ill-clothed from birth, and die prematurely. To perceive it is to desire action which perhaps no state can perform. But that we perceive it is something. Read the complacent rhymes of Lord Tennyson about ' freedom slowly broadening down ' and then turn to contemporary literature, to Jean Richepin or John Galsworthy, and you will acknowledge that a common ideal of social reform has come into existence. We are at least restless in face of a social organization which wastes humanity during long years of peace almost as completely, though not so recklessly, as during a few months of war.

Something has been already done—English writers and English experience have given a motive power to Hungarian, Russian, Finnish, Turkish, Persian, and Indian democracy. Groups of men have claimed, for example in South America, their right to free development. And everywhere during the period of European peace the contact between nations was teaching every nation the force of its own character, while the new complexities of society were weakening the old dividing lines of caste between individuals.

In all these matters we seem to be moved by a desire for a freer social atmosphere. Whether law or administration changes or not, it is clear that most European nations have undergone in the years of peace from 1871 to 1914 considerable social changes. How far they are effective in all nations and in all classes it is very difficult for a contemporary to judge. It may be that the social structure of the decorative upper fringe or of the bedraggled hem of society is much the same as it was before communication was easy and transit rapid. But the central body of European society is certainly changed; and, after all, between the scum and the dregs is the good soup.

Such are the changes which have been introduced into social life owing to the interdependence of nations. But we should not understand what has happened if we accepted the mere record of achievements. The future is built not only upon what we have done, but upon what we hope to do. Reforms accomplished do not make us more satisfied to endure evil not yet reformed—for always working in the achieved present is the ideal which transformed the past into what we now see.

We may turn, then, to consider some general features of the force working in social reform which is not yet achieved. And for that purpose we put aside established law and custom to consider the implied attitude.

Now that political privilege and inequality before the law are more or less removed, there is a greater concentration upon the underlying social injustice. We all accept it as good that the activities of government should not be for the benefit of the few, or that the money should not be drawn from one class. We suppose at least that there should be one law for rich and poor.

To any one with a knowledge of history this seems an immense step since small classes in every nation held political privilege, made law for others, and forced tribute from the majority. Not that all is justice and liberty. The law still, with noble impartiality, forbids both the millionaire and the pauper to steal bread. Of course it is not directed against the poor. The law never forbids the poor man to cheat the state out of more than £3,000 a year. Again, political power still depends on the social position of your cousins and your aunts. But something has been done.

SOCIAL REFORM

We hear much more nowadays about social than about political or legal reform. That, in itself, is a sign of a change of attitude. In the revolution of 1381 the crowds came marching to London swearing, in the words of the old chronicle, that there would be no peace in the land till each and every lawyer was slain. In the revolutions of 1830 and 1848 it was 'death to the politicians'. Now—it may be that we despair of lawyers or politicians, dead or alive. In any case the attention of those in every state who are moved by enthusiasm for a better society is concentrated less upon votes and laws than upon the distribution of well-being.

Secondly, there has been a transference of enthusiasm of the religious or poetic kind from the sphere of contemplation or aloofness to that of earthly and even material action. Ideals of social reform do not any longer involve a neglect of food and clothing : we are all more and more convinced that it is idle to preach culture to a starving man, or to talk of liberty to one whose whole life is a bestial struggle for bare food and covering. I speak of normal times. In England, France, and Germany, social betterment means giving to a greater number security of bare life, upon which alone the good life can be built.

It will be seen that I imply a disagreement with the Tolstoian conception of reform ; in so far as that involves a neglect of food and clothing and generally of what are called material goods. That conception is not perhaps powerful among those who deal with what is usually called social reform. It is not 'modern', and it is also dependent upon a mistaken argument in ethical theory. An unfortunate confusion made by what is called Eastern, Stoic, or Mediaeval asceticism led to the idea that because the mind is more important than the body, the body has no importance at all. But we need not deal with this theory in detail, especially as the general attitude of to-day is opposed to it. There is undoubtedly a concentration upon the bare necessities of human life with a view to discovering how these can be shared more generally.

We are fully aware of the immense social danger in the desire for riches; but that is no objection to the desire for bread and clothing and the bare necessities of human life. And the seemingly materialistic enthusiasm which will gradually transform our semi-bestial civilization is no less poetic or religious than any Eastern aloofness or Tolstoian simplicity. Poetry is not all rhyming couplets: religion is not all for the intellectually or artistically incompetent. So, a world in which twenty per cent. of humanity did not slowly starve to death would not necessarily be less worthy of admiration. Nor would religion disappear if every one were healthy, unless religion means the result of neurasthenia or dyspepsia or premature ageing. No doubt there is some exaggeration in this element of the common social ideals. Not even a poor man lives on bread alone; and it is indeed possible to have a perfectly well-fed society which would be quite barbarous. But we must regard the fine flower of culture as purchased at too high a price if, for the sake of a few connoisseurs and courtiers not to say bourgeois plutocrats, the majority in every nation must lack a bare human life. Some declare that the division between nations is more important than that between the rich and the poor. It may be so; but the only reason must be that what the few have, the many, however dimly, may hope to share or may be induced to think they do share. Humanity is infinitely gullible. But in every nation there is rising a murmur which may yet become an articulate cry.

The writers of modern Utopias in their detailed conception of what is desirable may speak only for themselves; but it is a sign of the common enthusiasm that they all attach so much importance to organization and to physical health. This indicates that we all, in every nation, look forward, however vaguely, to a society in which human life shall be less difficult for the majority to obtain. We speak sometimes of the redistribution of leisure—August Bebel made it one of the chief articles of his creed. But this as an ideal does not indicate any desire that the dock-labourer should have time to loaf in a club, or his wife time to play bridge, except in so far as time to loaf is an opportunity for some other employment than the mere struggle for food. There is nothing inevitable in a situation which makes the development of most of the human faculties a privilege of a few and an impossibility for the greater number. Nor is it correct to suppose that the half-starved and the ill-clothed should be satisfied with being 'virtuous', and leave it to others, possibly wicked and certainly far from simple, to cultivate art and science.

Nor again is it absurd to hope for a world in which all should have at least the opportunity for the development of any faculties they may possess. The social gain would be immense. It would be like the change from a harmony which is produced by a few amateurs to one of a full orchestra.

Thirdly, it is increasingly evident that no one state or nation can act effectively in social reform unless it acts in concert with others. Treaties of commerce, common prison legislation, and common measures for sanitation and medicine have proved effective because they are in the nature of things. They are necessary means for the desired prosperity even of the most selfish and segregated state.

But ignorance and prejudice and irrational violence spread as easily as disease or crime. Knowledge is not secure until it is widespread; and civilization perishes, which is segregated in a world of barbarism. Therefore education also, in its widest sense, must be contrived in common. Not merely school systems influenced by foreign ideas, but the very atmosphere of thought must change in harmony among all nations, if we are not to go toppling down into the abyss from which by painful centuries we have ascended.

This ideal of social reform then seems to be agreed upon between some men of all nations, that more common action should be taken. It is not a vague sentiment for the abolition of conflict between states ; nor is it a pious aspiration for peace. It is the clear perception that the state cannot fulfil its functions in modern life if it continues to act as isolated or segregated. That for which the state itself stands cannot be attained even within the frontiers of one state by any state acting alone.

This is not the place to distinguish those subjects upon which states should act together from those on which they should act separately. That is simply the problem as to the limits of political regionalism. The fact which is sufficient for our argument here is that certain forces, chiefly economic, have come into existence in recent years, which disregard state boundaries. In concrete terms, these are international trusts and international labour interests. But it is increasingly evident that these cannot be effectively dealt with by any one state acting separately. The isolated sovereign state of earlier times is simply helpless before the elaborate world-system of economics ; and control can only be secured by an established world-system of politics. The states, one supposes, exist for justice and liberty. Divided, they will perish or become mere playthings in the hands of non-moral economic ' interests '.

To save itself and all it stands for, the state must cease to pose as a possible opponent to any other state, and must deliberately co-operate in an increasing number of reforms.

It is better to put into the coldest terms a conception which has too often hitherto proved futile, because it arose rather from vague discontent, than from the perception of a definite evil. The fire of enthusiasm must indeed work upon that conception before any effective change can be made in the attitude of governments or of peoples. But enthusiasm will be wasted if we cannot pause to see against what we are contending.

We are struggling with the greatest of all obstacles to social reform when we attack the isolation of nations. Unless that is overcome we shall perhaps patch and prop; but, time and again, we shall be enslaved to the immensely powerful non-moral forces, in the midst of which humanity finds its way. I cannot speak more clearly—βοῦς ἐπὶ γλώσσῃ. The nations face each other in conflict, while death, disease, violence, bestial indolence and docility corrode every state.

But when war was at its brutish worst Grotius spoke with effect of a moral bond which survived between men who in physical conflict had been trying to take their 'enemies' for beasts and stones. And humanity began once more its long struggle with the beast in man. So now—I leave it to your imagination.

We have made immense progress by assisting each other across the frontiers of states in such science as may provide high explosive and submarine warfare. In these the nations have co-operated. The guns which kill the English at the Dardanelles were made by Englishmen. There may yet come a time when high explosives will be out of date, and the state will use the careful dissemination of disease among its enemies. The only reason, I think, why it is not now done, is that no group can be certain of making itself immune from the disease it may spread among its enemies.

Our conclusion, therefore, is that one of the elements in the present attitude towards social reform is a tendency to co-operation between nations. We have seen that this has already had effect in various details of law and administration; and there is every reason to suppose that the method will be carried further.

But the problem cannot be left there. Co-operation as a word is a mere charm, like Evolution. There has been, and there may be co-operation in doing wrong. That action has become common does not prove that it is right; and an ideal implies at least some ethical judgement. Therefore, in every nation there are some few who are convinced of the necessity for more deliberately moral action in common between men of different races. If there can be so much co-operation in the making of armaments or the defrauding of shareholders, there may yet be more co-operation in the elimination of disease and poverty. And not only may there be such co-operation, but it must be. The situation no longer exists in which most of the effects of an evil régime are confined within frontiers. The social distress of European nations must be dealt with as a whole because it is a whole. Therefore whatever militates against the unity of western civilization destroys the possibility of social reform.

Many times before it has been seen that there are nobler conflicts than the struggle for markets or for the political domination of one clique or one nation. Many times before it has been felt, at least by a few, that man is deceived when he imagines that man is his enemy. And many times when the deliverance seemed near we have been enslaved again by an evil magic. A hundred years ago, at the end of the Napoleonic wars, the dreamers imagined that humanity would have done with its false prophets and lay the ghosts which have haunted it since it began to shake off the manners of the beasts. But a dismal succession of new falsehoods and new blind guides appeared. And now, in this so advanced age, we have to face the same possibility. There is much to excuse a despair; from which nothing can free us but a new enthusiasm. The evil magic must be overcome by magic of another kind, and how acute the crisis seems it is hardly possible to indicate.

The quality of our age was its expectancy. For that reason men of every nation were moved to desire a transformed society. But perhaps that quality of expectancy was the quality of youth. For the first time in history, in the early twentieth century, age was giving place to youth in the political equilibrium of the generations. Now—I dare not speak too plainly. The young men of the western world are already, since August 1914, noticeably fewer. Death may have made no difference to them. It has made an immense difference to the future. It means that the eager expectancy of youth, which is the source of so much enthusiasm for a better world, is being lost. The crisis is here. As yet the common ideals of civilized nations still survive; but the desire for a better future is at ebb and flow with a tired acquiescence in the established order. It is in our hands to decide which shall overcome. No generation has faced a greater issue. We cannot tell what will be the outcome ; but to hope too much is at least a more generous fault than to despair too soon.

Books for Reference

C. D. Burns, *Political Ideals*. Clarendon Press.
P. Geddes, *Cities in Evolution*. Williams & Norgate.
J. A. Hobson, *Towards International Government*. Allen & Unwin.
P. S. Reinsch, *Public International Unions*. Ginn & Co.

XII

POLITICAL BASES OF A WORLD-STATE

WORLD-STATE is a term likely to be offensive in its arrogance, if it be taken to mean the substitution of a single political community and government for the numerous separate national states which have hitherto existed. I therefore hasten to say that I intend no such meaning, but use the term as a convenient expression to cover any body of political arrangements, to which most of the principal nations of the world are parties, sufficiently stable in character and wide in scope to merit the title of international government.

Towards such a possibility the nineteenth century has made three great contributions. During that century great advances have been made in the settlement of political government upon a basis of nationality. This process has been accomplished partly by throwing off the dominion of some foreign power, as in the case of Belgium, Greece, Montenegro, Bulgaria, Rumania, and Serbia, and the South American colonies of Spain; partly by the closer federal union of independent states, as in the case of Germany and Switzerland; partly by a blend of the two methods as in the case of Italy; and partly by the peaceful dissolution of an unnatural union, as with Norway and Sweden. Though much still remains to be done before the identification of statehood with nationality even for Europe is completed, and some backward steps have been taken, the growing acceptance of the conception of nationality as a just and expedient basis of government is a powerful guarantee for the persistence of this joint work of

XII POLITICAL BASES OF A WORLD-STATE   261

liberation and of union. If, as the result of the settlement following this war, political readjustments are made which fairly satisfy the remaining aspirations after national autonomy, the more pacific atmosphere will favour all opportunities for co-operation between nations.

The second contribution of the nineteenth century towards political internationalism is of a more positive character. It consists in a series of inchoate and fragmentary but genuine attempts of the Great Powers to work together upon critical occasions in the interests of ' justice and order ', as they understood those terms, and to embody in acts or conventions some policy which is the result of their deliberations. This flickering light, called the Concert of Europe, first kindled at the Congress of Vienna, has reappeared fitfully throughout the century. The treaties, declarations, and conventions, proceeding from these conferences or congresses of the Powers, have marked important advances, not only in the substance of international law, but in the method of legislation. For whereas, before the Congress of Vienna, all the treaties between states which helped to form the body of international law were the acts of two or, at the most, a small group of states, since that time law-making treaties of general application and of world-wide importance have come into being. The most noteworthy examples of these general treaties are the Final Act of the Vienna Congress in 1815, the Declaration of Paris in 1856, the Geneva Convention of 1864, the Treaty of Berlin in 1878, the General Act of the Congo Conference in 1885, and the two Hague Conferences of 1899 and 1907. Having regard to the general character of many of the rules laid down at these conferences, as, for instance, the abolition of the slave trade, the neutralization of certain lands and waters, and the regulation of the rules of war, it is clear that we have to recognize throughout last century the existence of a rudimentary organ of international legislation, very irregular in its operation, very imperfect in structure and authority, but none the less a genuine experiment in international government.

Hardly less significant for our purpose has been the prominent assertion of the principle of federalism in the formation or growth of national government. The great example of the United States has been followed by Switzerland and Germany, by Mexico, Argentine, Brazil, and Venezuela, and by the dominions of the British Empire in Canada, Australia, and South Africa. I must not in this brief survey even touch upon the different forms of federalism. It must suffice to remark that, whether as a a principle of devolution, as in the case of the proposal of Home Rule for the constituent parts of Great Britain, or as a principle of closer union, as in the proposal for a federated British Empire, federalism is very much alive. It furnishes a hopeful mode not only for reconciling demands for local autonomy with effective central sovereignty among the provinces or districts of a single national state, but even for harmonizing the claims of separate nationality with those of wider racial, linguistic, and traditional sympathy. But even more important than these distinctively political movements and events, as a pledge of the coming world-state, is the manifold structure of industrial and commercial internationalism which has been growing during the last few generations at an ever accelerating pace. The network of material, financial, and intellectual communications, connecting all parts of the developed world, and establishing quick, constant, cheap, and reliable modes of transport for men, goods, money, and information, form the actual basis of what may not improperly be called an economic world-state. Though much of this machinery, with the great work of international trade and capitalistic co-operation which it assists to perform, lies outside the sphere of politics, there are innumerable points of political contact and pressure. The realities of foreign policy in every state are more and more concerned with issues of trade, communications, and concessions, and the treaties and other formal arrangements between states are to a growing extent the instruments and the expressions of the internationalism of economic interests. The imperialism and the colonial policy of each great Power, though composed of various ingredients, are mainly directed by commerce and finance. Most of the disagreements and conflicts between governments relate to interferences with the free play of economic internationalism by states whose policy is still dominated by foolish and obsolescent rules of a narrowly national economy. An enlightened interpretation of the needs and interests of modern man demands that all such national economic barriers be removed and replaced by governmental co-operation to secure, by free trade and an open door, for capital and labour the fullest and best development and distribution of the economic resources of the world.

While, therefore, the most impressive political events of the nineteenth century have been the expression and the successful realization of nationalism, many powerful undercurrents of internationalism have been gathering force. The pressures of civilization have been more and more towards extra-national activities. Thoughtful men and women in our time recognize the urgent need of closer international communion for three related purposes: First, the consolidation, extension, and effective sanction of the existing body of international law; secondly, the establishment of peace on a basis of reliable methods for the just settlement of differences; thirdly, the provision of regular accepted means for the co-operation of nations in all sorts of positive constructive work for the human commonwealth.

These general considerations I will ask you to regard as introductory to the grave practical question which confronts us. Is this essential work of internationalism consistent with the preservation of the sovereignty and independence of the present national state, or does its performance involve some definite cession of these national state-rights to the requirements of an international government?

The terrible events which are passing to-day ripen and sharpen this issue. They bring into powerful relief the inherent defects of an international polity based upon the absolute independence of the several states, and the futile mechanical balances and readjustments by which foreign policy has been conducted hitherto. But how far do they offer assistance or security for the achievement of organic reform? After this war has come to a close, will the nations and governments be enabled to lay a sound basis for pacific settlement of disputes and for active co-operation in the common cause of humanity for the future? No confident answer to this question is possible. For nobody can predict the composition and the relative strength of the feelings and ideas which will constitute 'the state of mind' of the several nations and their statesmen. As regards immediate or early policy, much will, of course, depend upon the definiteness of the victory and defeat, and the consequent distribution and intensity of the passions of elation and depression, anger and revenge, which peace may leave behind. It is, of course, part of the fighting strength of every belligerent to persuade himself that an overwhelming victory for himself affords the best security of peace and progress in the future. But this conclusion, based on the prior assumption, equally liable to error, that one's own cause is entirely right and one's enemy's entirely wrong, is unlikely to be sound. A peace which brings the least intensity of triumph and humiliation, the most even

XII A WORLD-STATE

distribution of gains and losses, would seem to give an atmosphere most favourable to the growth of pacific internationalism. This, of course, will be sharply contested, and those who contest it will exhibit the usual excessive confidence of those whose mind moves in a shut oven of heated but unmeaning phrases about fighting to a finish, crushing German militarism, and 'a war to end war'. But there is no stronger evidence of the intellectual and moral havoc of war than the easy acceptance of what Ruskin called ' masked words ' in lieu of thinking.

" There are masked words abroad, I say, which nobody understands, but which everybody uses, and most people will also fight for, live for, or even die for, fancying they mean this or that or other of the things dear to them. There were never creatures of prey so mischievous, never diplomatists so cunning, never poisoners so deadly, as these masked words; they are the unjust stewards of all men's ideas; whatever fancy or favourite instinct a man most cherishes, he gives to his favourite masked word to take care of for him ; the word at last comes to have an infinite power over him—you cannot get at him but by its ministry." In war-time this domination of 'masked words' is all-powerful, and is likely to leave the thinking powers of all Europe seriously impaired when the war is over.

There are those who hold that sheer exhaustion, nervous and economic, will compel the nations to seek concerted action against the recurrence of so shattering an experience, that some sheer instinct of self-preservation will find expression in adequate political arrangements. I should be the last to deny the reality of the collective instinct. But remember that, as an instinct, it works blindly, and is liable to be diverted and frustrated in a thousand ways by the conflicting streams of narrow passion amongst which it moves. Mere exhaustion and a general feeling of insecurity cannot yield a sufficient motive and directing force for the work of international construction. It is necessary to rationalize this instinct of self-preservation and co-operation, in order to make it of effective service. Here lies the heart of our difficulty. War is the most intensely derationalizing process, and the long steeping of European civilization in the boiling cauldron will have twisted and blunted the very instruments of thought. As Professor Murray points out in a powerful essay, war rapidly undoes the slow secular process by which liberty and capacity for individual thought have grown up, and plunges the personal judgement into the common trough of the herd-mind. It is, I take it, the recognition of this peril to the human mind, this necessity of safeguarding the powers of individual thought and personal responsibility, that brings us here. We seek to fortify the separate centres of personal judgement, to inform the individual mind, because the work of making a positive contribution to the unity of civilization depends upon the vigorous independent functioning of many minds.

This consideration brings me directly to confront the enemy, that is to say, those who contend that a world-state or any real international government is now and must always remain an impossibility, an unrealizable Utopian dream. The process of social evolution on its political side ends with the national state. It is a final product. National states cannot, will not, and ought not, to abate one jot or tittle of their inherent sovereignty and independence, and the experience of history shows that all attempts at international federation or union are pre-doomed to failure.

It is evidently quite impossible for me to present here a full formal refutation of these positions. I will therefore content myself with brief demurrers. To the argument from social evolution I would reply that evolution knows no

XII   A WORLD-STATE   267

finality of type, and that the presumption lies in favour of those who hold that the centripetal or co-operative powers, which have forged the national state out of the smaller social unities, are not exhausted, but are capable of carrying the organizing process further. To those who rely upon the authority of history, citing the collapse of the experiments in federation which followed the Congress of Vienna as proof that similar experiments will similarly fail to-day or to-morrow, I reply that this view is based on a false interpretation of the statement that 'history repeats itself'. A psychological or sociological experiment is not the same when fundamental changes have taken place in the psychical and social conditions. We have already recognized that the nineteenth century has seen a series of vital changes in the economic and spiritual structure of civilization. The evidence of 1815 cannot, therefore, be conclusive as regards the possibilities of 1915. To those who insist on the sovereignty and independence of the national state as an eternal verity, I will make no further reply than to say that such language has for me no more meaning than talk of 'the divine right of kings', 'the natural rights of man', or any other phrase of the abracadabra of metaphysical politics. The actual world in which we live knows no such absolutes. Sovereignty and independence, like all other legal claims, are subject to modification and compromise. Every bargain made by treaty or agreement with another state, every acceptance of international law or custom, involves some real diminution of sovereign independence, unless indeed the liberty to break all treaties and to violate all laws is expressly reserved as an inalienable right of nations. Moreover, within the limits of a single nation, sovereignty is itself divided and distributed. Alike in the United States of America, the Swiss Republic, and the German Empire, the constituent states as well as the nations are recognized as sovereign, possessing certain rights or powers safeguarded by the constitution against all encroachments of the central or federal government. So again within the state itself, the sovereignty is often no longer concentrated in a single person or a single body of persons, but is exercised by the joint action of several organs, as in Great Britain, where the king and the Houses of Parliament are the joint administrators of the sovereignty of the state. Sovereignty thus becomes more and more a question of degree and of adjustment. International lawyers will doubtless insist that neither treaties nor international laws involve any derogation of sovereign powers. But when the substantial liberties of action are curtailed by any binding agreement, the unimpaired sovereignty is an idle abstraction.

When, therefore, we ask whether it is not possible to extend and consolidate the agreements between so-called sovereign states into some form of effective international government, we broach a proposition less revolutionary in substance than in sound. If all the separate treaties, conventions, and other agreements, existing now between pairs of nations for the performance of specific acts and the settlement of differences, were modified and gathered into the forms of general treaties signed by all the treaty-making states; if all international laws and usages were codified and brought under the surveillance of some single representative court or council,—we should discover that there existed already the substance of an international government, not indeed adequate to our needs, but far ampler than we had suspected. In the Hague conventions and courts, again, and in certain other intergovernmental instruments, such as the Postal and Telegraphic Bureaux at Berne, we already possess the nucleus of the general forms required. We possess already the beginnings alike of the legislative, judicial, and administrative apparatus

XII A WORLD-STATE 269

of international government. But it is slight in substance, fragmentary in its application, and exceedingly imperfect in its sanctions. Moreover, it has just shown itself quite inadequate to perform the first function of a government, viz. to keep the public peace.

The task of converting so feeble a structure of government into an effective instrument of international peace and progress is evidently one of great magnitude and difficulty. But it is the task which lies persistently before us, and upon its performance the safety of civilization itself depends. It is, therefore, well not to exaggerate its difficulties, but to measure them as closely as we can. This can best be done by means of a brief survey of the principal lines of advance which have been proposed. In this country, in America, in Holland, and elsewhere, the air is thickening with schemes for obtaining better international relations after the war. All of them have this, I think, in common, that they concern themselves primarily not with ideal or practical plans for the general co-operation of nations in advancing the welfare of the world, but with methods of preventing future wars and securing relief against the burden of armaments. All agree that some general formal arrangements between nations must be substituted for 'the clash of competing ambitions, of groupings and alliances and a precarious equipoise', and that only by such stable agreement can disarmament be got and peace rendered secure. All agree that the instrument of this international government must be a general treaty to which a number of states must be parties and that the terms of this treaty must require them to submit all forms of disputes to some pacific mode of settlement. Nearly all, moreover, accept the distinction drawn between justiciable issues, relating to the application or interpretation of laws or to the ascertainment of facts by means of legal evidence, which are suitable for settlement by a judicial or arbitral process, and those which, not being capable of such settlement, are better suited for a looser process of inquiry and conciliation.

But the proposals differ widely, both as regards the scope they assign to the work of preventing war, and as regards the measures they advocate for securing the fulfilment of international agreement. They may be grouped, I think, in three classes on an ascending scale of rigour. The first class envisages a general treaty, by which the signatory states shall undertake to submit all differences between them to processes of arbitration or conciliation conducted by impartial courts or commissions, and to abstain from all acts of hostility during the progress of such investigation. This principle has recently found an important expression in the treaties signed last year by the United States with Great Britain and France, and other nations. The first article of these treaties reads as follows: 'The High Contracting Parties agree that all disputes between them, of every nature whatsoever, other than disputes the settlement of which is provided for, and in fact achieved, under existing agreements between the High Contracting Parties, shall, when diplomatic methods of adjustment have failed, be referred for investigation and report to a Permanent International Commission to be constituted in the manner prescribed in the next succeeding article; and they agree not to declare war or begin hostilities during such investigation and before the report is submitted.' The objects of this method of pacific settlement are three: first, to provide impartial and responsible bodies for a reasonable inquiry into all disputes; secondly, to secure a 'cooling off' time for the heated feelings of the contestants; thirdly, to inform the public opinion of the world and to make effective its moral pressure for a sound pacific settlement.

The efficacy of any such arrangement evidently depends

upon two conditions, first, the confidence of the signatory states that each and all will abide by their undertaking, and, secondly, the uncovenanted condition that they will accept and carry into effect the awards or recommendations of the arbitral and conciliation commissions. These proposals, however, furnish no sanctions or guarantees other than those of conscience and public opinion for the due performance of the treaty obligations, and make no attempt to bind the parties to an acceptance of the decision of the commissions. Moreover, regarded as a means of securing world-peace and disarmament, all such proposals appear defective in that they make no provision for disputes between one or more of the signatory states and outside states which are no parties to the arrangement.

Such considerations have moved many to seek to strengthen the bond of the alliance, and to make it available for mutual support against outside aggression. The vital issue here is one of sanctions or the use of joint force, diplomatic, economic, or military, to compel the fulfilment of treaty obligations and the execution of the awards. Many hold that, while most civilized states might be relied upon to carry out their undertakings, some powerful state —Germany, or Russia, or Japan—could not be trusted, and that this want of confidence would oblige all nations to maintain large armaments with all their attendant risks and burdens. To obviate this difficulty, it is proposed by some that the signatories shall pledge themselves to take joint action, diplomatic, economic, or forcible, against any of their members who, in defiance of the treaty obligations, makes or proposes an armed attack upon another member. This is the measure of stiffening added by Mr. Lowes Dickinson in his constructive pamphlet *After the War*: 'The Powers entering into the arrangement' are to 'pledge themselves to assist, if necessary, by their national forces, any member of the League who should be attacked before 'the dispute provoking the attack has been submitted to arbitration or conciliation.' A state, however, by Mr. Dickinson's scheme, is still to remain at liberty to refuse an award, and after the prescribed period, even to make war for the enforcement of its demands. Other peace-leaguers go somewhat further, assigning to the league an obligation to use economic or forcible pressure for securing the acceptance of the award of the Court of Arbitration, though leaving the acceptance of the recommendations of the Conciliation Court to the free option of the parties. This is the proposal made by Mr. Raymond Unwin, and by the League of Peace.

Now a definite halt at this position is intelligible and defensible. While binding by strict sanctions the States to submit all disputes to the pacific machinery that is provided, to await the conclusion of the arbitral and conciliatory processes, and even to accept the legal awards of arbitration, it leaves a complete formal freedom to refuse the recommendations of the Commission of Conciliation. Yet it must be borne in mind that most of the really dangerous disputes, involving likelihood of war, are not arbitrable in their nature, and will come before the Commission of Conciliation. If no provision is made for enforcing the acceptance of the recommendations of this body, what measure of real security for peace has been attained? An incendiary torch, like that kindled last year in the Balkans, may once again put Europe in flames. The defenders of the position we are now considering have three replies. They admit that their proposal still leaves open the possibility of war, but they contend that if a sufficient cooling-off time or 'moratorium' is secured, the likelihood of an ultimate recourse to war by rejection of the award will be reduced to a minimum. They urge that no scheme which can be devised will preclude the possibility of a strong criminal or reckless State violating its treaty

XII A WORLD-STATE 273

obligations and seeking to enforce its will by force. Finally they urge that many self-respecting States would refuse to abandon the ultimate right of declaring war, in cases where they deemed their vital interests were affected, and that any invitation to take this step might wreck the possibility of a less complete but very valuable arrangement.

Now it would be a considerable advance towards world government, if all or most powerful States would consent to abandon separate alliances, or subordinate them to a general alliance binding them to submit all disputes to a process of impartial inquiry before attempting to enforce their national will by arms. It may be that this is as far as it is possible to go in the direction of securing world-peace and international co-operation in the early future. If States will not carry their co-operation so far as to agree upon united action to put down all wars between their members, and to take a united stand against all attacks from outside, it would be necessary to respect their scruples, and to rely upon the softening influence of the moratorium and informed public opinion to render a final recourse to arms unlikely among civilized States. But, in considering the measure of security thus achieved, we must remember that we must look to the weakest link in the chain of the alliance and ask ourselves how far the plan of conciliation represented in the recent treaties between the United States and several friendly European nations can be considered equally secure in dealing with Germany, Russia, or Japan. If our international arrangement is to dispense with all forcible pressure in the last resort, and to rely upon purely moral pressure, it seems evident that the validity of the arrangement depends upon the degree of confidence which other States will entertain as to the bona fides and pacific disposition of the least scrupulous of the powerful signatory States. For if the opinion held of any one or two powerful States is that under the stimulus of greed or ambition they would be likely, in defiance of an award or of the public opinion of other States, to enforce their will upon some weaker neighbour, such an opinion will keep alive so strong a feeling of insecurity that no considerable reduction of military preparations will be possible.

In assessing the early value of all proposals for better international relations, the best practical test is afforded by the question, 'Will the proposal lead nations to reduce their armaments?' For it will be admitted that any settlement or international agreement, which leaves the claims of militarism and navalism upon the vital and financial resources of the several nations unimpaired, affords little hope of a pacific future. A return to the era of competing armaments will destroy the moral strength of any formal international agreements, however specious. The importance of this consideration has led many to insist that an explicit agreement for proportional disarmament should take a prominent place in any settlement. This proposal, however, seems to me defective in that it presumes in all or some of the nations a persistence of the motives which have hitherto led them to strengthen their fighting forces. Now the primary object of such international arrangements as we are discussing is to bring about a state of things in which the past motives to arm will weaken and tend to disappear. If nations, actuated either by arrogance or greed or fear, continue to desire to increase their fighting strength, no arrangements for proportionate disarmament are likely to be effective. On the other hand, if the basis of a really valid league or federation can be laid, precluding the most ambitious State from any reasonable hope of indulging dreams of successful conquest, while relieving timid States from the apprehensions under which they have lived hitherto, the natural play of political forces within each State will favour disarmament. An international arrangement that meets our requirements must be strong enough to reverse the motives, aggressive and defensive, which in the past have caused nations to arm. Nations will not pile up armaments if they believe that they will have no need or opportunity to use them. To produce this belief in the uselessness of national armies and navies is therefore a prime object of international policy. The successful establishment of this belief involves, however, a change of disposition among national governments amounting to the process known in religious circles as conversion. They must be induced to forgo that right of war which according to past statecraft has been the brightest jewel in the crown of sovereignty.

Thus we are again brought round to our vital issue, that of the amount and kind of cession of sovereignty required for an effective International Government. It may be the case that it will be impossible to induce a sufficient number of the great States to transfer the ultimate right of waging war to a representative International Government, or to cede to such a Government the right to legislate on international relations with power to enforce obedience to these laws. There are, however, many of us who hold that these powers are essential to an international arrangement which shall effectively guarantee the peace of the world. The abandonment of the sovereign right to make war is essential for the future security of peace. Legislative and executive powers for an International Government are essential to obtain by pacific means those changes in the political and economic relations of peoples which hitherto have only been attainable by war. No merely statical settlement will suffice. Great new issues of national controversy or of economic needs will certainly come up afresh for settlement, and until some stable method of government is established with power to determine and enforce the equities and the utilities they represent, recourse to the arbitrament of war will still be likely.

But granting that national government does not represent a final form of political structure, and that some federal internationalism is now practicable, is it possible to hope or to expect that by a single stride, or by a series of rapid strides, the sovereignty of national states will submit to so much diminution as is involved in the more advanced scheme of international government? Most historians, statesmen, and political philosophers will, I think, hold that so large and rapid a process of development is impracticable, however desirable in theory it might be. It will be necessary, they insist, to take one step at a time, to preserve as closely as possible the principle of continuity, and not to attempt to move further and faster than circumstances and the necessities of the time compel.

But do circumstances and necessities always compel us to move slowly and to take one step at a time? Though normal growth is slow and continuous, modern science tends to lay increasing stress upon discontinuous and sudden larger variations in the production of organic changes. Biology distinguishes these mutations by which new species arise from the normal process of evolution by insensible gradations. There is, as I understand it, no real breach of continuity, no miraculous creation, but a sudden removal from a structural position which by slow accumulation of prior changes had become unstable, or to a new position of stability, involving a swift readjustment of organic parts. May not similarly important mutations occur in the evolution of political institutions, when a similar stress of circumstances makes itself felt? Nay, we may further ask, whether the special function of man's reasonable will is not to bring about these changes in the direction of individual and collective conduct. The power of making new quick and complex adaptations to new environments is the essential economy of the human brain. Freedom of thought and of will are continually producing new judgements and new determinations for action which contain this quality of sudden mutation. Quick conversions of thought and will are of the essence of our conscious life. When they carry important consequences to our conduct they appear to be, and in fact are, breaches of the normal conduct of our life which proceeds by custom, repetition, and insensible modifications.

In politics, as in religion, sudden conversions under the stress of circumstances are not unknown, and they may be genuine and lasting. And what holds of individual wills and judgements holds also of the collective mind. That human nature in its fundaments of thought and feeling, its primary needs, desires and emotions, will not be appreciably changed even by this shattering experience of war must be conceded. But what we may call the general state of mind, or the moral and intellectual atmosphere, will be profoundly affected. This will be in part the result of the great economic and political disturbances which are occurring, and which will have undermined and loosened the old ideas and valuations in relation to such important institutions as property, the control of industry, the activities of woman, the party system, the State itself. But more profound still will be the direct reaction of sorrow and suffering of war, the revelation of the power of the organized destructiveness and cruelty, and of the inadequacy of reason, justice, and goodwill as defences of civilization. The very foundations of organized religion in the hearts of men will be shaken. The patent failure of the State to perform its primary function of safeguarding life and property is likely to feed currents of revolutionism in every country. The sudden changes produced in the balance of age and of sex by the destruction of so large a proportion of the young and energetic men of every nation, will affect all processes of thought and policy. Some of these changes will seem favourable to conservatism, timidity, and reaction. Everywhere, at the close of the war, military and official autocracy will be enthroned in the seats of power, and the spirit of political authority will be stoking the fires of fevered nationalism which war evokes. But other forces will be making for bold political experiments. Not only the fear of restive and impoverished workmen, who have recently acquired the use of arms and perhaps the taste for risks, but the havoc wrought upon industry and commerce, and above all the crushing burden of taxation, will dispose the controlling and possessing classes to seek alternatives to a return to the era of competing alliances and armaments. Mild and conservative measures will be obviously unavailing. During the years of exhaustion following the war, resolute leaders of public opinion will be setting themselves everywhere to frame schemes of international relations which shall yield adequate guarantees of peace. For the first time in history great reading and thinking communities will give their chief attention to international politics. They will recognize the urgency of the work of building the society of nations upon a basis of genuinely representative government. Behind this reasonable process of constructive thinking, carried on in every country by politically convinced individuals and groups, will be the powerful support of the unthinking, suffering masses, motived by no clear conception of causes or remedies, but by that collective instinct of self-preservation which impels the herd to avoid destruction and to follow leaders who point the way to safety.

BOOKS FOR REFERENCE

The International Crisis in its Ethical and Psychological Aspects.
   Humphrey Milford.
G. Lowes Dickinson, *After the War.* Fifield.
C. E. Hooper, *The Wider Outlook beyond the World-War.* Watts
   & Co.
F. N. Keen, *The World in Alliance.* Southwood.
Norman Angell, *Prussianism and its Destruction.* Heinemann.
Allison Phillips, *The Confederation of Europe.* Longmans.
The New Statesman. Special Supplement. Suggestions for the
   Prevention of War.
J. A. Hobson, *Towards International Government.* Allen & Unwin.

XIII

RELIGION AS A UNIFYING INFLUENCE IN WESTERN CIVILIZATION

THE argument of these essays has been to prove that even now, in the greatest armed conflict of the world, the term ' Christendom ' is not inapplicable to Europe. There is a real unity in Western civilization—a unity due in large measure to the influence of religious faith and organization. The mediaeval Church gave the Teutonic peoples of Northern Europe, and the barbarians who overran the Roman Empire, their first momentous introduction into the great inheritance formed by the uneasy blending of Christian faith and literature with Greco-Roman civilization. The spiritual achievements of Greek and Roman, Jew and Christian have remained the common possessions of the West, the foundation of what is still Christendom. In so far as it exists Christendom witnesses to the formative power of a religious faith : in so far as it remains a dream, we may suspect it demands the renewed impulse of a faith enlightened and chastened by all the experience of the past.

If, however, we ask, Is there any likelihood that a common religious faith and life will contribute to raise Western civilization to a yet higher unity ? modern as contrasted with mediaeval history seems at first sight to demonstrate the futility of any such inquiry.

Since the Reformation, religion has made for division rather than co-operation. The modern period of European history begins in disruption. Not only was Europe rent by the conflict of Catholic and Protestant, but the dream

XIII RELIGION A UNIFYING INFLUENCE

of an international reformed Church which at one time floated before the mind of Cranmer was dissipated by the strength of nationalism and the cleavage in the ranks of the reformers themselves. In our own country, what is euphemistically termed the Elizabethan Settlement proved to be the source of further dissension, and reform appeared as the prolific mother of sects and schisms. The Protestant Churches were organized on national and state lines. They ceased to retain any international character in their constitution, while international intercourse became a diminishing influence. The Church of Rome in the conflict with Gallicanism found herself at grips with the spirit of nationalism, and to-day the strength of national feeling within Roman Catholicism hinders the Pope from exerting a moral authority over sovereign states that would parallel the judicial functions successfully asserted by Innocent III. No Christian Church to-day so rises above the national states of Europe, as to control or even adequately to criticize the claims of those states. The Churches no longer serve to embody and express an European conscience.

The break-up of a common ecclesiastical organization was not perhaps the most serious loss of unifying power which religion in the West suffered at the time of the Reformation. If it be true that the Bible and the Greek spirit are the great common factors of Western civilization, then we must recognize that these two great influences tended to fall apart and even to oppose each other in the sixteenth and seventeenth centuries. The humanist element in the Reform-movement grew less and less, while humanism itself became more definitely secular. The European mind has ever since been conscious of a disturbing division between religion and culture. A development of religion which should render to Western civilization services comparable to those rendered by the mediaeval Church demands not only a heightened international consciousness among Christians, which shall be able to find organized expression, but also some fresh synthesis of religion and culture, some reunion of the spirit of Hellas, the Greek delight in beauty and faith in reason, with the moral strength and religious insight of Hebrew prophecy.

Those who are concerned for the future of our civilization will look eagerly for signs of any such development in the religious life and thought of our time. Do recent history and present experience discover any influences at work which may yet restore a unifying power to religion? Naturally any answer to such a question will be of a subjective character. The personal equation cannot easily be eliminated; we may be duped by our hopes or deceived by our fears. In the last analysis we cannot safely predict the future of religion. We may, however, take stock of our present situation, and survey its significant elements, even if our value-judgements as to their relative importance will inevitably vary.

While religious divisions have not vanished from the West, and indeed show no prospect of immediate reconciliation, and while the formation of new sects, of which the Christian Science Movement offers an example, has not altogether ceased, there has been an admitted decline of the dogmatic and sectarian tempers, and this decline has opened the way for knitting up severed friendships. The revolt against the dogmatic attitude of mind and even against religious dogma itself is widespread. The sense of loss involved in the isolation of any sect, and the wish to pass beyond the limits of any denominational tradition, are both appreciably affecting the religious situation. In England Matthew Arnold's somewhat unhappy criticism of Dissent expressed a dislike both of dogma and sectarian narrowness. His profounder contribution to the better understanding of St. Paul derives its worth precisely from his elevation of the mystic and the saint in Paul at the expense of the doctrinal theologian of Calvinist tradition. The wish to be rid of dogma continues to find vigorous intellectual expression, of which Mr. Lowes Dickinson's *Religion, a Criticism and a Forecast*, may be taken as an example. In another direction the Brotherhood Movement and the Adult School Movement represent the search, if not for an altogether undogmatic faith, yet at least for a broader basis of association than is compatible with the insistence on definite statements of belief. Both would unite in the prayer

> God send us men whose aim will be
> Not to defend some outworn creed,

and some members of both entertain the suspicion that all creeds are outworn.

This dislike of dogma may cloak an unwarranted scepticism as to the possibility of reaching truth in religion, but it is symptomatic of the longing for larger sympathy and broader fellowship. It is but the extreme expression of a temper which has reduced the angularity of those who are very far from surrendering or belittling definite beliefs and doctrines. The denominationalist who used to have no hesitation in claiming a monopoly of the truth for his particular Church now falters where he firmly stood. We are more ready to recognize our limitations. A growing number of thoughtful minds appreciate Lord Acton's position when he wrote to Mary Gladstone: 'I scarcely venture to make points against the religion of other people, from a curious experience that they have more to say than I know, and from a sense that it is safer to reserve censure for one's own which one understands more intimately, having a share in responsibility and action.' This more chastened mood opens the way to fresh understandings in the religious world. Whence does this change in atmosphere originate?

In tracing out the causes of this new temper in religion, a first place may legitimately be assigned to the growth of the scientific spirit. In considering science as a source of unity, it is a mistake to dwell exclusively on the creation of a body of common knowledge. To know the same thing may do little to unite men. To attack problems in the same way, and to share the same spirit of free inquiry, the same reverence for fact, the same resolute endeavour to surmount prejudice, issue in a far closer bond of union. Science unites men even more closely by its spirit than by its achievement. The application of scientific method to the literary and historical study of the Bible, as well as in the psychological analysis of religious experience, has called into being in every Church and every land, groups of people who approach the subject-matter of their faith from the same angle and under the guidance of the same mental discipline. As a result of the critical movement a man finds his foes in his own and his friends in his neighbours' ecclesiastical household. The study of religion renews international contact and requires international co-operation as much as any other branch of science. It is possible to detect differing characteristics in the scholarship of the leading nations, though it may be doubted whether these are fundamental differences. The volume of critical work published in Germany is so considerable as to foster the illusion that it constitutes a self-sufficing world. Thus it is possible for Dr. Schweitzer in his brilliant survey of research into the life of Jesus, to represent the whole inquiry as the work of German genius and as the endeavour of German liberalism to picture Jesus in accordance with its own half-unconscious bias. Yet even so the cloven-hoof of international interdependence makes its appearance, for he has to devote one unsympathetic chapter to Renan, even if he contrives to ignore Seeley's *Ecce Homo*. But the debt of English scholarship to Germany is undeniable, and must not be repudiated in war-time. Nor is the debt entirely on one side. It is worth recalling that Adolph Harnack, perhaps the greatest living German scholar in the realm of New Testament criticism and Church History, derived no little inspiration from the work of Edwin Hatch. At any rate the acceptance of the critical method associates scholars in all lands, produces International Congresses for the study of Religions, and fosters personal friendships which even war will not destroy.

Beyond the internationalism of scholarship, we must remember the reaction of criticism on popular religious thought. Slowly but surely the judgements of believers, lay and clerical, are being permeated with some sense of historical perspective. The mere attempt to recognize the literary character of the various books of the Bible has effected a liberation. The variation of the different parts of the Bible in literary quality, in evidential value for history and in spiritual significance, are at last being freely recognized outside the study and the lecture-room. Men are ceasing to regard the Bible as a series of legal enactments or common-law precedents of equal authority. This is leading to a revision of inherited traditions, that were based on a view of the Bible which is no longer tenable. In general this development favours a more modest assertion of one's own beliefs and a more charitable consideration of other people's. When we continue to differ, we differ with a more sympathetic understanding of those from whom we differ.

It is impossible to trace here in any detail the influence of the critical movement on traditional beliefs or even on the conception of authority in religion. It may, however, be worth while to point out that the psychological study of religion has tended to broaden sympathy by promoting the frank recognition of the varieties of religious experience. More allowance is made for temperament, and there is less anxiety to force all spiritual life into the same mould or scheme. The sacramentalist and the non-sacramentalist, the mystic and the intellectualist, the man of feeling and the man of action, those who experience sudden changes and those who are the subjects of more gradual growth—each receives his due, and neither need despise the other. There are dangers associated with our constant reference to temperament. It is really a condemnation of a Church to say that its position appeals to a particular temperament, while it is often no real kindness to an individual to be excused from attempting to enter into a particular phase of religious life on the ground that he is temperamentally disqualified. But it is clearly a gain to challenge an over-rigid standardization of religious life. It is pathetic to hear people protest that they have no religious experience, when they are simply blinded by too narrow an interpretation of the term. In so far as the psychology of religion throws into relief the manifold appeal of religious ideas to different minds, it helps to create a new sense of unity in difference.

Accompanying the growth of the scientific spirit and in part stimulated by it, more distinctly religious and philosophical influences are at work quickening the desire for wider and deeper fellowship. Considering first the problem within the borders of the Christian Church, I think we may claim that there is a growing willingness to co-operate and a revival of the hope of reunion. We may further claim that certain advances in thought, in the understanding of Christianity itself, have already been made, and render co-operation if not reunion less Utopian than before. Of these I would put first the acceptance of the principle of toleration as an essential element of

Christian faith. It has been suggested by Mr. Norman Angell that the religious wars of the seventeenth century came to an end through economic exhaustion and through rationalism. Toleration was accepted as a state-principle on the strength of a common-sense calculation as to the uselessness of repression. I am not disposed to ignore the forcefulness of the argument, ' You will starve or go bankrupt, if you do not cease to persecute heretics or fight Protestants,' nor would I underestimate the influence of common-sense in closing the era of religious wars, but I cannot help thinking that an intense religious conviction of the duty of toleration and a kind of philosophic liberalism, though entertained by few, contributed to the triumph of the principle. For the Christian, the duty has become clearer through the influence of the gospels. Some of the Churches have begun to take to heart the rebuke of Jesus to the disciples who wished to call down fire on the Samaritans. Nor is it a question of a particular incident. A deep respect for individuality is found to lie at the centre of the gospel. For the Christian, the attitude of toleration, the reliance on persuasion, on the appeal to every man's conscience, has become more and more clearly the indispensable qualification of the ambassador for Christ. As the acceptance of the principle of toleration is by no means universal in the Church, its fuller recognition in some quarters may serve at first to intensify division. It may emphasize, e. g. the continued necessity for Protestantism, by bringing into clearer light the moral obstacle to reunion in the Inquisition and disciplinary methods of the Church of Rome. But in the long run, this development of thought must make for better understanding and wider fellowship.

Still confining our survey to the Christian Church, there has been a significant fastening of attention on those parts of the New Testament in which the idea of Catholicity is fully developed. The epistle to the Ephesians and the seventeenth chapter of John are beginning to haunt the Christian consciousness as never before since the days of the Reformation. It is clear that the present position of the Church, in which divisions have crystallized into separate organizations, does not reflect and envisage the ideal that 'they all may be one'. The unity of the Church appears to be a condition precedent to the success of its testimony. The scandal and the impotence of division are more acutely felt. Unless the Church of Christ can heal herself or find healing for herself, it is little enough which she will be able to contribute to the healing of the nations.

There is hope then for closer fellowship within the Church, because the problem is being more and more definitely laid upon the consciences of her members. A further advance in thought which makes possible a closer approximation of the severed fragments of the Christian Church, is to be found in the process of sifting the essential from the accidental in the Christian tradition. It would be idle to pretend that the process has reached its conclusion, or that there is any large measure of agreement as to what constitutes the essence of Christianity. No one indeed believes any longer in the whole Bible from cover to cover—not even those who say they do. The fight for the creeds is more strenuous, while Rome cannot afford to admit that any article of faith which has been authoritatively defined may be treated as non-essential. But if I may venture a personal judgement, I cannot see that even the Apostles' creed will be able to retain its place as a summary of essential Christianity. The articles which deal with the Descent into Hades and the Resurrection of the Body, and perhaps those which deal with the Virgin-Birth and Ascension of our Lord, are dubious, if not false, and cannot fairly be regarded as indispensable. If I may attempt to forecast, I would say that the ultimate cleavage is coming not over particular articles of the Apostles' Creed, but over the value we set on the history and person of Jesus. The choice will lie between a conception of God for which the story and character of Jesus are final and determinative, and a vaguer spiritual theism for which Jesus has no supreme significance. This is not even the division between Trinitarian and Unitarian. The ultimate parting of the ways turns on the question whether a man's faith in God is Christ-centred or not. The significant cleavage of the future will come between those who believe that Christianity—the belief in the Fatherhood of God through Jesus Christ—is the final religion, and those who hold that Christianity in this sense is destined to be swallowed up in some still broader faith in God for which other revelations, through nature and through other figures in history, are as significant as the creed embodied in a tale in Galilee and on Golgotha nineteen centuries ago. But whatever cleavage may appear hereafter in the religion of the West, the search for the essence of Christianity, even when it works through controversy, will contribute to lop off idle dissensions and reveal fellowship in fundamentals where men had previously supposed themselves to be hopelessly divided.

It is a little invidious to choose out any particular movements for special reference, and in so doing I may merely betray personal bias rather than critical judgement. Yet it is perhaps permissible to point out that the genesis of the Adult School movement is the natural development of the Quaker respect for that of God in every man. It represents the longing for a religious fellowship which does not force opinion but offers the most favourable conditions for the formation of independent judgement and the growth of individual faith. How far the movement realizes its ideal, I forbear to inquire, but its very existence affords some evidence of the belief in the positive virtue of toleration as an essential element of the Christian character. Another powerful factor making for co-operation and better understanding among Christians may be found in the Student Christian movement. For this country its value has been enhanced if not created by the opening of the older Universities to Nonconformists. The future leaders of all our Churches are now being educated together, and through the Student Christian movement, they are educating each other and facing together old controversies and inherited problems at a time when their judgements are least hampered either by tradition or responsibility. What this may mean for the religious life of this country, we cannot yet tell, but it is certain that a new temper will be brought to bear on our divisions. The men who learn to appreciate one another through this association, tend to hold together when they pass out of the Universities into their life-work. There are springing up through the Student movement new associations or fellowships which conserve and continue the unifying impetus of the movement itself. Nor is that unifying power confined to this country. It forms a world-wide federation whose lines of communication have not been cut even by the present war. In every land, the Student movement intends to resume international intercourse at the earliest possible moment. I think it is not simply the bias of a student in favour of his own class, which makes me regard the Student Christian movement as one of the most hopeful developments in the religious life of our age.

Perhaps the influence of this movement itself may be traced in the growing demand for co-operation in the missionary task of the Church. This demand has no doubt arisen in part through the changes in the means of transport and communication which have made the world a smaller place. Missionary effort is less sporadic than it was. The Churches are developing a *Weltpolitik*. The exact proportions of the task before them are now more clearly grasped. The difficulty of overtaking the task even when united, and the impossibility of discharging it effectively while divided are also more apparent. But the demand for unity and the power of co-operation have also been strengthened by the men and women who have gone abroad under the influence of the Student Volunteer Missionary Union. High Churchmen and Nonconformist having learnt to work together on a Christian Student executive do not find it difficult to co-operate, where opportunity offers, in India or China. A half-involuntary revolution of sentiment is proceeding under our eyes. The strength of the new spirit of co-operation was revealed in the Edinburgh Conference of 1910. That date will stand out as supremely significant in the growth of a new Catholicism in the West.

We have so far been concerned with influences making for a deeper sense of unity within the Christian Church. But if we attempt a wider survey, we shall discover that religious thought and feeling in the West, whether definitely Christian or no, possess some common characteristics, bear the impress of convictions which are ever struggling for expression.

First among these characteristic features of religious thought in the West I would place faith in the solidarity of mankind. The origin of this faith probably passes beyond our analysis. I should suspect that there is a universal impulse stimulating this belief which I should be inclined to regard as instinctive. Yet it has certainly found fuller expression in the West than in the civilization of India or China. It is possible to point to traditions, to philosophies, and to particular events which have carried this faith in human solidarity deep into the consciousness of the West. Dr. Prichard, whose scientific labours, we were told in an earlier lecture, refuted the heresy of polygenism, was moved to undertake his inquiries by a desire to maintain the accuracy of the Mosaic tradition as to the common origin of mankind. It is a little curious to reflect that illusory anthropology, accepted on the authority of Moses and of Rousseau, the belief in Adam, and the belief in the free and happy savage, have perhaps done more than scientific research into primitive culture to maintain our faith in human brotherhood and equality. We must not, however, attach too much weight to the story of Adam. The Western sense of the dignity of ordinary manhood owes much more to the great Stoic conception of humanity, as Mr. Barker reminded us in his lecture on the Middle Ages. Perhaps even more significant is the feeling for humanity engendered by regarding all men as the objects of a common redemption. The poorest of men have been protected from their fellows where they have been recognized as brothers for whom Christ died. It would be worth while, if one had the time and the knowledge, to follow the growth of this sentiment in modern times, to trace the influence of the doctrine of Natural Rights, of the French Revolution, of the philosophy of Comte, and of the Evangelical Revival, upon its development. But whatever the sources and phases of its growth, the existence and strength of this faith in humanity are undeniable. It is this faith which compels us to refuse to think of Western civilization as merely Western. For we believe that the West holds in trust for mankind, not only a right knowledge of nature, not only a correct scientific method, but also an essential conception of the worth and unity of human life. Whatever we are to gain from the East, this is one of the gifts we bring to the other half of the world.

In speaking of this faith in human solidarity as Western, I am aware that I am making broad statements which badly need qualification. I am far from wishing to suggest that there is no such sentiment of humanity in the great structures of Asiatic civilization, particularly in the ethical systems of China. But I am persuaded that there is a broad contrast between West and East in this respect, and that in particular there is a significant gulf between the West and Hinduism. In the West, this often inarticulate faith in humanity has acted as a spring of progress. It inspires our faith in democracy, it acts as a perpetual challenge to privilege and oppression, as a constant denial of permanence to divisions of class, nationality, and race. The very difficulty which the orthodox Hindu experiences in appreciating the spiritual meaning of democracy—his feeling that the democratic movement is an irrational blindly selfish confusing of a divine appointed social order—discloses the existence of this gulf. It is not for nothing that the religious traditions of Hinduism trace the four castes back to divine appointment and regard them as coeval with the race. Nor is it without significance that India rejected Buddhism—a movement which challenged caste and whose missionary enthusiasm embodied a broader sentiment of humanity than has yet been woven into Indian civilization. The influence of the West is now renewing the attack on caste which Buddha initiated and failed to accomplish.

Without serious injustice we may claim that this faith in human solidarity has attained clearer expression and exerts greater influence in the West than in the East. To detail its influence is impossible. It underlies our hopes of social reform, it refuses to believe in the sub-human—at least it refuses to believe in the necessity of his continued existence. It inspires the religious enthusiasm with which men embrace Socialism as a hope for mankind'. It turns the brotherhood of man into a 'masked word.' As a character in one of St. John Ervine's novels puts it, 'Brother'ood of man, my boy—that's my motter. Brother'ood of man! the 'ole world, see! Not a little bit like England! the 'ole world! all of us! see? No fightin or nothink! Just peace an' 'appiness! Takes your breath away when you think on it. It do, straight.' The same religious impulse is at work in that disease of humanitarianism which distresses Chauvinists—the humanitarianism which Bernhardi denounces in Germany and Mr. Moreton Fullerton deplores in France. It is reflected in the religious life alike of Russia and of France. Paul Sabatier's book is largely concerned with following out the influence of this sense of solidarity in all philosophic and religious schools and in all classes in France. He notes, for example, the anti-clericalism of the French peasant, which does not, however, lead him to embrace the dogmatic negations of Free-thought. The peasant still clings to the rites of the Church through 'the perhaps unconscious desire to perform an act of social solidarity, to meet our fellow-men elsewhere than on the field of material interests and distractions, to accept the rendezvous which they offer to us and we to them, that we may draw together and, more than that—unite and unify'. In another quarter we may witness a new feeling for humanity resulting from the throwing together of diverse racial elements in the melting-pot of the United States. Zangwill's play might be cited as a document of this larger faith, while Jane Addams has sympathetically described its genesis in her *Newer Ideals of Peace*. Yet another expression of this instinctive faith may be discovered in the broad human interest of much of our modern literature and art. For the standard of orthodoxy in this connexion requires not only that we respond to a grand conception of humanity as a whole, but that also in particulars we are loyal to the Terentian tag, 'Homo sum: humani nil a me alienum puto.' The worthier side of modern realism has done full justice to this motto.

The expressions of this faith in human solidarity are so various, and its influence so pervading, that it is not surprising to find some modern thinkers looking to it as the essence of religion. In the sociological theory of religion, it is suggested that to become aware of society and its claims constitutes religion itself. A man is converted when his soul is ' congregationalized '. There is even a tendency to find the highest element in religious experience in a strong feeling of one's unity with one's fellows. Such a feeling of endless sympathy and tolerance is so large a part of love that it is easily mistaken for the whole. For this starting-point, we might readily imagine a Western faith in humanity with Walt Whitman as its prophet. But a second characteristic of Western thought about religion forbids any idealization of humanity as we know it, and draws us beyond the indiscriminate catholicism of ' The Open Road '. This characteristic may be defined as our faith in the worth of activity and in the reality of progress. We believe in the unity of mankind much more as a task to be achieved than as an accomplished or given fact to be enjoyed. Nietzsche says somewhere, ' if the goal of humanity be wanting, do we not lack humanity itself ? ' We look for the ultimate unity of mankind in the pursuit of a common end. The search for such a goal, and the effort to achieve it, lend worth to history and to present action.

This faith, often blind and unreasoned, is distinctly Western and modern. We do not derive it even from Greece. It comes to us through Christianity and modern science. The absence of any such faith in activity and progress creates the pessimism of the East. Hinduism and Buddhism are alike in their bankruptcy on this side. The majestic religious philosophy of India sees in history only an endless and meaningless repetition. Thucydides and Plato assume the same view, if I mistake not. As Eucken says, 'Ancient views of life bore throughout an unhistorical character. The numerous philosophical doctrines of the procession of endless similar cycles, which continually return to the starting-point, were only the expression of the conviction that all movement at bottom brings nothing new and that life offers no prospect of further improvement.' When Paul discovered that the law was a schoolmaster to bring men to Christ, he enunciated a profounder philosophy of history than Plato ever knew.

The very fact that Christianity sprang out of Judaism means that it enshrines and suggests the idea of progress in the very circumstances of its origin. But its hold on the idea is something deeper than its connexion with Judaism. Christianity claims to be the final religion, but its claim differs in kind from the parallel claim of Mohammedanism. The world of Islam is held in mortmain by the prophet. It cannot advance beyond the forms in which he embodied his message without denying the claims he made for himself. But to the early Christians the synoptic gospels were the record of all that Jesus *began* to do and to say, while the highest development of Christian experience and reflection in the New Testament, the gospel of John, contemplates the greater things which the followers of Jesus shall accomplish and the fuller revelations which shall come as the disciples are able to bear them. The claim of Christianity to finality rests on its opening up endless possibilities of spiritual growth to mankind. To some of us it seems that part of this fuller revelation has come through modern knowledge and discovery. The faith in progress which Christians have often held falteringly and have sometimes denied, appears to be confirmed and clarified by all that we are learning of creative evolution. In any case, the influence of modern science has tended to produce a faith in progress in the West—a faith which some regard as essentially different from the Christian view of the world and history, but which for others seems more and more to coalesce with that earlier if in some respects cruder Christian conviction. No doubt when the facts of evolution were held to point to gradual and continuous development, they favoured a view of steady progress which was antagonistic to the Christian belief in the sudden introduction of new elements into history. But the later advances of evolutionary theory seem more akin to the early Christian attitude. The element of apocalyptic is seen not to be so alien from nature as had been at first supposed.

However it arises and whatever form it takes, this faith in progress is characteristic of the Western outlook, and gives a positive answer to the question, Is life worth living? That such a faith is strange to India may be evidenced by the reception accorded to the poet Tagore in India itself. Mr. Yeats gives us the judgement of a Bengali who said of Tagore, 'He is the first among our saints who has not refused to live, but spoken out of Life itself, and that is why we give him our love.' Now Tagore's genius is thoroughly Indian, but his originality in this respect is due directly or indirectly to contact with the influence of the West. It is our belief in action and in the worth of human achievement which is voiced in his poems and in his philosophy, and the note is new in India.

Illustrations of this belief in progress and activity are superfluous, though I may remind you of the prevalence of this temper in the realm of philosophy as well as of religion at the present time. Perhaps it is worth recalling that Harnack's great history of dogma ends with this significant sentence from Zwingli : 'It is not the part of a Christian man to be for ever talking grandly about dogma, but always to be attempting big things in fellowship with

God.' This represents as well as anything our Western insistence on the worth of effort. As an admirable embodiment at once of the faith in humanity and the faith in progress, the close of Matthew Arnold's poem 'Rugby Chapel' recurs to the mind. You remember how he conceives the function of great men to lie in preserving the union of mankind, and how he conceives the life of mankind as a journey towards a city that hath foundations.

These two characteristics, faith in the oneness of mankind and in the reality of progress, do add a sense of common aspiration to the civilization of the West. But of themselves they do not create a very close unity. Men may believe in human solidarity and in the worth of effort, and yet be following divergent ideals and divisive enthusiasms. These beliefs are surrounded by haze and indefiniteness. In themselves they scarcely constitute a religion that will satisfy, much less one that can effectively unite us. However fully we share them, they will not enable us to meet and surmount the present crisis. So far as I can judge, these vaguer beliefs in humanity and progress are largely the deposit of Christian faith, and to be rendered effective they need to be ever reconnected with the central elements in that faith; in particular, with the Christian judgement on sin and with the Christian devotion to the historic Jesus.

The sense of sin has received a peculiar impress in the West. We owe it largely to the religious experience of the Jew and to the seriousness of the Latin mind. There is a curious coincidence of the seventh chapter of Romans with a famous quotation from Ovid. The Latin fathers, particularly Augustine, have developed, not to say overdeveloped, the analysis of sin. The concept of sin never had the same significance for the Greek, and humanism has always resented the severity of the tradition that comes from Paul through Augustine and Calvin. Mr.

Holmes's stimulating books on education are inspired by a theological polemic against the doctrine of original sin He not unnaturally takes refuge in Buddhism, for Buddhism makes suffering, not sin, the root trouble of human life. ' The division between the will and the power, the struggle of the senses against our better judgement, the falling below the moral ideal—none of all this comes within the horizon of Buddha.' Now it may freely be confessed that the Calvinist view of sin led to a distrust of human nature, and incidentally of child-nature, which had a not altogether healthy reaction on home discipline and school-life. It is very difficult to maintain the right balance, and the danger of morbidity through emphasis on sin is undeniable. Yet it seems to me that the worst errors of Calvinism and Evangelicalism in this regard have lain in a tendency to theological formalism and a failure to keep in touch with real life. In consequence, those who most deplore our waning sense of sin try us by a perverted or antiquated standard, and fasten often on changes of sentiment and habit which are by no means necessarily or largely sinful. They are least conscious of the want of a sense of sin, in modern society, where that want is most serious. But I do not doubt that our often old-fashioned friends are right on the main issue. I do not believe that we shall see the progress we desire, unless we recover a heightened sense of sin. I hold with Lord Acton that our internal conflicts are due to indifference to sin and not to a religious idea. We judge ourselves and our race too lightly. We quench our hope of progress by a leniency and indulgence towards our failings which involve an underestimate of our powers and responsibilities. The present crisis will not issue in a hopeful reaction through regret but only through repentance.

The sense of sin which Christianity has brought to the West is not, I think, to be found elsewhere. It only appears where men feel they have an assured knowledge of God's will. It is intense only where men are conscious of God's presence. The vision of the Holiest reveals to Isaiah that he is a man of unclean lips. Such a conviction of sin seems to me inexplicable apart from contact with the living God. Two things are required to bring home to men a true estimate of their moral failure, first a right standard of judgement, and, second, a conviction of the reality of God. Is it too much to say that we are not likely to reach either, apart from Jesus of Nazareth? 'It is through Jesus and not from Adam that we know sin.' It is through Him that men discover their moral ideal and learn not simply to believe that there is a God, but to say, O God, Thou art my God even for ever and ever.

Surely there is something providential in the resolute endeavour of the last century to get back to Christ. The whole movement has succeeded in disentangling the authority of Christ from that either of Moses or of Paul. We are almost where the disciples were when they saw no man save Jesus only. Some things in the traditions remain obscure and baffling. But we see enough to measure afresh our distance from Him. And when the peoples of Europe are thoroughly weary of the work of destruction, it may be they will turn to Him again for the secret of rest, and find that He alone can guide their feet into the way of peace.

BOOKS FOR REFERENCE

Sabatier, *L'Orientation religieuse de la France actuelle.* Armand Colin : Paris.

W. K. L. Clarke, *Facing the Facts ; or, an Englishman's Religion.* Nisbet.

E. C. Moore, *Christian Thought since Kant.* Duckworth's Studies in Theology.

XIV

THE GROWTH OF HUMANITY

THE preceding chapter has recalled attention to the need of deeper elements of unity in civilization than can be afforded by any commercial, financial or political ties. Plans for a political union of nations, common tendencies in social reform, even the essential unity of commerce and science, will be of no avail, unless there is a basis in common sentiments of a religious kind, in the consciousness that we are all members one of another and can only advance and realize ourselves by the help and sympathy of other members of the same body. It is to this point then that we will address ourselves in the concluding section of the subject. The mechanics of unity need both earnest advocacy and careful study. But beneath and beyond them a motive force has to be found in ideals and sentiments by which alone in the end the working of all such mechanical arrangements is rendered possible. Right sentiments are not a sufficient safeguard, but they are an essential foundation, and it is of the first importance to realize the things to which the mass of mankind are most deeply attached, how they are affected towards one another, the channels through which the tide of feeling most naturally flows and is extended. Looked at from this point of view the problem becomes primarily an educational one. We study mankind as we find it in order to effect an improvement in the direction which we desire.

We find then in the first place that men as a rule are most strongly attached to the localities and the people with whom they are first brought closely in contact. Here in the family is the first true microcosm, the first community in which the individual is developed by association with his fellows. On the value of this earliest social training there are hardly two opinions, and we need not dwell upon it. It is at the next stage that divergence, both of definite opinion and still more of emphasis, begins to be apparent. How far is attachment to country a valuable thing, how far should it be cultivated, what are the necessary limitations and controlling ideas? As to the reality of the sentiment every man can examine himself. We know, most of us, with what intense satisfaction we return to the country, the district, of our birth and home. The feeling is one of the strongest and deepest things in us, even if our reason deprecates and disallows the claim. As Englishmen, perhaps even more as Scotchmen and Irish, we love with an indefinable and ineradicable passion our sea-coast, our hills and valleys, the fields and cottages, even the sometimes sordid, nearly always ill-assorted, congeries of houses which we have thrown together as towns. We fight among ourselves, we have more religious, political, and social differences than any other people. Yet when we need companionship for work or pleasure at home or abroad, we would sooner have an Englishman at our side than any other man. Men and country—'dear souls and dear, dear land'—these are the elements which make up the real thing called patriotism and which, in spite of all our curses and all our self-seeking, lead us in millions to work or die for our country, and will, while life lasts, bring us home at last.

To those who know the local narrowness, the jealousies and pettiness of much of our own national life, it will seem a primary duty in education to present the country as an object of education and service, imperfect indeed and limited by larger ends, but yet supreme over the selfish interests of trade, town, or individual. This, with all its terrible losses, the war is doing for us with mighty and irresistible strokes, and it is a tragic truth that in our present imperfect social state, it is only a war, hurling us against other great and really co-operating communities of men, which can make us bear with comparative ease and cheerfulness the most serious burdens of loss and suffering. We act instantly as one people in war, we haggle and hesitate about the most moderate sacrifices to secure an advance in peace. It is this quality in patriotism, and in war as its stimulus, which largely and naturally biases our view. But to the ideal of a united Western civilization or a united mankind it is only one step. We cannot do without patriotism, but we must immediately proceed beyond it. We cannot reform the troubles and conflicts of mankind by attempting to root up some of our most tenacious passions; we progress by mastering and not mutilating our being. We have to advance beyond the limits of patriotism by wider sympathy, by seeing analogies, by recognizing the facts of common interests and co-operation in the world.

But here again, looking at the question from an educational rather than an abstract point of view, we have to recognize that actual realization of the life and services of other nations is a slow, difficult, and, at best, a limited process. It was really easier for the travelling student of the Middle Ages to enter into the simple and similar life of universities abroad than for the modern traveller to grasp the complex relations of a great foreign city or state. We have therefore, in practice, to select and concentrate. For the modern Englishman a knowledge of one or two other countries and languages is as much as the pressure of life will permit, and it is greatly to be regretted that poverty and hard work limit even this acquisition to very few. A *Wanderjahr* for the working-man would do much to cement the unity of western civilization.

Until the recent acute rivalry with Germany developed, English sympathies were fairly evenly divided. Your Liberal, as a rule, was a Frenchman, and your Conservative a German. George Meredith and John Morley sang the praises of France, Coleridge and Carlyle would have us learn from Germany. Now for many years the die is cast. We shall face the settlement and the dangers of the future side by side with France.

This becomes, then, one of the fixed points in our orientation. History and geography both dictate it. Just as in the building of our fatherland and its attendant sentiments, the process is not a purely logical one, but comes to its completion by most irregular courses, with all sorts of bypaths due to the odd configuration of our nature and the world we live in, so in widening out from patriotism to humanity we have to follow a line given, for the most part, by external facts. The French as our nearest neighbours have always had a special interest for us. They, like ourselves, have inherited a mixed race and a mixed civilization, partly Teutonic, partly Celtic, partly Roman, but with elements variously combined. To us a more predominantly Teutonic stock and an insular position have given a more independent and unique character, history, and constitution. France, as being continental and more central, was also more completely Romanized, and has at all periods of her history been more in touch with the general stream of thought than ourselves. Often she has led it, always she has reflected it more quickly and perfectly. Our traditional rivalry has been a chivalrous one, marked by many episodes of real admiration and close friendship. To Elizabeth, to Cromwell, to the Crusaders of the twelfth and the philosophers of the eighteenth century, France and England seemed as naturally allied as they are now in repelling a common aggression on their homes and liberty. But for the future the strongest links will be the two great

XIV THE GROWTH OF HUMANITY

common ideals, self-government and individual freedom at home, and the community of free peoples abroad. In the practical democracy already realized at home, and in the ideal of a humanity built up of such self-governing and co-operating states, France and England stand for the unity of western civilization in the sense in which it has been traced in this volume, the only sense which makes it worth the sacrifice of wealth and toil and life.

The unity of which we believe ourselves to be now the champions must therefore be a real thing based on freedom and realized by conscious effort; but it must also be truly comprehensive, not exclusive of any willing co-operator, not aimed against any one but for the whole. It is not intended in this volume to discuss any burning questions of the day, and therefore the briefest indications must be given of how the nucleus of western culture has been formed and how it must reform itself after the war. France, Germany, and England have been for many years, collectively far the most important centres of science and social progress in the world, and it would have been the ideal policy for them to give a united lead to the rest of the world. The war has altered that, but it cannot abolish the fundamental facts on which the civilization of the West is based, science, power over nature, and social organization? In these the same three countries will still have a certain primacy, though the position of the United States will be enormously strengthened. No peace can, of course, be permanent which contemplates the excommunication of a leading member of the human family.

Italy in science, philosophy, and literature, is a worthy colleague, and Russia makes a great stride forward by allying herself with the forces of progress and European unity.

Now it is clear that there are two distinct lines of approach to our goal of a united mankind. We may cultivate for ourselves, as an ideal based on love and reason, the notion of all men as brothers working together, helping one another even when unknown, strengthening one another's powers, and gradually advancing towards a higher goal. This, though not a complete religion for most people, at least partakes of the nature of religion. The other line is concerned with the practical task of reconciling actual difficulties, bringing nations together for various purposes—arbitration, international trade, boards of conciliation and the like. This is the slow and thorny path, and on account of its very difficulty is apt to engross the thoughts and energy of the best brains which devote themselves to the cause. But the first line, of self-cultivation and the promotion of a favourable spirit among others, though open to any one and easy of approach, is apt to be neglected. Such 'mere idealism', like pure benevolence, runs some risk of being choked by the multiplicity of details and agencies and organizations which beset the modern world. Humanity, as an idea, was perhaps more easily apprehended in the days of Turgot and Condorcet than it is with us when the implements of a united mankind have been immeasurably augmented and improved. All the greater, then, the need to re-integrate the notion. Just as in science the dispersive effect of specialism has led many thinkers to desire another order of minds specially devoted to generalism, to knitting together the results of the detailed investigations of others, so in conduct, morals and politics, it is more and more imperative to recall men's minds, and, in the first place, our own, to the large governing ideas by which after all our lesser rules and objects must stand or fall. For who will dispute that all our alliances and international action and the war itself can only be ultimately justified if they are seen to serve the highest interests of mankind as a whole?

A volume, and a very valuable one, might be written on the evolution of this idea of Humanity in history. We should need in the first place to analyse, with some care, in what sense it is in each case used. There is the simple sense of brotherhood such as we know to be deeply felt among our allies in Russia. Of this there must have been germs from the earliest appearance of mankind upon earth. It is one of those most precious things which the development of wealth and class and distinctive culture has tended to blunt in more elaborate civilizations. But when we consider that the full conception of Humanity involves a knowledge of man's evolution, his growth in power, and organization throughout history, as well as the simple but indispensable sense of man's brotherhood, we shall see how long a road the Russian moujik—as well as multitudes of his fellows in all other lands—must travel before he comes in view of the goal. In the fuller sense of a self-conscious and developing being, the idea of Humanity first appears with the Stoics, after the Greeks had put their leaven of abstract thought into the world. The whole inhabited world as the City of Man was the Stoic ideal, and it embraced both the idea of the πόλις which Platonic and Aristotelian thought had reached in the fourth century B.C., and the extension to the rest of mankind which was in the air just before the Christian era. Christianity affected the conception in a twofold manner. On the one hand it limited it, for the Stoic City of Man became the City of God, who was to be sought and worshipped in one prescribed order. On the other hand it deepened it, for the springs of a common humanity were found to go beneath the superficial facts of a citizen life into the depths of souls which have identical relations with eternal things, with sin and suffering and hopes of the future.

It is not till after the outburst of science in the fifteenth and sixteenth centuries, after that reawakening of the hopes of human powers which takes our minds back to the Greeks, that we find the conception of Humanity appearing in something like the form in which we can now imagine it. It will have been gathered from our chapter on Science and Philosophy how essential is the growth of organized thought to the realization of any unity in a progressive world. For the realm of thought is the only one in which no distinctions of race or nation are possible, but it must be thought in which agreement is reached. So long as men can differ, as they still do, on questions of human affairs, politics, social arrangements, or even archaeological matters where race or national predominance is involved, so far science does not exert her unifying sway. But in mathematics, physics, chemistry, all the matters in which it is impossible for a man to take another view because he is a Frenchman or a German—here we reach a haven of intellectual peace; and these calm waters are spreading over the world, in spite of the tempests.

To return to the educational point from which we started, we can see now another line of approach to unity in training our own minds and those of others. In some respects it is a surer way, though less direct. When studying the political life and history of other nations, even if we do so deliberately in order to find out what we owe to them, we are bound to be arrested here and there by things that we do not like, even among our best friends. The French may seem frivolous or less self-restrained than ourselves; they have had their sanguinary outbursts of revolution. Where they have impeded our own movements, as in colonization, we are the more conscious of their faults. Or we may feel that Americans have their materialistic vein. And so on. This with our best friends, who, no doubt, feel the same about us. But on the other line of approach, the study of the things on which men now agree without question, which they have built up steadily with co-operating hands, the mental effect is quite different. The opening vista leads us on, with growing admiration and confidence in the unbreakable solidarity of mankind. We know that Newton who completes Galileo, Maxwell who follows Laplace, Helmholtz who uses the results of Joule, can have no conflicting jealousies. Here quite obviously and indisputably all are fellow-workers, and before the greatness of their work the passions of rival domination in material things, the differences of national taste and habit, the quarrels of the past or the future, appear contemptible and insignificant.

They are not insignificant, as we know to our cost. But by dwelling on the things of greater moment and solidity, we train ourselves and others to reduce the elements of discord to their true proportion and allay the storm. The progress of a united mankind is thus an ideal, slowly realizing itself in time. But its realization is quickened and rendered wider and more beneficent, the more we think of it and believe in it. A blow comes, such as the present war, and seems to shatter the whole picture which so many hands have limned and so many eyes admired. Those who have followed its growth through the ages, know well that no such blow can finally destroy a living growth or even go very deep in injuring its features.

It is surely a commonplace that in proportion as western populations, from statesmen downwards, are animated by sentiments of comradeship which arise from considerations such as these, the danger of war must diminish and the possibilities of fruitful common action increase. Yet there is probably no country in Europe where any deliberate attempt is made to instruct the people in ideas which would most surely broaden their sympathies and lay the foundations of peace.

The argument takes us back for a moment to the essay on education. We left off there at a point where the old unity based on Greco-Roman culture was seen to be disappearing in a confused mass of new studies, partly suggested by modern languages and history, still more by the growth of science and the application of science to the problems of contemporary life. It may well be that in this conception of humanity, the co-operation of mankind in a growing structure of thought, we shall ultimately find the *idée-mère* under which all the other subordinate ideas in education may be grouped and inspired. This might take place if the notion were grasped in no narrow sense, but so broadly that all human thought, religion, and philosophy, art as well as science, might find their justification in it.

The advantage of putting the educational issue first has been already indicated. We can all get to work on it at once for ourselves, and it is a far more fundamental and, in some respects, easier thing to introduce a new idea into the minds of others than to alter the boundaries and political conditions of States. If we once achieved a general atmosphere of co-operation and goodwill in the world, the practical problems would be already more than half solved.

Discussion will take place, with more and more vigour as years go on, as to the various measures which have been described collectively as the establishment of a World-State. At what point could it be said that a World-State is in being? How can such a World-State be reconciled with the independent sovereignty of the several States comprised in it? What is to be the sanction imposing the decisions of the larger community on its constituent members? Such are a few of the problems involved in any advance towards the Kantian ideal of cosmopolitanism. None of them admit of a single definite answer. They do not belong to questions of pure theory, and we shall have to solve them slowly and with difficulty, seizing every favourable opportunity of a slight advance, avoiding grave obstacles, compromising with every possible friend.

But for the moment we seem likely to be overwhelmed by unchained passions which are the practical denial of everything that the ideal of humanity implies. Instead of

XIV THE GROWTH OF HUMANITY 311

co-operation we are faced by schemes of conquest and domination, and the simplest notion of brotherhood is limited to comradeship in arms for defence or attack. Many will be found to ridicule the idea that any real progress in unity has ever been made, or that the world can ever be envisaged except as an irksome enclosure of rival armed forces thirsting for the fray. But to those who are not prepared to accept this as the last word in human association the argument of this volume may have some weight. It will lead those who follow it to a quiet but well-grounded belief that the forces tending to unity in the world are different in quality, incomparably greater in scope than those which make for disruption. Discord is explosive and temporary, harmony rises slowly but dominates the final chord.

Like the great common purposes of science, the common tendencies of human action have in recent years suffered some eclipse through the bustle of our activity and the multiplicity of its detail. The colours, too, of a conflict of any kind are so much more vivid and arresting than the quiet and monotonous tones of a long piece of harmonious and co-operative work. The labours of such a bureau of international effort as is described in Chapter X appear to our pressmen and publicists so little interesting that they are practically ignored, and the results of scientific congresses, being of a highly specialized kind, are left perforce to those who can understand them. Yet it is precisely in these things, if our diagnosis is correct, that the most characteristic features of the age are to be found. For in them and in similar movements we see united the two fundamental human traits from which we started, reason and sympathy: reason winning triumphs over nature, sympathy realizing itself at last in a community of men devoting their powers to mutual aid. 'Idle dreams', it will be said, as we hurl more and more millions of our best youth to destruction by the most highly developed resources of science. Yes, but the same nations were only yesterday celebrating the services of Pasteur, Virchow, and Lister to a common humanity, and will do so again to-morrow or the day after.

It is in truth one of the most poignant features of the tragedy in which we are manfully and rightly bearing our part, that the community-sense in the world had never been so highly developed, or found so many channels in which to diffuse itself, as just at the moment when the blow fell. The socialist movements in all civilized countries have always had this as a leading motive ; comrades and poor among themselves, these men have always been eager to stretch out a hand to those of like mind abroad. And in the last chapter we saw how among Christian communities throughout the world there has been in recent years a growing approximation. Neither the cause nor the effects of such forces can die away. They will reappear when the storm has passed and rebuild the wreck.

One large aspect of the united action of the western world has received no notice in this volume, though it might very well be the subject of a detailed study in itself. This is the relation of the more advanced and powerful nations of the West towards the weaker and less progressive peoples. It might, indeed, be treated as the touchstone of our civilization, just as the education of the young is a good, perhaps the best, test of the advancement of any single people. For it involves some joint action of the western nations ; it shows how far they are disinterested and how far skilful in their treatment of the less advanced.

The record is not a good one, but it confirms, on the whole, the view we have suggested that a growth of the sense and conception of humanity may be traced from the time when modern science was born in the sixteenth century. The Middle Ages hardly furnish us with any examples of the

XIV THE GROWTH OF HUMANITY 313

action of Christendom towards heathen and weaker people until the Crusades, in which, with rare examples of personal chivalry, the earlier attitude was one of contempt and hatred of the unbeliever. In the conquest of the New World, which was to some of its earliest conquerors a new Crusade, there is the same general savagery marked by rare cases of Christian kindness, such as Las Casas showed. But after the Reformation, when the Church itself had been purified and more human tolerance and care and interest in life prevailed, we find the enlightened Jesuit missions to China and Paraguay, St. Francis Xavier's work in India, and the Quaker dealings with Red Indians in the New World. From the middle of the seventeenth century, slavery, which had fallen into abeyance during the Middle Ages as a domestic institution, began to be denounced as a trade. We are on the threshold of the great humanitarian outburst of the eighteenth century. It is impossible to believe that this growth of human feeling in dealing with other men is unconnected with that new gospel of human power which Bacon and Descartes had just proclaimed. Except for the occasional superman, the greater the powers a man possesses and the higher he rates human capacity at its best, the more careful he is to cherish and develop the germs of humanity in the young and weak.

This was undoubtedly the case with the 'philosophers' of the eighteenth century; it is equally true of the nineteenth century, an age wonderful alike for its unexampled development of science and for the rise of activities, national and international, for the betterment of the race. Jointly the western nations have in this period put down the slave trade, and in the Brussels Conference of 1890 we see the highest point yet reached by the united humanity of the West expressed by the assembled states in regard to backward people. The point therefore is a notable one, and Englishmen will be glad to remember that it was Lord Salisbury, then Foreign Secretary, who took the first step. The previous Conference at Berlin, in 1884, had secured freedom of trade for the basins of the Congo and the Niger, and in 1889 Lord Salisbury, through the Belgian Government, called the Powers together to consider questions relating to the slave trade in Africa. For Africa, home of the black race, last exploited of the continents, discovered after the white man had discovered science, was pre-eminently the part of the world where the co-operation of leading peoples in civilizing backward races was most needed and most to be expected. The Congo, the Herreros, Morocco, Tripoli, Omdurman, offer a blood-stained record in reply.

But the general act of the Brussels Conference is clear and adequate as to what the purpose of the Powers should be. " To put an end to the crimes and devastations engendered by the traffic in African slaves, to protect effectively the aboriginal populations of Africa, to ensure for that vast continent the benefits of peace and civilization ", is in fact the whole duty of a united western civilization when dealing with the less civilized. The results achieved may well seem small compared with the magnitude of the purpose, but those who know most about it do not despise them. Slave-raiding and tribal wars have been diminished and some check put on importing arms and spirits.

It is not a topic on which it is easy to keep a cheerful mind. Some Putumayo will constantly occur to remind us of the fierce brutality of strength unsupervised and unrestrained. We compare the actual performance of mankind when free to try their best or wreak their worst on comparatively defenceless folk, with the noble rivalry which we can imagine between the nations of the world in leading the weaker people to develop their resources and themselves, on paths which may tend to the greatest prosperity and happiness of all, advanced and backward together:

and the comparison leaves us sick at heart. But a sober judgement will not deny that even here advance is being made. The ideal has been admitted. The rights of smaller States are being made, as in the present conflict, the subject of the concern of their strongest neighbours. Steps are being taken all over the world to preserve and ameliorate the remnants of primitive people. Horrors when revealed are more strongly reprobated. Missionaries are pursuing their labours with more enlightenment and zeal, and in wider spheres. In spite of cynics and doubters, it is true in this as in the other activities of a united mankind, *e pur si muove*. And as the work moves on it is seen to involve the same guiding thoughts that inspire us in the case of the young and feeble at home—pity for their weakness, love for their humanity, hope for the future.

Ugr
CB
5
M3
1970